NIGHT

+

MARKET

NIGHT + MARKET

DELICIOUS THAI FOOD TO FACILITATE DRINKING AND FUN-HAVING AMONGST FRIENDS

KRIS YENBAMROONG

WITH GARRETT SNYDER

PHOTOGRAPHS BY MARCUS NILSSON

FOREWORD BY ANDY RICKER

CLARKSON POTTER/PUBLISHERS

NEW YORK

LIBRARY OF CONGRESS CATALOGING-IN-PUBLICATION DATA
HAS BEEN APPLIED FOR.

ISBN 978-0-451-49787-1
EBOOK ISBN 978-0-451-49788-8

PRINTED IN CHINA

COVER AND INTERIOR PHOTOGRAPHS BY MARCUS NILSSON
BOOK AND COVER DESIGN BY JULIETTE CEZZAR

10 9 8 7 6 5 4 3 2 1

FIRST EDITION

CONTENTS

4 — USING WHAT YOU HAVE *201*

5 — T.G.I.F. *249*

6 — BASICS THAT ARE WORTH MAKING YOURSELF 294

SARAH, KRIS

FOREWORD

I admit, at first, I didn't "get" Night + Market.

I'd heard of Kris Yenbamroong and his restaurant in Hollywood probably via an article in a food rag; I recall photos of a rather bare white room with a few long tables and a menu of what the writer described as "street food," which I immediately recognized as Northern Thai and Isaan dishes, such as *laap*, *sai krawk*, *sai ua*, *naam phrik mengda*, and even *luu*, the raw blood soup prized by rural folks in the northern provinces, not on the streets of Bangkok. He is a kindred spirit, I thought, except (unlike me) he's a young Thai realizing the beauty of the food of his ancestral home and celebrating it in an unadulterated form for the good people of Los Angeles. In part, my assumption was right: we are kindred spirits in some ways. In part, I was dead wrong; what Kris was doing was far from my idealized fantasy.

We met, finally, a couple of years later when a beer company brought us together to prepare a Songkran (Thai New Year) meal at Night + Market. Kris has described it as a kind of blind date and we hit it off right away, though neither one of us were exactly what we thought the other to be. I expected exacting replicas of family recipes from Chiang Rai, like subtly spiced laap and sai ua, but he was serving something else. The laap was salty, wildly spicy, huge in portion, not nuanced, or herbal like my favorite versions. The sai ua had a sweet flavor, and the naam phrik mengda was over the top smoky and hot. It was confusing to me and I wasn't sure I liked it, hidebound as I was to my preferences for the old ways and recipes.

The dinner itself was a big success; food critics, actresses, Thai dignitaries, Yenbamroong family members, musicians, Angelenos of all stripes packed the dining room. It was truly Bacchanalian. (You could describe Kris that way as well. The man loves bottle upon bottle of wine, huge sushi feasts, steak house carpet bombing, bone marrow mac and cheese at midnight, meals before meals.) I noticed that the hits of the night were not the Pok Pok offerings; our tame *kaeng hung leh* (mild Burmese pork curry), *phat khanom jiin* (a stir-fried rice vermicelli often served on special occasions, its long and golden strands signifying long life and wealth), and *yam jin kai* (a northern chicken soup with laap spice) came back to the kitchen only partially eaten. It was Kris's heavily spicy, funky, and powerfully seasoned dishes that people were there for.

I came away impressed with Kris. Here was a young chef, with very little cooking experience, totally going by the seat of his pants. His menu had food I had not seen stateside, with dishes that I had not dared to serve at my own place for fear westerners would not eat them. But what gave me pause was that though the names of the dishes were familiar to me, the execution was not. To my taste, they were too wild, too hot, too sweet, too big, just too MUCH.

But something has happened over time. Kris matured as a chef; his vision and aesthetic gelling as his chops got better and, finally, after hanging with Kris both in LA and in Thailand and eating at Night + Market a bunch more times and living in LA for a spell myself, my view of what he is doing has changed. I finally get it (I think)! What he is doing is actually nothing short of revolutionary in the Thai food game. And it's also part of a much larger discourse around "ethnic food," "immigrant food," "tradition," "authenticity," and other potentially incendiary topics. You see, just calling Kris a Thai chef would be doing a disservice to him and to other young chefs who are shaping the future of Asian American food.

Yes, Kris is Thai. Yes, he has deep cultural connections to Thailand. But he is also an Angeleno, an American born and bred. The city and his life experience have shaped him as much as his ancestral heritage, and what has emerged is at once as American as apple pie and as deeply rooted in the teachings of his Thai grandmother.

Thai food has always been a dynamic cuisine, influenced by its neighbors and visitors, changing as the taste and habits of the Thai people change, adapting to the environments it is exported to. Usually, when Thai food is sold outside of Thailand, it is engineered to take advantage of what raw products are available and what the local populous will buy rather than a slavish adherence to old recipes. As a child of Thai immigrant restaurateurs, Kris witnessed this firsthand. But he also had the benefit of a college education in New York City, an exposure to the food and arts both in NY and in LA, and his travels to Thailand. Unfettered by his parents' reasons for opening a restaurant ("because it was necessary" is how Kris has described it to me), inspired by the teachings of his grandmother and the city he lived in, he set out to do his own thing. The result is a new way of approaching Thai food. But while pushing the boundaries, he is actually carrying the torch for Thai cuisine in a very recognizable way: no matter what the influence or origin of a dish, Thai people end up making food that is recognizable as uniquely Thai. The food of Night + Market is Thai, make no mistake, but it is also LA food, and by extension American food. It personifies the chef that helms the kitchen.

Witness the traditional Americana tattoos that cover Kris and his Instagram account showing dinners at fine-dining spots in LA or at taco carts, him hanging with his cousin in rural Chiang Rai, the Hispanic Catholic imagery candles on the tables at his joints, and the hoopla surrounding his celebrity in a city that is all about celebrity. But most of all, witness the menu at Night + Market Song, his second restaurant: a fried chicken sandwich with *som tam*, tacos, dim sum with caviar on top, boldly flavored versions of the Northern Thai canon that appeal directly to the soul of the dining public of LA, all accompanied by natural wines! This is not the reverent homage to specific regional Thai recipes and dining experience Pok Pok has ascribed to, and I was wrong to have been looking for that when I first ate at Night + Market. This is something way more exciting, way more vital and modern, way more visceral.

—Andy Ricker

About two decades ago, at a film conference in Minnesota, Werner Herzog—probably the greatest documentary filmmaker of all time, and an iconic director in general—explained his theory about the best way to achieve truth in documentary film. According to him, in creative work there are two kinds of truth—objective truth and ecstatic truth. Objective truth is an illusion, he argued, because although it might act as a record of facts, it is ultimately superficial in describing truths. It misses the greater point. Objectivity is for accountants (and politicians, hopefully). "There is just very shallow truth in facts," he said. "Otherwise, the phone directory would be the Book of Books."

The other type of truth—the ecstatic truth—is different. "There are deeper strata of truth in cinema," Herzog said, "and there is such a thing as poetic, ecstatic truth. It is mysterious and elusive, and can be reached only through fabrication and imagination and stylization."

What does this have to do with Thai food? Well, to start, I should tell you that if you're looking for a cookbook dedicated to the objective truth of Thai cooking, this isn't it. There are other chefs and authors out there who have done a far more intensive job of cataloging the thousands (if not hundreds of thousands) of recipes and techniques and foods that make up the giant sprawling patchwork of what people eat in Thailand.

I didn't realize it at the time, but when I opened Night + Market in 2010, what I was after was the ecstatic truth behind Thai food. We set up inside a blank room next door to my parents' Thai restaurant in the middle of Hollywood's Sunset Strip, pouring two dozen or so wines I was into and serving a handful of cheap drinking snacks like fatty grilled sausages and fried pig tails. I'd project movies like *Shampoo* and classic tennis matches like Sampras vs. Agassi at the US Open in 2001 on the wall during dinner. I ate in front of the TV a lot as an only child; in those early months, the restaurant was often empty, so I tried to fill the void by re-creating that same effect. At that point I couldn't really decide whether Night + Market was an actual restaurant or a half-finished piece of performance art. If it failed (and for a while it seemed like we would), I figured, at least I could meet some chicks out of it.

But people came, and I saw something about how they were eating and drinking and socializing together at Night + Market that was inherently Thai, at least in the way that I saw it, how it was casual and fun and not the least bit precious. So as Night + Market grew, I doubled down on this idea that I was channeling some elusive Thai spirit. I put a note on the menu that read, "I didn't create anything on this menu, I'm presenting recipes as they are found in Thailand." When my dad opened Talésai, the restaurant next door, in the early '80s, his goal was to have a Thai restaurant where non-Thai people would come to eat, the ultimate American Dream for an immigrant. Thirty years later, my barometer for success in the early days was if Thai people were coming into Night + Market. I kept prices low to the point of absurdity, figuring I had to compete with the hole-in-the-wall places a couple of miles away in LA's Thai Town. I had a chip on my shoulder, one that came out of a need to prove how Thai an unlikely little place on the Sunset Strip could be, and how authentic we were.

But then, in a process so subtle and gradual that I only realized it once I sat down to write this book, the more I tried to cook "authentic Thai food," the more it became apparent that I was curating and synthesizing and translating certain things, just based on my own personal preference. I'd been slowly veering away from the way things were done in Thailand, or the way my grandmother taught me, because whether it was slicing a cut of pork in a certain way or adding lemongrass to a curry paste that wasn't supposed to include lemongrass, the changes made sense to me somehow, or I found the final product improved in some way.

I started thinking about all the compelling foods that I had tasted when I visited my aunt and uncle in rural Northern Thailand, or the back-alley street foods I ate as a high school kid living in Bangkok, dishes that were probably obscure or unremarkable in the larger universe of Thai food, but ones to which I had an oddly intense

personal connection. How could I translate those dishes, and the party-friendly ethos behind them, to people who would probably never fly into Chiang Rai or Bangkok? How could I show Thai food as this weird fun-house mirror of culture that I saw it as?

Around the time we opened our second restaurant, Night + Market Song, I started to become paranoid that I was allowing our food to be experienced in a way that I felt involved the wrong attitude. I was worried every time I saw a table that looked overly serious or contemplative, as if they were quietly studying the food for "Thai-ness" rather than enjoying it. When people compared the food with what they ate in Thailand, it no longer sounded like a compliment. It sounded like the joy was being sucked out of the room, like the only metric that mattered was how closely something resembled another similar thing a thousand miles away. Of course, it could've all been inside my head—maybe those people I worried about were actually having a great time in their own way. But it got me thinking about how the best part of eating at a restaurant is that sense of surprise, that sense of unexpected and subverted expectations. Maybe that includes serving really good versions of the takeout Thai-American food some people consider passé. Why were the good versions of Thai takeout classics like *pad see ew* scarfed on your couch out of a paper carton any less meaningful than a Northern Thai salad? Why was something like our sea urchin fried rice, which isn't necessarily a part of Thai culinary tradition, looked down upon if people liked it? The more I thought about it, the more I decided that looseness was a good thing. It was how to make Thai food fun again.

The first explicitly non-Thai dish we ever served was our fried chicken sandwich. Now the words "World Famous Fried Chicken Sandwich" are painted on the side of our building in big bright letters (a man can dream). The longer Night + Market has been in existence, the more that line between Thai food and everything else has begun to blur. The grand commonality—more than any specific combination of lime, fish sauce, chiles, and herbs—is this idea that food should be delicious enough to jolt awake your senses, and addictive enough that like Pavlov's dog you start to associate certain tastes with loud music and loud friends and a party that never really starts or ends. That's the ecstatic truth of Thai food.

Since this is an actual cookbook, you're probably wondering how you will go about achieving that sort of Thai-induced bliss in your own kitchen. Well, most important, it's not about fitting your life into Thai food, but rather Thai food fitting into your life.

I'm a chef, and I am not a chef. I am in the sense that I run a restaurant and can be found behind the stoves most nights, but I'm not in the sense of someone who went to culinary school or worked their way up from fry cook to become chef de cuisine. I'm the kid who goofed around at NYU film school, hung out with jazz majors but didn't play music, tried to scrape together a living taking pictures of naked girls, then quit and moved back to LA to almost run my parents' restaurant into the ground. I'm a firm believer that the journey makes the person (no matter how peripatetic) and that without those trying experiences our restaurant wouldn't have ended up where it is now. As LA Times food critic Jonathan Gold so flatteringly put it: "Night + Market has become the restaurant New Yorkers want to visit when they come in from out of town, new restaurants copy its menu, and Yenbamroong may show up in more national magazines than Ryan Gosling these days."

As someone who grew up in and around Thai restaurants, I have the built-in advantage of knowing flavor. I have the hubris to claim that I know how to season better than most culinary school graduates—the good palate part is in my blood. I am the product of my grandmother, the tough and resourceful chef behind my parents' restaurant, but also my grandfather, a Thai pharmacist who enjoyed his wine, women, and song. I'll be the first to admit that while knowledgeable, I'm also a lazy cook (generally speaking), but only because I think that brings its own advantages: Another way to put it is that I believe in working smarter, not harder. Every dish at Night + Market is streamlined with a simple question: How minimal can we go and still come up with the best product? No style of cuisine, especially Thai cooking, needs to be overcomplicated, either for a business or for someone who cooks at home. The recipes in this book are meant to be simpler and easier than whatever terrifying, labor-intensive notion you have of cooking real Thai food, but that doesn't mean they are neutered of flavor. Once again, it's about subverting expectations: I'm telling you that you can make brilliant, mind-alternating, true-to-life Thai food while still embracing shortcuts and work-arounds that will make your life easier. This might sound like a late-night infomercial pitch, but I promise it's not.

In life, nothing exists in a vacuum. Every single day, in countless different ways, you make tiny calculations weighing time, effort, and how much pleasure can be squeezed out of a situation. You could probably launder your own dress shirts or wash your own car, but there's a reason people take them to someone else. My philosophy is that if you're going to make the effort to cook anything the traditional, hard-core, you-have-nothing-else-to-do way, the results have to be a noticeable upgrade over doing it in a way that's more direct. One of my great passions in life is shooting the breeze with old Thai chefs, asking them why they do the things they do—why they massage the pork a certain way before it goes on the grill, why they use this fresh herb but not that one. In my experience, nine times out of ten, the answer you end up with is some variation of "Well, that's how I was taught to do it." And to be clear, that way might actually be the best way. But the hard thing we've done at Night + Market (and by extension in this cookbook) is to break down those traditions, retaining the ones that really make the difference, and leaving out the rest. The more you cook these recipes, the more you'll realize that you have plentiful opportunities to simplify, alter, or tweak in ways beyond what is presented. That's cool, that's what you should do. Your job is to adapt these recipes based on your life; there's a whole chapter, called "Using What You Have," that is all about taking the recipes on the page and figuring out how to implant the ideas behind them in your brain, so that you can always make something like a Thai cook would, even if it's just that half head of cauliflower and box of spaghetti lying around in your kitchen. The point is, do whatever is fulfilling and gratifying for you and the people you're cooking for.

That last part is especially important. You could, of course, eat any recipe in this book on its own, and in certain cases there are dishes specifically called out as one-plate meals. But Thai food lends itself well to big dinner parties where the table is covered in dishes. That's because Thai people think of balance not just in terms of seasoning a dish, but balancing a meal with an array of dishes. That usually means a spread that includes a soup or curry, a stir-fried dish, rice, and maybe some sort of salad. Don't overthink it. If you want your party to include noodles and chicken wings, or spicy meat salads and chile dips, you can build it however you want. But there is one more important aspect to achieving that balance: alcohol. All of the food in this book is drinking food, and by that I mean it's food conducive to socializing and sharing, food that whets the appetite even as it satisfies it, and food that often demands something refreshing or fizzy to wash it down. Once again, figuring out that part is up to you—I am especially partial to certain types of wine, as you'll see in the next section—but that process starts by expanding your field of vision to see food, drink, and company as playing equal roles in determining how pleasurable a meal can be.

One last piece of advice: My senior year of college I remember reading something in *Vice* magazine's *Guide to Everything* in the "Dos & Don'ts" issue. The rule was "never say never: don't ever say no to a reasonable invitation to do something that might be fun. This is a W.A.S.P. rule, and one of the reasons why rich white people rule the planet." It meant something to the effect that a common outlook among successful people from all walks of life was, if an opportunity arrives that has even a *1 percent* chance of being rewarding or enjoyable or meaningful to you in some way, do it. For much of my adolescence, I was always looking for a reason to say no. It could have been that I was posturing, or that I was scared, or that I was just close-minded. But I realized I needed to say yes more.

That mantra has led me to interesting places, and it's part of why I'll never turn down an opportunity to visit the motherland. When I travel to Thailand, I realize how much more there is to learn about a country I call home, and how much can be revealed when you view things with the curiosity and enthusiasm of a shameless tourist. I hope this book helps you approach Thai cooking in the same way. If nothing else, remember this: Food does not have to be precious. Make it fun.

DRINK WINE WITH THAI FOOD: A CALL TO ACTION

Since the first day we opened, I've had this persistent fantasy. In it, someone comes to the restaurant, orders a bottle of wine, and doesn't eat anything at all. It hasn't happened yet, but I'm holding out hope.

The reason it occurs to me is because Night + Market was conceived as a wine bar as much as it was a restaurant, and in my view it still functions that way. Wine has always been a major part of the story we tell: the idea of encountering things in an unexpected context, and the joy of discovering combinations that are as appealing as they are unlikely. In fact, when we first started, we had more wines by the glass on the menu than we had food items.

So why does Thai food and wine make sense? Well, in some ways it works because you have total freedom. There is no tradition of wine drinking or winemaking in Thailand and thus no orthodoxy, no right or wrong answers about what you should or shouldn't drink. The robust and very essential drinking culture that *does* exist revolves around supercold, watery lagers and whiskey, which is usually drunk with soda water or something bubbly. The unifying element is that you're drinking things that are refreshing and thirst quenching in a way that matches with assertively seasoned Thai food.

Like a lot of people, I used to not link the idea of refreshment with wine. I thought of it as this contemplative, heavy thing that you sipped and swirled by the fireplace out of big round glasses, which of course it can be in certain contexts. But then I was introduced to another kind of wine. I realized that it could be a beverage that was energizing and uplifting. It was something you could drink frequently and copiously—chug, even—without feeling like it was precious, or reserved for special occasions.

What types of wines am I talking about? Here's how I like to think of them:

WINES THAT ARE MEANT TO BE DRUNK NOW

I haven't had the privilege of enjoying many wines with age, that is, wines that have been sitting in the bottle for more than a couple of years. Part of that is a function of price—older wines tend to be more expensive. Part of that is just a function of those wines not being widely available. Those constraints are what actually led me to discover the wines that would make up the bulk of what we pour at Night + Market as well as what I drink at home: wines that are *meant* to be enjoyed young. What that provides is a wine that is fresh and light on its feet. I've been fortunate enough to work some harvests in France's Loire Valley, and what impresses me most is how distinct and vibrant a wine can be right when it's put into the bottle, sometimes even before it's finished fermenting. It's important to remember that wine is at its core an agricultural product from the countryside, made by farmers who like to party. They want their wine to facilitate fun-having as much as you do.

WINES THAT SHOULD BE CONSUMED WITH ABANDON

Thierry Puzelat, a winemaker hero of mine and a legendary figure in the wine community, is credited with saying something to the effect of, *My favorite wine is the bottle I can drain in ten minutes or less*. It might seem obvious, but wine should first and foremost be drinkable. In fact, it should entice you to drink it quickly. Part of what makes wine culture seem so snobby and off-putting to outsiders is that it prioritizes deep, contemplative wines and downplays the role of wine as a *beverage*, something to quench your thirst and make you happy. It's party fuel. An offshoot of seeking out fresh and vibrant wines is that they tend to have lower alcohol in exchange for more liveliness. There are gently sparkling wines that literally smell and taste like the world's greatest strawberry wine cooler (without the saccharine aftertaste) and astoundingly, the only thing that makes them taste that way is grape juice and yeast. What I'm saying is, start thinking of wine as a daily, gulpable pleasure rather than something that collects dust in a cupboard. If that means seeking out wines that are affordable enough to buy two of rather than splurging on one, that's a good thing—you'd be amazed at the immensely enjoyable bottles you can pick up for between fifteen and twenty-five dollars. A budget should be an asset rather than a liability.

WINES ENJOYED FAMILY-STYLE

At Night + Market, we serve our food family-style. Dishes come out of the kitchen in big waves and are meant to be enjoyed together. With that, it seems only logical that wine should be approached family-style as well. Another by-product of a too-restrictive wine culture is that most people overemphasize food pairings. Not to say that pairings can't be important—that's exactly what I want if I'm having a tasting menu where each course is a pristine single bite whose flavors have been honed to an empirical essence—but in general it's too confining to worry about matching certain wines with certain foods. What's more important is to find a wine you can enjoy drinking throughout the meal (which is really an extension of the second point about finding refreshing wines that keep beckoning you back for more). This is especially true in the case of Thai food, where a full meal is usually going to include a wide range of flavors and intensity levels, and you might hop back and forth between dishes throughout the evening. The traditional concept of pairings breaks

down in those situations. The best advice is to find something you'd want to consume while eating any type of food, but especially wines with enough obvious and bright character as to not get lost against bold and flavorful food. Also along those lines—open more than one bottle at a time. More is more.

WHERE TO START

Once you're aware of these wines, the next step involves locating them, and depending on where you live, that might involve a wine bar, a wine shop, or maybe just the Internet. At some point, you're going to want to deal with a person when you're learning about wine (unless you just stay on the Internet) and in that regard it's a good thing to have someone with whom you can build a relationship. If a sommelier is truly good at what they do, they'll approach wine as an enthusiast rather than a scholar. One of my biggest influences in thinking about wine is my friend Lou Amdur, who runs what I believe to be the greatest wine store in Los Angeles. The Lou philosophy when talking to customers is to not rely on geeky terms like tannins or acidity or dryness, but to communicate in ways that are visceral and sensory; words like *refreshing, spicy, tangy, ass-y, Thanksgiving-y, sweet, juicy, mineraly, salty, wild, fragrant,* etc. When you strip down the overwrought, complicated language of wine into simpler, more expressive terms, it ends up better for everyone involved.

WHAT TO DRINK AND WHY

This section of the book isn't intended to be a Thai wine-pairing bible. Ultimately wine—just like food—is subjective, and it's your job to decide how, and if, it could enrich your life. But since there are still so many barriers when getting into casual wine drinking, I want to do my best to open the floodgates. Those cold beers and whiskey sodas? They still work wonderfully with everything in this book, and if you were so inclined, washing everything down with icy Singha and Miller High Life would still provide oceans of pleasure. But to peer into the world of wine is to open yourself up to another dimension of enjoyment and fulfillment.

Consider the suggestions that follow not so much as pairings, but as small interesting experiments to mess around with. The general thought process behind them is to either match similar flavors and heighten a particular taste or contrast different flavors so that they achieve a level of balance. Sometimes you can achieve both with the same wine and different dishes. If one combination strikes you as memorable, you can follow the thread further by reading more specific wine pairings peppered throughout the book.

Lightly Chilled Light Reds with Grilled Pork Products

Next time you open a bottle of red wine, throw it in the fridge for thirty minutes first. The fruitiness will jump out at you while the spicy qualities of the wine (tannins) will be toned down. That matters because the fruit and the freshness are what make wines thirst-quenching, while spice sort of does the opposite. Generally speaking, the lighter the wine, the more chilled it should be.

Try this with any Gamay-based wines, particularly ones from the Loire Valley. My favorites have a wildness to them that makes sense with the extra-porky taste of grilled pig parts (this pairing was one of the original ideas Night + Market was based on).

Pét-Nats (Sparkling Wines) with Anything Fried (and/or to Begin/End a Meal)

Pétillant naturel is the French term for naturally sparkling wines, and in general they're more rustic and straightforward (and cheaper) than Champagne. With complex and robust foods, you don't necessarily want a complicated and multilayered beverage. The tingly bubbles of a pét-nat do just enough to enhance the experience of fried or generously seasoned foods while providing refreshment that is direct and exuberant. They are perfect to begin the meal because they cleanse your palate, which is another way of saying they reset your tongue and tell your taste buds to get ready for what's coming. Think of pét-nats as snapshots of the wine as it transitioned from grape juice into an alcoholic beverage. Or think of them as rustic wine coolers. Either way, drink them. Also, try a sweeter pét-nat in lieu of dessert. The heavy-hitters of French pét-nats are producers such as Les Capriades, Olivier Lemasson, and Hervé Villemade, though there are also great domestic pét-nats from California wineries like Donkey & Goat and j°brix.

Chenin Blanc with Pretty Much Anything

Chenin Blanc is what I suggest when people ask me at the restaurant, What should we drink? It is rarely the wrong answer. It is a white wine that can assume many guises, in terms of minerality and aromas, sweetness vs. dryness, and body. It can make great sparkling wines. All of the things I mentioned can also be said about Riesling, which is traditionally the "go-to" pairing for all foods Asian. But I feel less of a kinship with Riesling. The wines it produces seem to always scream out "I am Riesling." It's like when a blockbuster movie star plays a regular person but you can't stop thinking, Oh, that's Tom Cruise.

Chenin Blanc, while it sometimes seems unmistakably chenin, can also be more mysterious and exciting.

Salty-Savory Whites with Pungent Fishy Things

Yes, some wines can have an intense savory, sometimes salty quality to them. Consider pairing these with foods of similar characteristics to enhance those qualities in each. This could mean a briny white from Greece with a food that has fish sauce as a key ingredient. Or try an orange wine (that's a white wine that's made like a red wine, by letting the skins stew in the juice, thereby imparting their flavor) from the Republic of Georgia with a salad of canned tuna.

Oxidative Wines with Pungent, Salty, and Fried Stuff

Wines that are exposed to some level of oxygen in the production process—things like fino and manzanilla sherry, or the notorious Jura wines that are aged in open barrels (wines are conventionally aged in closed containers)—take on very complex flavors and smells. That can mean yeasty, savory, nutty, or candied aromas. Try contrasting these characteristics with foods that have sharp, bright, or salty notes like the Shrimp Paste Chile Dip → 197 with fried eggplant, or with nutty foods like the Seasoned Fried Peanuts → 309 with lemongrass and garlic. Pair more delicate dishes, like the Royal Tuna Tartare → 281, with wines that have gentler levels of oxidation.

GET THE NECESSITIES

I've always believed that, rather than scrap a particular dish because you're missing a few things, it's better to work with a substitution or adjust with similar ingredients to fill in the gap. The most important trait in a Thai cook is resourcefulness, which means making something delicious out of what you have at hand. In an ideal world, my dream would be to have you pick up this cookbook and start cooking right away, and most of the recipes in this book are designed with that level of immediacy and simplicity in mind.

That said, unless you're a Thai home cook, or your pantry looks like that of a Thai cook's, there's a good chance you might not have everything you need to start cooking Thai food right off the bat. By that I mean the fundamental, irreplaceable stuff, things that can't really be substituted for because they make Thai food, well, taste like Thai food.

Some of these essentials have recipes that are in the last chapter of this book (consider taking a peek there before you start cooking), but others are best store-bought. The good news is that these things last forever in your pantry, are cheap, and are relatively easy to find at an Asian grocery, the Asian section of a supermarket, or online (check out importfood.com, templeofthai.com, or grocerythai .com). Thai brand products are always

CHEF TING GETTING READY FOR SERVICE

preferred (check if it says "Product of Thailand"), but in many cases you can find a Chinese or Southeast Asian brand that makes the same product. Here's what to have on hand:

SEASONING SAUCE

Despite its generic-sounding name, and the fact that fish sauce is famously a key Thai ingredient, *this* is the stuff that makes your stir-fry taste like a Thai stir-fry. The main brand I use is Golden Mountain, but there's also a popular label called Healthy Boy. It's made from fermented soybeans like soy sauce but it has an extra dimension to it, with a little bit of sweetness and umami flavor to balance out the salt.

OYSTER SAUCE

This is the other half of the equation for Thai stir-fries. It's a thick brown sauce with a distinctive sweet/briny flavor that comes from cooked-down oyster extract. You'll find it in the Asian section of most supermarkets.

THIN SOY SAUCE

This is your basic Chinese-style light soy sauce, which is on the thin and salty side. Finding a bottle shouldn't be difficult; just make sure you don't use a Japanese brand like Kikkoman, which has a sake flavor to it that works for sushi but not for Thai food. Look for Thai brands like Kwong Hung Seng, Healthy Boy, or Maekrua. If you can't find a Thai brand, then use a Chinese-style light soy sauce instead.

BLACK SOY SAUCE

In Thai cooking, black soy sauce is a soy sauce that has been thickened with sugar and caramel to produce a dark syrupy sauce. Avoid Chinese thick soy, which is more like a finishing sauce. Thai brands to look for are Kwong Hung Seng, Healthy Boy, and Maekrua. In a pinch, you can also use Indonesian sweet soy (*kecap manis*), which is thicker and more sugary; but before using, thin it out by adding 2½ teaspoons Thai seasoning sauce for every 1 tablespoon kecap manis.

FISH SAUCE

Finding fish sauce shouldn't be a problem in most supermarkets with an Asian section. I like the sharp saltiness of cheaper brands like Squid and Tiparos for basic salads and stir-fries, and the softer flavors of slightly more expensive brands like Three Crabs or Red Boat when I'm dealing with pristine raw seafood like prawn sashimi.

SHRIMP PASTE/DRIED SHRIMP

Chances are you're not going to grind, salt, and ferment shrimp to make your own shrimp paste (*gapi*) from scratch, so the smartest option is to buy a small tub—a little goes a long way—which you can dollop in when making curry paste and a few other dishes. If you can find Thai shrimp paste, that's preferred, but any Southeast Asian brand will work. Just make sure you don't buy shrimp paste in soybean oil, which is a different product. You want the uncut stuff, which is a thick gray-purple paste that smells very pungent. Look for Thai

or Vietnamese brands specifically. As for dried shrimp, for our purposes you can buy whichever size you prefer—the smaller ones are usually cheaper. They're common in most Asian markets, and you can occasionally find them at Latino markets as well.

COCONUT/PALM SUGAR

In Thailand, this type of brown sugar is made from the crystallized sap of palm trees. It usually comes in hardened discs that look like Mexican *piloncillo* or Caribbean jaggery. Though you can find palm sugar at almost any Asian market, you can also use coconut palm sugar found at most natural foods stores these days. They're essentially the same thing. As a somewhat general rule, I prefer coconut sugar for when I want a subtler molasses-y sweetness, like in sauces and curries, and palm sugar when I want a brighter, sharper sweetness in things like salads and stir-fries. If you do find the Thai palm sugar that comes in rock-hard discs, warm it up for about 20 seconds in the microwave first so that it is easier to work with.

COCONUT MILK/ COCONUT CREAM

Not to be confused with coconut water, you'll find this stuff in boxes or cans. *Always* buy the 100 percent pure unsweetened variety. You might see it labeled as coconut cream as well, which in Thai cooking means a thick "first pressing" of the coconut that's slightly richer and creamier. But for our purposes, both coconut milk and

coconut cream serve the same function. I like the brands Chaokoh and Mae Ploy, but a good rule of thumb is to pick out the coconut milk that has the highest fat content (avoid the "lite" stuff, which is thickened with additives). Sometimes the oils will separate inside the package, and often the fat will have congealed at the top, so before using coconut milk in cold recipes like salads, empty the container into a saucepan over low heat and stir until it has emulsified.

BIRD'S EYE CHILES

You'll find these in the fresh produce section of Asian markets. Thai bird's eye chiles (or "rat shit chiles," as they're called in Thai, because that's what they resemble) are small and intense. In fact, they're the most intense source of spiciness in this book. Anytime you see them used, you can always scale up or down to your heat tolerance. If you can't get ahold of

bird's eye chiles, substitute habanero—it's the closest chile I've found in terms of intensity and flavor (use 1 part habanero for every 3 parts bird's eye).

SAWTOOTH/RAU RAM/ THAI BASIL

Sawtooth (also known as sawtooth coriander, or culantro) and *rau ram* (also known as Vietnamese coriander) are two herbs that are important in various *larb* salads and other Northern Thai dishes. Choose them the way you would other fresh herbs, i.e., they shouldn't look too wilted or droopy. With sawtooth, you'll want to cut off the bottom two inches of the stems before using. For rau ram, use only the leaves and discard the rest. Thai basil looks just like regular basil, but with purple stems and a sweet licorice smell to it—use just the leaves.

If you can't find any of these herbs, the best option is to substitute

with an equal amount of other fresh herbs, such as cilantro, mint, or green onion.

GALANGAL

Galangal looks like a bigger version of ginger, but it has a much more complex and intense piney/citrusy flavor to it. Unlike regular ginger, it doesn't have a thick papery skin, so you don't have to peel it before using (though since we only use it finely minced, in a paste, or sliced into soups, this isn't much of an issue). Ideally you should look for the fresh kind, but it's sold frozen as well.

LEMONGRASS

You've probably seen these long stalks before, but here's the way to prepare them for use: Peel off the outer, dry layers until you see the bottom is a smooth, creamy, pale green color. Use just the white and very light colored part, about the bottom one-third of each stalk, or until the purple rings inside disappear when you're slicing. The upper portion beyond that will be too tough and fibrous to eat, though you can use it to flavor stocks and infusions.

DRIED CHILES

There are two categories of dried chiles in this book. The first is small hot ones. These are used to make chile powder, which is the other source of spiciness in this book, and for certain *nam priks* (see → 190). In Thailand most people use sun-dried bird's eye chiles (often labeled as dried Thai chiles), but if you can't find those, then dried *pulla* or *árbol* chiles work as well. The second type of dried chile is large mild ones, and in this application you have a little more leeway in choosing a variety. New Mexico or California chiles are the best bet, but other fleshy mildish chiles like guajillo or ancho will work too.

PICKLED MUSTARD GREENS/ MINCED SWEET RADISH/ MINCED SALTED PRESERVED CABBAGE/PICKLED GARLIC

You won't see these preserved ingredients in this book very often, but when called for they do add a certain salty or sweet tang that is necessary in certain stir-fries and curries. Rather than making them yourself and waiting for the pickling process to finish, I'd suggest finding them in an Asian supermarket or buying them online. Most come packed in jars or sealed in small plastic bags, and even a small container will last a long time. As

usual, Thai brands work best. Note: Since the pickled mustard greens are preserved in salty brine, make sure to rinse them thoroughly before using.

JASMINE RICE/STICKY RICE

You'll be using a lot of rice for this book. If you've eaten Thai food before, you'll probably know that rice provides the perfect canvas for soaking up spicy, sour, and pungent flavors as well as providing balance. I tend to not obsess over the particulars of rice too much, but it's important to use white rice. Although it pisses off the occasional health obsessive, we don't serve brown rice at Night + Market. The nuttiness and chewiness is too much of a presence and it doesn't absorb or balance flavor very well. There's only one dish in the book that I would suggest eating with brown rice (see if you can find it). If possible, use long-grain jasmine rice from Southeast Asia, which has a nice fluffy texture and a subtle fragrance to it. The best jasmine rice comes from Thailand, so if you can find Thai jasmine rice,

even better. Flip to the last chapter → 294 for instructions on how to make consistently solid steamed rice at home.

As for sticky rice, it's mostly served with dishes from the north and northeast of Thailand. Preparing sticky rice is its own process (don't worry, it's still easy) and is also detailed in the last chapter. At the store, look for stuff labeled glutinous rice or sweet rice. Thai glutinous rice is preferred since it tends to be a little longer grain, although you can also substitute sticky rice from other Southeast Asian countries if that's what is available.

KOSHER SALT

For this book, I use Diamond Crystal brand kosher salt as the standard for all recipes. If you're using Morton's brand kosher salt, which has a more concentrated saltiness, decrease the amount of salt called for by a third. At the restaurant I tend to salt my food pretty assertively, so if you're concerned about amounts you can always scale back and gradually adjust the salt level to your taste.

BUILDING (AND SEASONING) A THAI MEAL

One of the central tenets in Thai cooking, or any type of cooking, is balance. Balance is a word that gets thrown around so much, though, that it's lost much of its meaning—at least when people talk about food. In the Thai school of thought, there are two important types of culinary balance. First is the idea of balance in seasoning. This doesn't always mean the seasonings are always equal to each other, just that they are applied in the correct ratio. If you wonder why many Thai dishes have the similar interlocking sensations of spicy/salty/sour/sweet, it is that from the Thai perspective something can be strongly seasoned and still achieve balance. The linchpin of this process is tasting and adjusting as you season, which means dipping your finger in the pot every so often to see where things are before you splash in more fish sauce or lime juice as needed. In the case of this book, follow the recipes as they're written, and when you feel you've developed a reasonable amount of comfort with them, begin to tweak them to your own tastes. But it's also important to take this into account: A majority of Thai dishes are intended to be eaten with bland starchy rice, which means they might taste borderline overpowering when eaten on their own. So season assertively.

The second aspect of this idea is achieving balance within the meal. In the more traditional Thai sense, that means arranging a spread that might consist of a curry, a salad, grilled meats, and a chile dip; the different textures, temperatures, and flavors of these dishes balance one another throughout the meal. At Night + Market, we blow out that line of thinking in three ways: The first is to eat some Thai foods with other Thai foods that might not be customarily paired together (stir-fried noodles and crispy rice salad, for instance). The second is to combine traditional Thai foods with things that aren't Thai, or are Thai-adjacent (Northern-style *larb* with a scallop tostada). The third, and perhaps most urgent, aspect is a borderline insistence we have on consuming all these foods with a copious amount of thirst-quenching adult beverages.

Ultimately how you interpret these guidelines is up to you, but in the Night + Market universe, there are no wrong ways to enjoy this food. Do (and eat) what feels right to you.

BURN AFTER READING

I'd imagine that a good portion of people who have eaten at Night + Market associate our food with mouth-scorching, tear-jerking, blow-your-face-off levels of spiciness. This isn't completely untrue, but it's not the whole picture, either. Thai food is about harnessing strong flavors, and the intense heat that comes from chiles is just one element. Chiles are used to make certain dishes taste brighter and more vibrant, or to bring a kind of lightness to otherwise rich or heavy foods. They also might nudge you to reach for a cooling beverage more frequently, which is important in its own way. But not everything is meant to be incredibly spicy. In fact, dishes that are mild, or ever borderline bland, are just as essential in a Thai meal as ones that make you sweat (and I've found executing those blander dishes really well can be harder to accomplish than with the searing-hot ones).

All that said, each person will have their own definition of pleasure versus pain, and with spicy foods the line between them is often perilously thin. That is why the spiciest ingredients in this book (fresh bird's eye chiles and roasted chile powder) can always be adjusted to taste. If a recipe calls for both types of chiles and you want to mellow the heat, reduce the amount of fresh chiles first since they're slightly spicier. If you still find the dish too hot, cut back on the chile powder after that.

A BRIEF HISTORY OF TALÉSAI, OR HOW GRANDMA HELD IT DOWN

I didn't come out of the womb ready to cook blood soup.

Before there was Night + Market there was Talésai, the restaurant that my dad, Prakas, and my grandma, Vilai, opened on the Sunset Strip in 1982, the year I was born. My dad was working for a Thai bank at the time and he had the idea to open a restaurant where he could take clients for business dinners. At the time, the restaurants that served legit Thai food were located in Thai Town, and for the most part they functioned as cheap "ethnic food" spots in the eyes of non-Thai people. You didn't go there for the ambiance, in other words. My dad's concept was to elevate what a modern Thai restaurant could be—there were white tablecloths, there were wine pairings, there was contemporary Thai artwork on the walls. The waitresses wore black leather skirts, and the kitchen was using ingredients like filet mignon, fresh crab, and rack of lamb with Thai sauce. This was all happening at a time when Wolfgang Puck opened Spago and Susan Feniger and Mary Sue Milliken launched Border Grill—the new era of LA fine dining was still in its early years.

Back in the eighties, no one knew that people would be interested in upscale Thai food. It just wasn't out there. The only chefs doing "Asian fusion" were white guys who put lemongrass in their beurre blanc. But my dad's ethos was "build it and they will come," although for the first year or two, they didn't. Their stylish dining room was empty most nights. They stared across the Sunset Strip, a block away from clubs like The Rainbow Room and The Roxy, at this Scandinavian restaurant called Scandia known for its rich and famous clientele and wondered why those people weren't coming into their restaurant. Slowly though, it started to happen. By the early nineties it was *the* place to eat Thai food in LA—celebrities like Jack Nicholson, Mick Jagger, Axl Rose, Harrison Ford, Chuck Norris, Annie Lennox, Michael J. Fox, Kareem Abdul-Jabbar, Quincy Jones, and Sharon Stone all passed through the doors to taste my grandma's cooking, and there were various starred reviews in publications like the *LA Times* and *Los Angeles* magazine. Warren Beatty once had his car stolen outside the restaurant (he refused to use the valet service after that). Bob Dylan and Annie Lennox would listen to demo tapes in a back booth. Somewhere, there is a photo of me as a gawky preteen with a parted bowl cut posing with Brooke Shields.

Growing up as a restaurant brat, especially at a Thai restaurant, is an odd thing. You are immediately aware that your parents do something different from other parents. They work later hours, so you eat dinner later than the other kids; you spend time sleeping in the supply room, or fall asleep on the long drive home after the restaurant closes. And at some point I realized there was a gap between what we served at the restaurant and what the restaurant staff cooked for themselves when off duty or between shifts. There might be tiger prawns with garlic sauce, fried wonton "Bags of Gold," or steamed seafood "Hidden Treasures" between the hours of five and ten p.m.; but before or after, the kitchen would be filled with the strong smells of sour fish curry, shrimp paste rice, and fermented sausages. I remember my grandma once making *nam prik gapi* (Shrimp Paste Chile Dip → 197) with high-quality shrimp paste she had just brought back from Thailand. It was so stinky that when it came time for dinner service, the stench was still lingering around the dining room. My aunt yelled at her to put the stuff away or else the *farangs* (white people) would think there was a dead animal in the kitchen. At that age I didn't fully grasp and appreciate what my family was trying to accomplish with the restaurant—which was to showcase the upper echelons of Thai food culture in a modern, stylized way yet to be seen in America—but I understood through the food alone that when my grandma cooked for paying customers, she was aiming for something different than what we all normally ate.

At Talésai, it was my grandma who held it down in the kitchen. My grandmother started selling noodles when she was about nine years old. She likes to joke that she's an 85-year-old fourth grader, since that was the year she left school to work. This was in pre-industrialized Thailand, in a rural village, so although she never worked in an official restaurant, she had a never-ending list of side hustles in order to scrape together a living. One gig was shuttling diamonds between the capital and her hometown, a process where she'd sew the stones into the hem of

Despite our differences, when I talk about my grandma, I refer to her as my "true north" in the kitchen. While every chef probably credits their grandma in some way, I'm assuming that most of their grandmothers never won a James Beard award, never spoke at a culinary conference in Napa, and never cooked green curry pizzas with Wolfgang Puck. As a chef, my grandmother was efficient, she was resourceful, and she was incredibly gifted at making Thai food that was beautifully composed and awe inspiring. I can't say that all these traits translated directly to how I cook—I definitely lean toward flavors that are a little more crass—but as far as laying the groundwork for how to conduct yourself in the kitchen without acting like a fool, my grandmother is the reason I've been able to build up a solid foundation of skills.

This chapter is an ode to my grandmother's greatest hits—both the dishes she cooked in Thailand, the ones she created at Talésai, and the recipes of hers that I've adapted into my repertoire at the restaurant. More than that, it's a road map to some of the iconic dishes you'd find at every Thai-American restaurant in the country, streamlined and synthesized in our own Night + Market way. Are my versions the pinnacle of authenticity? Not really. Are they all made the exact way my grandmother made them? No. But if you want to school yourself in the fundamentals of Night + Market cooking, these recipes, which are straightforward and delicious, are the best place to start.

her pants in case bandits hijacked the bus she was riding. But the overarching theme of her life centered on food. She sold pork stir-fries out of her parents' shophouse when she was teenager. After she got married, she sold dim sum and fish curry as a street vendor in Southern Thailand while my grandpa studied to become a pharmacist. By the time the eighties rolled around, she and my grandpa were running a boarding-house in Bangkok. They got a call from their son living in America, and he invited her to come out to Los Angeles (for the first time ever) and help him run the restaurant he was opening. I'll take care of everything, he told her, and all you have to do is cook.

For my grandma, Talésai was a chance to showcase not only the Thai perspective she brought with her, but a chance to flex her creative muscle, honed and developed after cooking for

most of her life. She had never worked as a chef in a restaurant before, but the role was one that came to her naturally. The sensibility of her cooking, and much of the food she created for Talésai, veered more toward the refined royal court cuisine found in Central Thailand—even when she cooked for herself or her family, she leaned toward milder and more nuanced flavors. The food I ended up serving at Night + Market was very different from that, and maybe in some ways a direct reaction to it—spicier, brasher, more intense—but the more I developed as a chef and picked up knowledge, the more I respected how skillful she was, even if our personal tastes aren't exactly the same (she often describes my cooking as *meun nak*, which is a Thai phrase that means to have a heavy hand with seasoning, or she'll joke that I'm an alcoholic who cooks food for drunkards).

HOW TO
STIR-FRY WELL

I know it's just the first chapter and already I've told you to go buy lots of stuff to cram into your cupboard, but here's one more: Go buy a wok. In terms of essentials for the Thai kitchen (or any kitchen), nothing is more baseline than a wok, no matter how cheap or fancy or shiny or worn it is. If you already own a wok, then I can say with 95 percent certainty that whatever you have on hand will work fine. There's a sense of mystification and fetishization in many cookbooks that will lead you to believe you need to track down a carbon steel, hand-hammered, well-seasoned wok instilled with magic Oriental powers; but the reality is that at a fundamental level, a wok is a frying pan with sloped edges. That's it. Rather than the material it's made from, its power comes from its conical shape, which forces the food toward the middle of the pan over the hottest part of the flame. Does a wok that has made two thousand pad Thais have better "mojo"? It could, but most of that comes from the thick patina that has developed along the surface over years of use (which reminds me, don't use steel wool or scouring pads on your wok. Just wash it out with water and dry it thoroughly with a paper towel right after you're done cooking in it. If your wok is still wet when cooking, the hot oil will sizzle and splash up). Woks

are like wood-fired pizza ovens: Old broken-in ones are really cool, but no one ever complains about a place with a brand-new one.

The other reason a wok is appealing—beyond being the best sautéing vessel for anything from pasta to vegetables to meats—is that it makes deep-frying much easier. Because of the shape, you'll need less oil to achieve the same depth as in a Dutch oven, the oil will heat up faster, and there will be less splatter on your stovetop.

So which type should you buy if you don't own one? At the restaurant we use woks from a Thai restaurant supply store, which get beat up fairly quickly, and at home I use a pre-seasoned, flat-bottomed wok from Le Creuset that's significantly fancier. Both do their job, and the same can be said for the wok you buy on Amazon, or at a home goods store, or wherever else. I would advise buying one with a rounded bottom, since it will better allow you to toss and stir in one continuous movement as you slide your spatula along the bottom. If you go that route, you will also require a metal wok ring so it will sit flat on your stove (they cost a couple bucks). If you want to go above and beyond that, pick up a shovel-shaped metal wok spatula and a tool called a spider (a wire-mesh strainer). These aren't strictly necessary (you can use a regular spatula or strainer that you have on hand), but picking tools designed to be used with a wok is something to consider.

The point is: Don't let the pursuit of the perfect wok keep you up at night. If you handed Eric Clapton a crappy cheap guitar he could still play "Layla."

When it comes to wok technique, the key phrase is *tactile feedback*. How do the noodles look in the pan? How do they smell? Every stove and wok is different—that's even true in the three kitchens at the different locations of Night + Market—so the best way to figure it out is to make a few honest attempts at a dish, see how it turns out, then tweak from there. If you're dealing with a brand-new wok, I would recommend heating it over high heat for five minutes or so, then adding a cup of cooking oil and giving it a quick swirl. Once the oil starts to smoke, remove from the heat, pour out the oil, and wipe clean with a paper towel. Your wok is now seasoned and ready to stir-fry.

Another thing to remember: Since you're dealing with a pan that is ideally super-hot, whatever you toss in will cook quickly. For the home cook with a gas or electric range, you'll generally turn up your burner as high as possible (the industrial burners used at most Thai restaurants are like jet engines). Make sure to give your wok enough time to heat up, and just when you think it's hot enough, leave it a bit longer. It's hard to have a wok that's too hot when you're cooking at home. Once you've achieved maximum heat and added the oil, you'll need to be vigilant in flipping and tossing whatever you add with a sturdy spatula. Always keep the food moving. This helps ensure that

things cook evenly instead of sticking to the pan or burning.

This quick cooking action also means it's crucial to have all your ingredients prepped and laid out beforehand. To borrow a cooking school term, get your *mise en place* together. You'll be cooking things in a matter of two to three minutes and there won't be any time to fumble with mincing garlic or slicing chicken. When you first start cooking with a

wok, you're better off using slightly more oil (so the food is less likely to stick), which is basically like choking up on a baseball bat in Little League. At the pinnacle of wok technique, there are cooks in Bangkok who can flash-cook pad Thai with only a tiny splash of oil over a bed of glowing red coals. I am not on that level, and I don't think you should expect to be either, so consider your cooking oil as a friend rather than something to be

skimped on. It is also smart to have a container of water off to the side. This will help regulate the temperature if you feel things are cooking too fast, or if the moisture level in the wok looks too dry. Think of adding a spatula's worth of water as pumping the brakes.

The last thing you should know about stir-frying is that you are never done figuring it out. As much time as I've spent behind the wok station at Night + Market, I'm still mesmerized when I watch my grandma cook. She works from pure muscle memory, and even when she turns to talk with me about something completely unrelated, she'll be stirring and tossing with a level of calibration that is second nature. That said, we disagree over tiny little details that no two normal people would quibble over, if only because I have my own way I like to cook. In this chapter, I'll show you the way I think is right, but eventually you're going to develop your own reality and if that ends up with delicious pad Thai, *pad see ew*, or *grapow*, that's what matters most.

Wait, there is one more thing: Pretty much all the stir-fry recipes in this book are scaled to serve one or two (while most other recipes are intended to serve two to four). If you want to scale any of the stir-fries up, cook in batches rather than trying to fit a double portion of noodles into a wok. More food in the pan means less heat, thus you're less likely to get that searing action you're looking for. If your dinner guests are impatient, tell them to be quiet and thank you later.

PAD THAI

Serves 1 or 2

4 ounces dried rice stick noodles (⅛ to ⅓ inch wide)

2 tablespoons sugar

2 tablespoons fish sauce

2 tablespoons distilled white vinegar

3 tablespoons vegetable oil

¼ pound Brined Chicken thighs → 313, cut into bite-size slices (or extra-firm or pressed tofu or large peeled shrimp)

1 egg

1 cup bean sprouts

2 green onions, cut on an angle into 2-inch slices

2 tablespoons crushed Seasoned Fried Peanuts → 309 or roasted peanuts

1 teaspoon Roasted Chile Powder → 304, or to taste

1 lime wedge

Here are my pad Thai ground rules: Some chefs like to keep the toppings separate. I don't. I toss in the green onions and bean sprouts right after turning off the heat so they are incorporated but remain crunchy. The roasted chiles and crushed peanuts are arranged next to the noodles for easy mixing access, along with a lime wedge to squeeze on top. This arrangement makes it easier to scarf down a plate once it hits the table, which is the best way to eat pad Thai.

I like my sauce to be direct and sharp, which is why I use white sugar and white vinegar as opposed to the subtler (and harder to find) palm sugar and tamarind water. I never use fresh noodles, only dried rice stick noodles soaked beforehand because I find them more consistent. I don't use an abundance of meat—the noodles should be the focus—and I prefer the egg to be cooked through but still soft, so that it can incorporate into the noodles as a distinct ingredient rather than as a coating, like with pasta carbonara. On the opposite end of the spectrum, don't cook the egg too much early on, or by the time the noodles are finished, it will look like rubbery scrambled eggs from a bad hotel buffet.

If you time everything right (which might take a few tries to master), you'll end up with chewy, sauce-infused noodles, soft bits of egg, and crunchy bean sprouts and green onion. You'll never need another pad Thai recipe again.

1. Soak the noodles in warm water for 30 minutes, until pliable enough to bend around a finger. (If you're not using them immediately, you can drain the noodles and keep them in the fridge until ready to use.)

2. In a small bowl, stir together the sugar, fish sauce, and vinegar to make a sauce.

3. Heat an empty wok over high heat until it begins to smoke, then swirl in the oil. Once the oil is shimmering, add the chicken or tofu and stir-fry until the meat turns opaque but isn't fully cooked, which should take about a minute (less time for shrimp—they

recipe continues

will cook a little more quickly). Add the noodles and sauce, then continue to stir-fry, constantly stirring, until the noodles absorb the sauce, about another minute.

4. Use your spatula to push aside the noodles and leave them there, making an empty space in the center of the wok. Crack the egg into the empty space and let it cook until the edges start to set, 15 to 20 seconds. Use the edge of your spatula to break up and roughly scramble the egg, then toss it back in with the noodles while the egg is still soft. Once the egg looks mostly cooked, remove from the heat and throw in the bean sprouts and green onions, tossing thoroughly to combine. Transfer to a plate and garnish with the peanuts, chile powder, and lime wedge.

THE POWER OF PAD THAI

Everyone has a recipe for pad Thai. Literally everyone. The Internet is fraught with more recipes promising "quick and easy pad Thai" than wealthy Nigerian princes or hot and horny singles in your area waiting to chat. As expected, most of these recipes are dubious at best. Which begs the question: Why open this book with one of the most overexposed and bastardized Thai recipes ever? Because pad Thai is a beautiful thing that has been misunderstood, and I want to take it back.

I didn't always feel that way. When I first came up with the idea for Night + Market, pad Thai represented the stuff I wanted to rebel against. To me it signified everything that was boring, safe, and bland—the height of dumbed-down Americanized Thai food. Since I was a teenager, my first obsessions revolved around the more aggressive flavors of Thai food— nam prik, larb, and sour fermented sausages. I was like a cheese nerd fixated on the ripest Époisses or stinkiest blue cheese. The thrill for me was in the extremes.

But the truth that I learned after a few years at the wok station is that when you make a really great version of pad Thai, it is exciting in its own way. There's the soft chew of the noodles, the starchy richness, the slight char from the wok. It's a showcase of technique over ingredients.

Underneath all the cultural baggage heaped onto a single noodle dish, there is something straight-up addictive about it, which is why it's probably still the biggest seller at 90 percent of the Thai restaurants in this country. It's true that in Thailand the pad Thai is generally less sweet and more savory that what you find in America, but the gap isn't as wide (or clear-cut) as you may have been led to believe. Having eaten pad Thai a thousand different ways—from my grandma, from Bangkok market vendors, from Thai-American places in LA—I've triangulated it down to how I think it is best prepared, which is not to say the most authentic, but extremely delicious in a simple and direct way.

PAD SEE EW

Serves 1 or 2

Any chef will tell you: Working the wok station blows. You're standing over a hot burner with the BTU power of a furnace, sweating from the heat, with smoke and chile powder dust stinging your eyes. You look at your watch after what feels like an eternity and it's been ten minutes at most. Why do chefs put themselves through that level of misery? The answer to that is there no method that can substitute for what a superheated wok achieves, whether that be with meat, vegetables, rice, or noodles. The technique of wok cooking arrived in Thailand via Chinese immigrants, but in the centuries (or however long) since it arrived, Thai cooks have embraced it as a centerpiece of their kitchens. Everyone has a wok, and everyone knows, at least, how to make a half-decent stir-fry.

If you want to see the difference legit wok cooking can have, a good demonstration is with the classic takeout noodle dish *pad see ew*. In a standard noodle stir-fry, the noodles caramelize and char slightly from the starchy sugars in the noodle and the added sauce, but with pad see ew you pour in a little black soy sauce (a sweetened soy sauce, basically) at the end. The extra sugar in the sauce clings to the noodles and exaggerates that caramelizing and charring effect even further.

Thus, a benchmark for success with pad see ew is when it looks borderline burnt, with a charred flavor that's smoky but not bitter. It should not be gloopy or saucy. The entire reason cooks stand over screaming-hot woks, questioning their career choices, is that we are compelled by a higher power to banish sad wet noodles at any cost. Thankfully, making this at home is less painful than cooking it in a professional kitchen, although you still need your wok to be as hot as possible.

In Thai there's a word, *hom*, which means "fragrant or good smell," like the scent you would get if you were roasting sesame seeds. If you pull pad see ew off right, your kitchen should be filled with the hom of caramelized noodles and slightly singed oil. That is the smell of victory. Once the noodles are browned, add a shake of white pepper, which has a zesty, nose-twitching quality that is brighter than what you get from black pepper. Ground white pepper is a crucial finishing move to almost every stir-fry dish in this book.

1 jalapeño or serrano chile, diced

½ cup distilled white vinegar

3 tablespoons vegetable oil

¼ pound Brined Chicken thigh → 313, cut into bite-size slices

8 ounces fresh wide rice noodles (chow fun), separated into strands (see Note)

1½ teaspoons sugar

2 tablespoons Stir-Fry Sauce → 306

½ cup Chinese broccoli (*gai lan*) or broccoli rabe, stems sliced on an angle into 2-inch lengths, and leaves sliced into 2-inch pieces

1 egg

1 tablespoon black soy sauce

Ground white pepper

If you're unable to find fresh rice noodles (look in the refrigerated section of Asian grocery stores), the dried ones are a decent alternative. Soak them in warm water for 30 minutes, until pliable. If you do find fresh noodles but they seem hard and rubbery, you can soften them up by soaking them in warm water as well.

recipe continues

1. In a small bowl, combine the jalapeño and vinegar. Set aside.

2. Heat an empty wok over high heat until it begins to smoke, then swirl in the oil. Once the oil is shimmering, add the chicken and cook until opaque but not fully cooked, about 30 seconds.

3. Add the noodles and sugar (it helps keep the noodles from sticking) and toss to coat. Add the stir-fry sauce and Chinese broccoli, making sure to fold the noodles on top of the broccoli pieces to help them steam and soften. After the noodles have absorbed the sauce and the broccoli begins to look softened, about a minute or so, use your spatula to push the noodles aside and leave it there, forming an empty space in the center of the wok. Crack an egg into the empty space and let it cook until the edges start to set, 15 to 20 seconds. Use the edge of the spatula to break up and roughly scramble the egg, then toss it back in with the noodles while the egg is still soft.

4. Add the black soy sauce and toss to combine. Let the noodles sit over high heat for slightly longer than you feel comfortable—about a minute total—while quickly tossing every 20 seconds or so. This is where the hom sensation should develop. Once the noodles have developed a slight char, remove from the heat and add a few shakes of white pepper. Serve the jalapeño-vinegar mixture on the side.

LUCY

CHICKEN FRIED NOODLES
KUAY TIEW KHUA GAI

Serves 1 or 2

I prefer to describe *kuay tiew khua gai* as deliciously bland, or blandly delicious. Flavorwise, it's sort of the Thai equivalent of mashed potatoes—except not a side dish, and a million times more interesting in terms of texture. Whether it's gloopy potatoes or chewy seared noodles, though, humans are programmed to crave that certain combination of starch and salt. It's just how we're built. At Night + Market, people usually think of our food as being spicy, sour, or otherwise intense, and while that's often true, there are also dishes that are intended to be simple and comforting on the most elemental level. That's kuay tiew.

Also important: Kuay tiew is the best litmus test there is for how skilled you are at stir-frying, since much of its appeal derives from the wok-kissed texture of the noodles. The seasonings are minimal—a hit of salt from the pickled cabbage and a little sweetness from the preserved radish—so there are no bold sauces to hide behind. In the back alleys of Bangkok you'll find hawkers selling noodles like these cooked over coal-fired wok stations where the flames leap high into the air and the cooks wear masks and goggles to protect themselves from the furnace-like heat. You're handed this heavily seared noodles-egg-chicken-sometimes-seafood mixture that's deliberately bland in comparison to most stir-fries. While you probably won't be able to achieve that same level of heat at home, you can produce noodles that have been transformed under the intense heat of the wok, charred and seared until they become crisp-edged and chewy, slicked with the perfect amount of singed oil.

I usually serve these noodles with a dish of sambal on the side, which provides an optional chile kick that contrasts with the minimal seasoning. You'll also often see these noodles laid over strips of crunchy lettuce, which serves to add another textural contrast.

3 tablespoons vegetable oil

¼ pound Brined Chicken thigh → 313, cut into bite-size slices

¼ pound peeled and deveined large shrimp or baby octopus, thawed if frozen

½ teaspoon minced garlic

8 ounces fresh wide rice noodles (chow fun), separated into strands (see Note → 39)

1 tablespoon sugar

2½ teaspoons Thai seasoning sauce

1½ tablespoons minced sweet pickled yellow radish

2½ teaspoons minced salted preserved cabbage

1 egg

2 teaspoons fish sauce

Ground white pepper

2 green onions, cut on an angle into 2-inch slices

1 or 2 romaine lettuce leaves, cut into long, thin strips

1 tablespoon sambal oelek, for serving

recipe continues

1. Heat an empty wok over high heat until it begins to smoke, then swirl in the oil. Once the oil is shimmering, add the chicken, shrimp or octopus, and garlic and stir-fry until the protein is opaque and half-cooked, a minute or so. Add the noodles, sugar, and seasoning sauce and toss to coat. Once the sauce has been mostly absorbed, add the radish and salted cabbage and toss again.

2. Use your spatula to push aside the noodles and leave it there, forming an empty space in the center of the wok. Crack an egg into the empty space and let it cook until the edges start to set, 15 to 20 seconds. Use the edge of the spatula to break up and roughly scramble the egg, then toss it back in with the noodles while the egg is still soft. Once the egg looks mostly cooked, remove from the heat and add the fish sauce, a few shakes of white pepper, and the green onions. Toss thoroughly to combine. Serve over romaine lettuce strips with the sambal on the side.

JAY FAI, ANN; BANGKOK NOODLE VENDORS

DRUNKEN NOODLE PASTRAMI
PAD KEE MAO

Serves 1 or 2

I don't think anyone quite knows where the name for "drunken noodles" originated. *Pad* means "to stir-fry" and *kee mao* is a great Thai phrase that means "someone who is prone to drunkenness," i.e., your uncle who usually shows up to the family reunion three whiskeys deep. Are they called drunken noodles because they're meant to feed people stumbling out of bars at night, or because some Thai cooks add a glug of Chinese cooking wine? I'm not entirely sure.

What I do know is that we sell a ton of pad kee mao at Night + Market, especially to the late-night crowd. This dish is not as iconic as *pad see ew* or pad Thai, but it does have many of the aspects people love about Thai food: It's spicy, fragrant, and carb-heavy enough to function as a post-drinking meal. At the restaurant we sometimes toss the noodles with short rib that's been pressure-cooked with soy sauce and aromatics until tender, but if you have leftover steak or roast beef on hand, then by all means slice that up and throw it in the wok.

This version, though, is my favorite. It's the result of an experiment inspired by the kung pao pastrami Danny Bowien serves at Mission Chinese. It involves going to the nearest deli counter and having them slice the pastrami extra thick (¼ inch), then tossing it into the wok at home. Something about the combination of salty deli meats and drunken noodles makes perfect sense.

3 tablespoons vegetable oil

1 tablespoon Prik Tum → 308, or ½ teaspoon each minced fresh bird's eye chiles and garlic

¼ large red bell pepper, cut into strips

1 jalapeño pepper, seeded and cut into strips

8 ounces fresh wide rice noodles (chow fun), separated into strands (see Note → 39)

1 tablespoon sugar

2 tablespoons Stir-Fry Sauce → 306

6 ounces sliced pastrami (¼ inch thick), cut into 1 × 2-inch ribbons

Fish sauce

Handful of Thai basil leaves

Ground white pepper

Crispy Fried Egg → 244, for topping (optional)

1. Heat an empty wok over high heat until it begins to smoke, then swirl in the oil. Once the oil is shimmering, add the *prik tum* and stir until it becomes fragrant, just a few seconds. Add the bell pepper and jalapeño and stir-fry until slightly softened, 30 seconds or so. Then quickly add the rice noodles, sugar, and stir-fry sauce, tossing to coat evenly.

2. Once the noodles have absorbed most of the sauce, add the pastrami and toss again. Stir-fry until the meat is warmed through and the noodles have developed a slight char, then remove from the heat. Add a splash of fish sauce, the basil leaves, and a shake of white pepper and toss again to combine. Top with the fried egg, if desired.

GRAPOW CHICKEN

Serves 1 or 2

3 tablespoons vegetable oil

½ pound ground chicken (preferably with dark meat)

2 tablespoons Prik Tum → 308 or 1 teaspoon each minced fresh bird's eye chiles and garlic

1 teaspoon sugar

½ cup cut green beans (¼-inch pieces)

1 tablespoon Stir-Fry Sauce → 306

1 tablespoon fish sauce

½ cup loosely packed Thai basil leaves (or holy basil leaves, if available)

Ground white pepper

Serve with Steamed Jasmine Rice → 296 and a Crispy Fried Egg → 244, topped with Thai seasoning sauce (optional).

Grapow is the quintessential fill-you-up meal in Thailand. When I was in high school, I would eat bowlfuls of grapow at these restaurant stalls clustered around the main infantry bases for the Royal Thai Army in Bangkok. My uncle was a four-star general, so I would occasionally bum around the base to play tennis, since those were the only courts where I could play for free. The vendors would set up near the barracks to feed the soldiers, mainly with a handful of stir-fries that could be cooked quickly and cheaply. The most popular thing was grapow, a spicy stir-fry made from bits of meat and basil that could be topped with a crispy fried egg for a few baht more. As with other Thai dishes, there are a million ways to make grapow. I have found the most pleasure in what some might consider the low-rent version, made with ground chicken (or pork) instead of larger slices of meat. In Thailand you usually find it made with holy basil, another variety that has a flavor distinct from Thai basil, but I wouldn't lose much sleep over using Thai basil instead.

Since ground chicken is leaner than pork, try to find some with a higher fat content, or ideally some with dark meat and skin mixed in. Consider asking your butcher. Don't try to sub in 99 percent lean ground turkey—trust me, it will not come anywhere close to this version.

1.   Heat an empty wok over high heat until it begins to smoke, then swirl in the oil. Once the oil is shimmering, add the ground chicken and stir-fry until mostly cooked, around a minute or so. Add the *prik tum* and sugar, stirring to coat. Add the green beans and stir to coat, then add the stir-fry sauce and fish sauce and stir-fry for another minute. The chicken should be cooked, the green beans should still be crisp, and the grapow should look wet but not soupy.

2.   Remove from the heat, add the basil, a dash of white pepper, and toss to combine. Transfer to a plate, serve with a side of steamed jasmine rice, and top with a crispy fried egg. Spritz the fried egg with a bit of seasoning sauce if you're feeling decadent.

CASHEW CHICKEN

Serves 1 or 2

My grandma is half Chinese (her dad was from Chiu Chow and came on a boat to Bangkok when he was eighteen), which meant that a lot of the dishes that later became her specialties at Talésai reflected her knack for quick Chinese stir-fries. This one in particular might be the quickest and simplest, but it somehow ends up far more satisfying than the sum of its simple parts.

Thai-style cashew chicken is very different from the gravy-intensive stuff you'd find at, say, a Chinese-American restaurant, and in my opinion it's much better—it's lighter, sweeter, and fresher, and there's a good chance you already have what you need to make it in your fridge.

1. In a container big enough to hold the chicken, combine the teriyaki, thin soy sauce, and 3 tablespoons of the black soy sauce. Add the chicken and marinate at room temperature for 15 to 20 minutes, or until the chicken develops a light brown color. Drain off any excess sauce that hasn't been absorbed.

2. Heat an empty wok over high heat until it begins to smoke, then swirl in enough oil to come 1 inch or so up the sides. Once the oil is shimmering, add the cashews and stir-fry until golden brown and fragrant, 1 to 2 minutes. Drain the cashews on a paper towel. Pour all but 3 tablespoons of the oil into a heatproof container (and save for a later use). Swirl the reserved oil in the still-hot wok and heat over high heat until shimmering, then add the chicken and onion and stir-fry for a minute or so until the chicken is opaque and the onion is soft. Add the remaining 1 tablespoon black soy, the sugar, and the cashews and cook until a thick sauce forms, another minute or two. Add a dash of chile powder and the green onions, then remove from the heat. Toss to combine and serve immediately with steamed jasmine rice.

3 tablespoons teriyaki sauce

3 tablespoons thin soy sauce

4 tablespoons black soy sauce

½ pound boneless, skin-on chicken thighs (unbrined), cut into bite-size slices

Vegetable oil, for frying

⅓ cup raw cashews

⅓ cup thinly sliced (root to stem) white onion

1 tablespoon sugar

Roasted Chile Powder → 304

2 green onions, cut on an angle into 2-inch slices

Serve with Steamed Jasmine Rice → 296 and a Crispy Fried Egg → 244.

CURRIED CRAB

Serves 2

1 egg

¼ cup half-and-half

1½ teaspoons fish sauce

1½ teaspoons oyster sauce

1½ teaspoons Thai seasoning sauce

2 tablespoons plus 1 teaspoon mild Indian-style curry powder (see Note)

¼ cup vegetable oil

½ medium sweet white or yellow onion, thinly sliced (root to stem)

1 tablespoon sugar

½ pound canned or frozen jumbo lump crabmeat

1 green onion, cut on an angle into 2-inch slices

Ground white pepper

1 heaping cup loosely packed pea shoots or baby spinach

A few cilantro stems

If the curry powder has been sitting in the cupboard for a while, consider toasting it on medium-low heat in a dry pan until fragrant before using. This will help revive the flavor of the spices.

Serve with Steamed Jasmine Rice → 296.

When you order curried crab at a big Thai-Chinese seafood emporium in Bangkok, it arrives as a giant whole crab bathing in puddles of lumpy sauce spiked with Indian-influenced curry powder—it's a good example of the sort of mild, fragrant Thai food that my grandma loves to eat (it also speaks to the influence of South Asian spices on Thai cooking). It's delicious, but also a pain to consume: cracking the shells, digging out small bits of meat, staining your fingers with curry. The slightly more elegant solution I worked out was to prepare this same dish but with shelled crab. Even though it ends up a little less visually impressive, you get all the satisfaction of the original dish in a much easier format.

It's important to use high-quality jumbo lump crabmeat and some type of sweet white onion, like Maui or Walla Walla if you can—you're going for a creamy, sweet flavor rather than a barrage of heat. Adding the egg binds everything together and mimics the buttery richness of crab guts you'd find in a whole crab. There is a Thai word, *mun*, which means "slick" or "fatty," and in Thai you actually call the guts "crab fat." This is an easy way of concentrating all that decadent fatty goodness into a single plate.

1. In a small bowl, whisk together the egg, half-and-half, fish sauce, oyster sauce, seasoning sauce, and 2 tablespoons of the curry powder.

2. Heat an empty wok over high heat until it begins to smoke, then swirl in the oil. Once the oil is shimmering, add the white onion, sugar, and remaining 1 teaspoon curry powder and stir-fry until the onion is soft and translucent. Turn down the heat, add the egg mixture, and continue to stir vigorously until it resembles a soft custard, about a minute. Add the crabmeat and toss to warm and coat with sauce. Remove from the heat, add the green onion and a dash of white pepper, then toss to combine.

3. Spread the pea shoots onto a plate or wide bowl and top with the curried crab. Garnish with cilantro and serve with steamed jasmine rice.

CHOP SUEY EGGPLANT

Serves 2 to 4

When I was on a health kick in college I tried to pull off one of my grandma's stir-fries with steamed eggplant rather than fried. It was a terrible idea. The eggplant was limp and gross, like a *wah-wah* trombone version of what is intended to be a gloriously rich vegetable dish. Don't make my sad mistake. The lesson I learned was that the only way to achieve that beautiful tender texture you get from stir-fried eggplant at a Chinese restaurant is to deep-fry those suckers first. If you're using a wok, it doesn't create much extra work, but the difference in flavor is extraordinary. If you can find a jar of Thai yellow bean paste for this recipe, use that, but any brand of miso paste will work in a pinch. Just make sure you're using the long skinny Chinese or Japanese eggplants, rather than the fat Italian variety.

2 Chinese or Japanese eggplants

Vegetable oil, for deep-frying

1 jalapeño pepper, thinly sliced into strips

½ large red bell pepper, cut into strips

1 tablespoon Prik Tum → 308, or 1 teaspoon each minced fresh bird's eye chiles and garlic

1 teaspoon sugar

1 tablespoon Stir-Fry Sauce → 306

1 tablespoon Thai yellow bean sauce (or miso paste, if unavailable)

½ cup Thai basil leaves

Ground white pepper

Serve with Steamed Jasmine Rice → 296.

1. Halve the eggplants lengthwise, then slice them crosswise on an angle into 1½-inch lengths.

2. Pour enough oil into a wok to come halfway up the sides. Heat the oil over high heat until it reaches 350°F. (Throw in a grain of uncooked rice; if it pops up and starts sizzling right away, the oil is ready. Or use a thermometer.) Working in two batches, fry the eggplant chunks until soft and just golden, a minute or so per batch. Drain the eggplants on paper towels.

3. Reserving 1 tablespoon of the oil, pour the frying oil into a heatproof container (and save for a later use). Return the wok to high heat, then swirl in the reserved oil. Once the oil is shimmering, add the jalapeño and bell pepper and stir-fry until they begin to soften. Add the *prik tum* and eggplant and toss to coat.

4. Add the sugar, stir-fry sauce, and bean paste, then stir-fry until completely incorporated. Remove from the heat and add the basil and a dash of white pepper. Serve with steamed jasmine rice.

PRAKAS'S RIB EYE

Serves 2 to 4

2 tablespoons black
soy sauce

2 tablespoons Thai
seasoning sauce

Ground white pepper

1 (16-ounce) boneless
rib eye steak (about
1½ inches thick)

3 tablespoons plus
2 teaspoons olive oil

1 tablespoon minced garlic

½ teaspoon minced fresh
bird's eye chiles, or to taste

¾ cup halved
cherry tomatoes

½ teaspoon sugar

1 tablespoon Stir-Fry
Sauce → 306

½ cup loosely packed Thai
basil leaves

2 ounces Parmigiano-
Reggiano cheese

Serve with Steamed
Jasmine Rice → 296.

Unbeknownst to me at the time, my dad began to develop a progressive way of thinking about food in the nineties. He's always been the entrepreneur of our family, the outside-the-box thinker. He realized no Thai restaurants in Los Angeles were using ingredients that would be considered fancy or high-end, and like most ethnic restaurants, even now, people expected the food to be cheap, so dishes were made with cheap ingredients. Once Talésai started to become famous and attract a wealthier clientele, he experimented with things like jumbo lump crab and rib eye steak. He learned about the concept of umami at a food conference, and became obsessed with first-press olive oil and aged cheeses. While I was a kid watching *Titanic* in theaters five times, he was connecting the dots about the next big movement in food culture; to him that meant cherry-picking luxurious food ingredients from other parts of the world and mashing them together.

So for Prakas's Rib Eye—the pinnacle of his culinary ingenuity—you start with a well-marbled and preferably dry-aged steak, give it a good sear, then finish it in the wok with a glug of good olive oil. Some people say you aren't supposed to waste quality olive oil in a stir-fry, but my dad didn't subscribe to that line of reasoning. If you use the best, it must make it better.

It's important to sear the steak in a skillet or on a grill first. You won't get a beautiful caramelized crust if you just cut the rib eye up and throw it in the wok. The steak then gets the Thai treatment in the wok, stir-fried with garlic, bird's eye chiles, a dash of sugar, and stir-fry sauce. Once you've cooked the steak to the desired pinkness, transfer to a plate and shower with Thai basil and freshly grated Parmesan-Reggiano, a fragrant combination that makes the whole dish explode. Think of it as a middle finger to anyone who thinks Thai food is only made from poor-people ingredients.

recipe continues

1. In a shallow dish, combine the black soy and seasoning sauces and add a dash of white pepper. Toss the steak in the mixture, flipping a few times to coat. The glaze is mainly meant to help form a caramelized crust, so the steak doesn't need to soak longer than a few minutes.

2. In a heavy skillet, heat 2 teaspoons of the olive oil over high heat until the oil begins to shimmer. Remove the steak from the marinade and let the excess drip off, then sear it in the skillet for no more than 2 minutes on each side. You'll want a dark brown sear on the outside, with an interior that is still pretty raw. Remove from the pan and let the meat rest for 10 minutes. Once rested, cut the steak into ½-inch-thick strips across the grain.

3. Heat an empty wok over high heat until it begins to smoke, then swirl in the remaining 3 tablespoons olive oil. Once the oil is shimmering, add, in this order, the garlic, chiles, tomatoes, rib eye strips, sugar, and stir-fry sauce. Toss and stir-fry until the steak is medium-rare, or pink in the middle.

4. Remove from the heat, add the basil, and toss to mix. Transfer to a large plate or shallow bowl, shower with finely grated Parmigiano-Reggiano, and serve immediately.

CHOOSING A NAME

In 1979 my parents had just moved to LA. My dad worked for Thai Farmers Bank, a job where he'd meet with Thai clients and take them out around town. A few years later, he started to mull over the idea of opening a modern Thai restaurant, one he could take clients to. He wanted to feature artwork from contemporary Thai painters and cutlery crafted by Thai designers. He wanted food that presented Thai cooking as elegant and refined.

So my dad called my grandma in Thailand and convinced her to move to the US. He had visited her often and watched her hawk curry at the market. He thought, *Why waste her talent for five dollars a day? Wait until they try her cooking in the States!* Together with my mom (who was pregnant with me at the time), they scraped together all their money to purchase a space on the Sunset Strip, just down the street from Geffen Records. At some point, my dad met an Italian restaurant designer named Nini. I never met Nini, but I like to picture him as Giorgio Armani—leather blazer, unbuttoned collar, fluorescent white teeth, well tanned. Nini had designed several notable restaurants in LA, but never an Asian restaurant, so he agreed to work with my dad as a sort of personal artistic challenge. Of course, he charged a hefty fee. My mom and grandma thought my dad was being brainwashed by a slick con man. But Dad was resolute: If they wanted to be in the same league as places like Spago and appeal to "the blue eyes,"

they had to look the part.

My dad and Nini start discussing the restaurant's name. My dad tells him they'd been considering "Heart of Siam," the sort of name you'd expect a first-generation immigrant to come up with. Nini hands the retainer check back and says, if that's the name you want, I can't design this restaurant. I thought you were trying to do something different, he says, but that sounds like every other Thai restaurant in town. My dad says fair enough, what do you think would be a good name? So Nini starts asking my dad the Thai translation for random words. Ocean? *Talay.* Wind? *Lom.* Desert? Talésai. "Say it again!" says Nini. Talésai. "That's it! That's the name!" decides Nini. It rolls off the tongue and it will sound good when the hostess picks up the phone. My Dad is skeptical. Naming your restaurant "desert" seems like bad feng shui, given the connotation "barren." But Nini was adamant. So after a day or two, my dad decides to go with Talésai. He still has to convince my mom and grandma though, who are set on Heart of Siam (they already had a sign made), and who are now more than ever convinced that Nini is a snake oil salesman. Yet somehow my dad convinces them. Who are we really trying to attract? If David Geffen comes in, is he going to care about what the name means in Thai or will he see a hip modern restaurant with a catchy name?

A few years later, at the height of the Hollywood '80s, David Geffen had a standing reservation at Talésai. Did

he ever wonder what the name Talésai meant? I have no idea.

P.S. In the same way that my parents concerned themselves over the way their restaurant name sounded, I was obsessed with how the name of my restaurant would look. For the record, although it's written Night + Market, it's just pronounced "night market." When I was running an unknown and virtually empty restaurant in the early days, I was concerned that a neon sign with just two words wouldn't look like it signified anything specific. It would have as much meaning as a sign that read "Pawn Shop." So I conceived this visually attractive icon, I guess you could call it, which had the words stacked atop each other with a "+" symbol in between. Then that name stuck. The result was that after almost seven years a lot of people don't know how to say our name, which I realize is a quirk I may have overlooked at the time. I've heard it called "night and market," "night plus market," and, for those who are unwilling to commit either way, "night 'n' market" read really fast.

GOLDEN TRIANGLES

Serves 4 (makes 12 triangles)

Things that were ahead of their time: Nikola Tesla, *Twin Peaks*, Pets.com, and Golden Triangles. What were Golden Triangles? They were an appetizer served during the heyday of Talésai, one that was extremely popular at the time but never fully entered the Thai restaurant lexicon like I felt it should have. I've brought them back to Night + Market on special occasions, and the best I could do in describing them was as a seafood mortadella pancake, which was a weird visualization for most people. But trust me, they're delicious. Like most fried foods, this one pairs really well with beer, and the best way to serve it is with a sweet plum sauce for dipping and a handful of deep-fried leafy greens on top as a garnish. My grandma would chiffonade whatever greens she had on hand (you can use kale, collard greens, spinach, etc.) and toss them in the fryer until crispy, then sprinkle them over dishes like fried soft-shell crab. In this case, I think it adds a touch of class.

6 ounces pork fat, ground or diced into ¼-inch cubes

½ pound peeled and deveined large shrimp

½ cup Garlic-Cilantro Paste → 308

½ cup Thai seasoning sauce

1 tablespoon sugar

4 egg roll/spring roll wrappers (8-inch square), thawed if frozen

Vegetable oil, for deep-frying

Handful of roughly chopped kale, washed and well dried

Sweet 'n' Sour Sauce → 308, for dipping

1. In a food processor, combine the pork fat, shrimp, garlic-cilantro paste, seasoning sauce, and sugar and blend until the mixture becomes a thick, whipped paste.

2. Smear a ½-inch-thick layer of the paste onto half of a wrapper and fold it over diagonally, as if you were making a triangle-shaped quesadilla. Wipe away any excess paste spilling out from the edges, but don't worry about sealing the wrapper. Repeat with the rest of the filling and wrappers.

3. Pour 2 to 3 inches of oil into a wok or deep saucepan with several inches of clearance and heat over medium-high heat to 350°F. (Throw in a grain of uncooked rice; if it pops up and starts sizzling right away, the oil is ready. Or use a thermometer.) Working in batches of a few at a time to prevent crowding, fry the triangles until they're puffy and golden brown, flipping once, for 2 to 3 minutes. Drain on paper towels. Deep-fry a handful of kale for about a minute until it's crispy, then drain on paper towels.

4. Once cooled, cut each folded wrapper into three triangles, which is about the size you want to serve as canapés (you can cut them larger if preferred). Arrange the golden triangles on a plate and top with the crispy fried kale. Serve with sweet 'n' sour sauce for dipping.

THAI DIM SUM
KHANOM JEEB

Serves 4

1 pound ground pork

6 ounces peeled
and deveined large
shrimp, minced

½ pound crabmeat, small
lump or claw

1 cup very finely diced
(⅛ inch) jicama

1 egg, beaten

3 tablespoons Thai
seasoning sauce

2 tablespoons Garlic-
Cilantro Paste → 308

2½ teaspoons sugar

½ cup finely chopped
cilantro, with stems

Dash of ground white pepper

1 (12-ounce) package 4-inch
square wonton wrappers
(with yellowish dough),
thawed if frozen

Vegetable oil, for steaming

Cured salmon roe
(ikura; optional)

Thai Dim Sum Dipping
Sauce (recipe follows)

Chile Oil → 303, to taste

My dad was born in Trang, a city on the southern Thai coast that used to be known for its huge rubber plantations. My grandparents were living there because the Bayer Corporation was paying for my grandpa to attend pharmacy school (and sell their drugs), and my grandma, who was young and living in a part of the country she had never seen before, decided to make some extra money by selling food as a street vendor. One of the things my grandma would hawk was *khanom jeeb*, the Thai version of shumai dumplings—the typical breakfast in Trang was usually a cup of sweet, condensed milk–heavy coffee and an order of dumplings—and the way my grandma learned the recipe was by befriending another local street vendor whose tiny diner stall was famous for their dumplings. This later became one of the classic Talésai dishes, called "Thai dim sum." You don't have to eat them for breakfast, necessarily—I could eat a steamer basket's worth at any time of day—but if you have the inclination to go fancy at your next brunch party, consider topping each one with a spoonful of salmon roe for extra decadence.

1. In a large bowl, combine the pork, shrimp, crab, jicama, egg, seasoning sauce, garlic-cilantro paste, sugar, cilantro, and white pepper and mix with your hands until a filling forms. Pinch off a small bit and microwave until cooked, about 20 seconds. Taste and balance the mixture with more sugar or seasoning sauce as necessary.

2. Remove the wonton wrappers from the package and trim to form a rough circular shape.

3. Spoon about 2 tablespoons of the filling onto the center of each wonton wrapper and spread it out evenly with the spoon. It's better to overfill than underfill here, since you can scrape off any extra filling with a spoon. Then, using your non-dominant hand, place your thumb and forefinger together like you were making an OK sign, with your thumb and finger parallel to the ground. Nestle

recipe continues

Minéral +, Frantz Saumon, Loire, France

Like the name suggests, this Chenin Blanc has a lot going for it in the mineral department. But beyond that, it offers an enticing window into the wide world of Chenin. It has brightness and tension and although it tastes dry, it has sweet citrusy aromas that make it very approachable. If I could sum up this bottle in one word: generous.

the wonton wrapper in the center of the "O" part of the OK sign, and use your other hand to gently fold the wrapper upward, so the formed wonton starts to fit into the O formed by your hand. Once the edges of the wrapper bunch up at top of the wonton, use a small spoon to gently crimp the edges so they resemble the top of a drawstring pouch. You don't want the dumplings fully sealed; there should be a little filling visible on top, but not too much. Use the bowl of the spoon to flatten or remove some of the filling if it squeezes out over the wrapper. Repeat until all the dumplings are formed.

4. Set up a steamer rack in a pot with a few inches of water at the bottom and lacquer the rack with a generous layer of oil. Bring the water to a boil over high heat, then reduce to a simmer. Place as many dumplings on the steamer rack as can fit in a single layer, cover, and cook until the filling is cooked and the wrappers look tender and glossy, 10 to 15 minutes.

5. If you're feeling decadent, dollop each dumpling with a spoonful of salmon roe as you plate them. Serve with dipping sauce and chile oil.

THAI DIM SUM DIPPING SAUCE

Makes about ½ cup

¼ **cup black soy sauce**

2 **tablespoons Thai seasoning sauce**

¼ **cup distilled white vinegar**

In a small bowl, stir together the black soy, seasoning sauce, and vinegar.

CRISPY SPICY DUCK ROLLS

Serves 2 to 4

One milestone in becoming a legitimate chef is admitting when you'll never be able to make something better than what you can buy. I find roasted duck to be one of those things, so here's my advice: Go to your nearest Chinese BBQ restaurant and buy a duck. Even if you spend hours trying to make it at home, it's just never going to be as good as the one you can get from a specialist in Chinatown.

That said, taking time to make duck-filled spring rolls *is* worth your time. These were one of the truly iconic appetizers at Talésai, and they're the perfect thing to serve to a party of people hanging out in your living room. Another piece of advice: Don't be the sucker who eats the roll by itself and skips out on the roughage. If you want the full communal experience, lay out the lettuce and herbs with the dipping sauce and let your guests roll away.

1. For the duck rolls: Remove the breast from the duck, trying to keep it as intact as possible. Slice the breast into ¼-inch strips, skin-on. Pick off the rest of the duck meat with your hands, or however you can, cutting the meat into ¼-inch slices. Reserve 2 cups of the meat for this recipe, and eat the rest however you'd like.

2. Heat an empty wok over high heat until it begins to smoke, then swirl in the oil. Once the oil is shimmering, add the cabbage, mushrooms, and celery and cook until the cabbage wilts, 4 to 5 minutes. Remove from the heat and transfer the cabbage mixture to a sieve to drain, squeezing out as much liquid as possible. Transfer the cabbage mixture to a large bowl and toss with the seasoning sauce, sugar, and white pepper. Wipe or wash out the wok once cool, since you'll be using it to fry the rolls later.

3. Use a knife to trim 1 inch off two opposite corners of the stacked wrappers, and position them so that the pointy ends go north–south. With one of the pointed ends facing you, place ⅓ cup of the cabbage filling on the bottom third of the wrapper in a horizontal line, top with a few slices of duck meat, a few slices of bird's eye chile, and green onion, layered evenly. You want there to be

DUCK ROLLS:

½ Chinese-style BBQ roasted duck (see Note)

3 tablespoons vegetable oil, plus oil for deep-frying

4 cups shredded green cabbage

4 dried shiitake mushroom caps, reconstituted in warm water until soft and cut into thin slivers

½ cup thinly sliced celery, cut on an angle

3 tablespoons Thai seasoning sauce

1 tablespoon sugar

1½ teaspoons ground white pepper

8 egg roll/spring roll wrappers (8-inch square), thawed if frozen

4 to 6 fresh bird's eye chiles (to taste), thinly sliced on angle

½ cup thinly sliced green onion

1 egg white

DIPPING SAUCE:

⅓ cup black soy sauce

⅓ cup hoisin sauce

1½ teaspoons sambal oelek

1½ teaspoons toasted sesame seeds

recipe continues

enough filling to give you a plump spring roll, but not so much that it's hard to contain. Leave about a ¼-inch gap between the filling and the edges of the wrapper.

4. Starting from the pointed end closest to you, fold the wrapper over and tuck it in under the filling. Fold the cut edges inward over the filling, as you would when making a burrito. Then tightly roll the wrapper upward, like you would imagine rolling a cigar. Try to keep it tight. Once you near the top, brush the other pointed end with egg white and fold it downward against the roll like you are sealing an envelope.

5. Pour 3 to 4 inches of oil (deep enough to bathe the rolls) into the wok and heat over medium-high heat to 350°F. (Throw in a grain of uncooked rice; if it pops up and starts sizzling right away, the oil is ready. Or use a thermometer.) Working in batches of a few at a time so you don't crowd the pan, fry the rolls until golden brown, 3 to 5 minutes (use a skimmer or spatula to keep the rolls from bobbing above the surface). Drain on paper towels. Once they're cooled, use a serrated knife to slice each roll crosswise at an angle. Try using a sawing motion with your knife, rather than pressing down, to keep the crispy wrapper from shattering.

6. For the dipping sauce: In a bowl, combine the black soy and hoisin, then top with the sambal and sesame seeds.

7. Arrange the lettuce and herbs on a platter along with the dipping sauce. To assemble, wrap each roll inside a romaine leaf along with Thai basil and cilantro. Dip the assembled package into the sauce.

ASSEMBLY:

16 romaine lettuce hearts, bottom ends trimmed

Thai basil leaves

Cilantro sprigs

If your local Chinese deli sells roasted ducks in halves, one should provide more than enough meat for this recipe. Serve any leftover meat over Steamed Jasmine Rice → 296 with a side of Chile Relish → 79 and a splash of black soy sauce for a quick snack.

THOUGHTS ON NON-NERDY CURRY

One of my favorite places to dine in Bangkok is Nahm, run by the iconic Thai food god David Thompson (the restaurant was No. 37 on the San Pellegrino World's 50 Best Restaurants list in 2016). As a chef, David is a hero of mine who has spent his life perfecting and cataloguing the dying art of traditional Thai cooking, even going so far as to re-create recipes pulled from 100-year-old local Thai newspapers. He has a particular knack for creating jaw-dropping curries, especially ones that are nuanced, complex, and really, really time consuming. He pounds, toasts, fries, and blends every element of his curries in painstaking detail.

It's fair to say, though, that I don't think he would exactly approve of my curry methods.

As opposed to stir-fries—where the order of adding ingredients to the wok is crucial—my opinion is that you can create a fantastic curry by throwing everything a pot and just letting it simmer. I'm not here to make a food nerd out of you; I'm here to enrich your cooking life. I think you should be at a bar trying to get lucky on a Friday night, not stuck at home sweating over the stove.

So when it comes to the soul of any curry—the curry paste—you should acknowledge that making your own curry paste in a blender is a highly rewarding and relatively painless process. As opposed to creating a specific curry paste for each curry recipe (which is how most curry specialists do it in Thailand), I've done my best to simplify things by creating an All-Purpose Curry Paste → 303 that is meant to serve as a baseline. From there you can use it on its own, or tailor it to fit specific curries by blending in certain other ingredients.

But if you decide that making any curry paste, no matter how simple, doesn't fit your busy lifestyle, that's cool too. Just buy a jar of red curry paste from the store and use that as your baseline, increasing or decreasing the amount of curry paste called for in the recipe to taste (since the potency of premade curry pastes varies). You will still end up with something delicious. If you do go that route, however, try to find curry pastes with Thai writing on the package. The three Ms: Maesri, Mae Anong, and Mae Ploy are all brands that are solid. Avoid anything labeled "curry sauce." Also, since canned curry pastes can generally be saltier and spicier than the fresh kind, I suggest hacking your store-bought paste by blending in a teaspoon or two of lime zest and sliced lemongrass if possible, which will add brightness that mimics the fresh stuff.

In Thailand, most curry recipes call for a step called frying the paste, which involves stir-frying it in fatty coconut cream to unleash the paste's aromatic flavors. While that process has its merits, half of the reason Thai cooks do it is because of orthodoxy. I find that it's better to do that frying step (in vegetable oil) when you're first making the curry paste, since it gets it out of the way early and helps the paste last longer in the fridge. If you're using store-bought paste, stir-fry a 4-ounce can of curry paste in 2 tablespoons vegetable oil for a few minutes (until fragrant) before starting the curry.

PANANG BEEF CURRY

Serves 4

½ teaspoon coriander seeds

½ teaspoon cumin seeds

1 teaspoon grated key lime zest

2½ tablespoons All-Purpose Curry Paste → 303

1 (13½-ounce) can coconut milk

1 pound chuck steak or shoulder steak, sliced across the grain into ¼-inch-thick strips (see Note)

1½ tablespoons fish sauce

1 teaspoon coconut or palm sugar

1½ tablespoons chunky peanut butter

Kaffir lime leaves, deveined and slivered, for garnish

1 Fresno chile, seeded and cut into thin slivers

Serve with Steamed Jasmine Rice → 296 or Roti → 314 and Cucumber Salad → 181.

Fresh-toasted coriander and cumin seeds give panang its trademark aroma. When selecting beef for curry, look for cuts that aren't too lean or completely trimmed of fat and connective tissue, which help keep the meat tender as it simmers.

My grandmother's *panang* curry is a menu workhorse for good reason. Rich and fragrant, it's the ultimate gateway for people who are more accustomed to creamy Indian curries. At Night + Market, I've tweaked her recipe into my own, which for the most part involves me trying to make it more addictive, for lack of a better term. For example, we serve *panang en neua*, which is made with sinewy cuts of beef shank. The thick tendons break down to rich gelatin as they simmer in coconut milk. In general, chewier, tougher cuts tend to offer a beefier flavor, but also take longer to simmer. A happy compromise is to use hanger steak, which is commonly available and has a fair amount of sinew but won't take forever to braise. The other tweak is peanut butter—traditionally panang is made with crushed peanuts, but my secret is a scoop of crunchy peanut butter that adds another layer of lushness. At the restaurant, we serve panang with steamed jasmine rice or roti bread for dipping. You can make your own roti → 314, but you can also buy the frozen ones if you can find them.

1. In a dry skillet, toast the coriander and cumin seeds over low heat, stirring occasionally, for about 2 minutes or until fragrant. Transfer the seeds to a small coffee or spice grinder and grind to a fine powder. In a small bowl, combine the ground spices, lime zest, and curry paste and stir until completely incorporated. Set aside.

2. In a medium saucepan, heat the coconut milk over medium heat, stirring occasionally, until bubbling. Measure out 1 tablespoon of the milk and set aside. Stir in the steak, curry paste, fish sauce, coconut sugar, and 1½ cups water. Reduce the heat to a gentle simmer, cover, and cook, stirring occasionally, until the meat is tender, 1 to 1¼ hours. Add some water if the mixture becomes too thick—the consistency should resemble a light gravy. At the last minute, stir in the peanut butter and remove from the heat.

3. Pour the curry into individual bowls. Garnish each one with a dollop of the reserved coconut milk, the kaffir lime leaves, and the sliced chile. Serve with a side of jasmine rice or roti bread.

PORK AND MORNING GLORY CURRY
GAENG KHUA PAK BOONG

Serves 4

1½ (13½-ounce) cans coconut milk

2½ tablespoons All-Purpose Curry Paste → 303

2 tablespoons coconut or palm sugar

¾ pound pork shoulder, cut into 2 × ½-inch slices

4 cups ong choy (aka morning glory or water spinach), cut into 3-inch sections

⅓ cup julienned *grachai* (Thai wild ginger) or peeled and julienned regular ginger

3 tablespoons fish sauce

1 tablespoon ground turmeric or grated fresh turmeric

1½ teaspoons freshly cracked black peppercorns

Serve with Steamed Jasmine Rice → 296.

If you can't find *ong choy* (aka morning glory or water spinach) for this recipe, you can substitute watercress, bok choy, or whole stem spinach.

In theory, a Thai curry is something you'd eat as part of a spread, like with a simple egg omelet, or roti bread, or with something crunchy and sweet like the Banana Blossom Salad → 87. If you're feeling inspired, turning a pot of curry into the centerpiece of a larger meal will win you friends and admirers. There is an alternate theory, however, and it's one of which I'm a follower: Curry is a one-pot meal (two pots if you count the rice). If you were to base a meal around one curry in particular, I'd point you toward this one, *gaeng khua pak boong*, an all-purpose staple curry made with soft braised pork and crunchy water spinach. It's lush and velvety thanks to an ample amount of coconut milk, but balanced with a mellow, glowing heat that comes from curry paste and black peppercorns. It's a curry with broad appeal, especially for those who are relatively new to Thai curries, which is partly why it's become a perennial favorite at Night + Market. In this case start with a classic curry paste and jazz it up with a dose of ground turmeric, which will turn the pot a pleasant seventies-era goldenrod color.

1. In a large saucepan, heat the coconut milk over medium heat until bubbling. Add the curry paste and coconut sugar, stirring until dissolved. Add the pork, reduce the heat, and simmer until the meat is tender, 45 minutes to 1 hour.

2. Meanwhile, bring a large pot of water to a boil over high heat. Add the ong choy and blanch for 15 seconds. Set the blanched ong choy aside, reserving 1 cup of the hot water.

3. Once the pork is tender, add the reserved hot water, the ginger, fish sauce, turmeric, ong choy, and peppercorns. Return to a boil, then remove from the heat. Serve with jasmine rice.

FISH CURRY NOODLES
NAM YA

Serves 2 to 4

The other dish my grandmother would sell as a street vendor was *nam ya*, a fragrant fish curry served with bundles of fermented rice noodles called *khanom jin*. She would carry a big pot of curry like a backpack, and wear a satchel on her hip filled with noodles. The original version, as my grandmother would make it, involved chunks of salted and fermented Thai fish and Thai wild ginger, both of which lend a sort of medicinal funk that makes this dish appealing in a murky, swampy, deep-flavored way. Substituting canned anchovies and regular ginger produces a version that is cleaner and simpler, but just as compelling in the end. Since you'll probably have a hard time finding khanom jin as well, I'd suggest using rice vermicelli, although it's pretty good with spaghetti noodles too.

Nam ya uses more curry paste than most other curries. Combined with the brightness of ginger and the saltiness of the anchovies, the result is kind of like spicy puttanesca sauce without the tomatoes. Serve this curry with noodles and fresh crunchy stuff and you'll end up with something that resembles an elegant pasta as much as it does a rustic Thai curry.

½ cup All-Purpose Curry Paste → 303

½ cup sliced *grachai* (Thai wild ginger) or peeled and sliced regular ginger

6 ounces *pla raa* (Thai fermented fish) or anchovies packed in oil, drained and roughly chopped

½ pound skinless catfish fillets

2½ tablespoons fish sauce

1½ tablespoons sugar

Handful of Thai basil leaves

2 cups cooked rice vermicelli noodles (follow the package directions)

1 cup bean sprouts

1 cup shredded carrot

1 cup store-bought Chinese pickled mustard greens, rinsed and roughly chopped

1. In a blender, combine the curry paste and ginger and blend until pureed (add a bit of water if needed).

2. In a large pot, combine 2 quarts water, the ginger-curry paste, and the pla raa. Bring to a boil, then reduce the heat to medium and add the catfish. Simmer until reduced by a third, about 20 minutes. Remove from the heat and let cool slightly.

3. Transfer the curry to a blender or food processor and process briefly, until the fish breaks apart and thickens the curry. (You can also do this with an immersion blender.) Return the curry to the pot and season to taste with the fish sauce and sugar (the curry should be savory and herbal, with a tiny amount of sugar to balance the salty funk).

4. Portion the curry into bowls and garnish with basil leaves. Serve with noodles, bean sprouts, carrots, and pickled mustard greens.

JUNGLE CURRY CLAMS
GAENG PA HOI

Serves 2 to 4

Compared to curries that are usually tamed with coconut milk, the intense flavors of jungle curry (*gaeng pa*) are intended to be a direct punch in the mouth. It's a dose of chile heat, wild herbs, and strong spices, which is exactly what makes it addictive in an endorphin-rush, make-your-neck-hairs-go-prickly sort of way. The amount of oil used in jungle curry is heavier than most, which creates an oily/spicy/salty slick similar to what you find in Sichuan hot pots, although you can scale it back slightly if desired.

Jungle curry can technically be made with any protein—you'll find it with roughly chopped waterfowl, murky-water fish, or boar ribs, as the strong herbs and spices help offset the gamy flavors of wild meat—but when I serve it at Night + Market, I prefer it with shellfish. My best results have been with clams and mussels, with a small amount of ground pork cooked in the broth to add heft. You don't necessarily need rice to go with this curry, but I do recommend pairing it with a cooling beverage.

1. Heat an empty wok over high heat until it begins to smoke, then swirl in the oil. Once the oil is shimmering, add the bell pepper, garlic, chile, and ground pork and stir-fry until the pepper is slightly softened and the pork is opaque, about 1 minute. Add the curry paste, stir-fry for a few seconds until fragrant, and then add 2 cups water. Let the water come to a boil, then add the fish sauce, sugar, a dash of white pepper, and the clams. Cook until the clams begin to open, stirring frequently (discard any clams that won't open). Once the clams are fully opened, remove from the heat and add the ginger, peppercorns, and basil. Toss to combine, then transfer to a large serving bowl.

2. Serve with an empty bowl for the discarded shells.

⅓ cup vegetable oil

½ red bell pepper, cut into thin strips

1 tablespoon minced garlic

½ teaspoon minced fresh bird's eye chiles, or to taste

2 ounces ground pork or uncooked Northern-Style Herb Sausage → 162, casings removed

1½ tablespoons All-Purpose Curry Paste → 303

2 tablespoons fish sauce

2½ teaspoons sugar

Ground white pepper

2 pounds littleneck clams or mussels, scrubbed

⅓ cup julienned *grachai* (Thai wild ginger) or peeled and julienned regular ginger

1 tablespoon brined green peppercorns or dried pink peppercorns

⅓ cup loosely packed Thai basil leaves

FIVE-SPICE PORK HOCK
KAR MOO PARLOW

Serves 4

2 whole unsmoked pork hocks, skin-on

1 cup sugar

2 teaspoons Chinese five-spice powder

¾ cup Thai seasoning sauce

½ cup black soy sauce

2 heaping tablespoons Garlic-Cilantro Paste → 308

4 soft-boiled eggs, shells removed

½ cup store-bought Chinese pickled mustard greens, rinsed and roughly chopped

Handful of cilantro sprigs, with stems (optional)

Serve with Steamed Jasmine Rice → 296 and Chile Relish (recipe follows).

Few things make me think of my grandma's cooking as much as sweet braised pork hock (*kar moo parlow*) does. It's a classic Thai-Chinese dish that functioned in my extended family as the Sunday potluck centerpiece. If there was a party going on, you could count on sweet-sticky pork hock and rice. Think of it as the most tender and decadent pot roast with the enchanting aroma of caramelized sugar and Chinese five-spice.

The first step is getting your hands on some skin-on pork hocks (pork shanks, a slightly meatier cut that also comes the front leg of the pig, will work too). Make sure they're the non-smoked kind—your butcher can probably help you out. These have the right balance of fat and cartilage to ensure a soft, melting hunk of meat at the end of the braise.

The next step is to char the outer skin over a stove burner. The charring gives the pork a slight smoky flavor and helps the syrup absorb into the skin. If you burn it a bit too much, just scrape off the blackened bits with a spoon as if you were scraping off the burnt layer on a piece of toast. I'd recommend doing the scraping under a running faucet to make the cleanup easier. Once you've climbed that hurdle, your main goal is ensuring the braising liquid doesn't become too thick while the pork is cooking, so keep the heat low and add water if the sauce level dips more than halfway below the pork hocks.

Once the meat is cooked, you can present it in a large casserole dish. Have everyone spoon it over steamed jasmine rice and serve with fresh herbs and a simple chile relish on the side to help lighten the richness. Don't be afraid of leftovers either: The sweet, deep flavors of this dish are only enhanced by a night in the fridge.

1. Turn a stove burner to high heat. Place the pork hocks on top of the burner grate and rotate the hocks with a pair of tongs to evenly char all sides, until the skin turns a very dark shade of brown. There will be smoke, so turn your oven fan to high. If the skin becomes too burnt (black), place the hocks under cold running

recipe continues

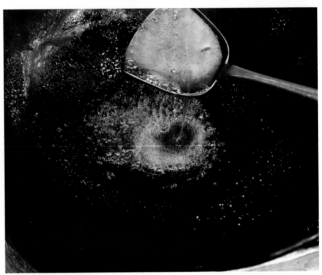

water and scrape off the blackened skin with a spoon. Try to scrape off only the outer burnt layer, not the skin underneath.

2. In a large, heavy-bottomed pot, heat the sugar over medium heat, stirring until the sugar begins to caramelize and turn golden. Then carefully add 1 cup water (it may sputter) and the five-spice powder. Stirring occasionally, let the mixture reduce to a thick syrup with a yellow-caramel color. Add the pork hocks, turn to coat, then cook for 5 minutes so the syrup can fuse with the skin. If the syrup becomes too thick to stir easily, add water as needed.

3. Add the seasoning sauce, black soy sauce, garlic-cilantro paste, and enough water to cover the pork hocks halfway. Increase the heat and bring the mixture to a boil. Reduce the heat to a simmer. Loosely cover and simmer until the skin is jiggly and the meat starts to come away from the bone, 1½ to 2 hours. Turn the hocks 3 or 4 times while cooking, and if the liquid level drops past halfway, add more water.

4. When the pork is nearly cooked, add the soft-boiled eggs and mustard greens and continue to simmer on low for another 10 minutes, uncovered. The liquid should reduce down to the consistency of brown gravy—thicker than a broth, but not quite a syrup.

5. Serve the pork hocks, greens, and eggs covered with the sauce until partially submerged. Top with cilantro sprigs. Serve with steamed jasmine rice and spicy chile relish on the side.

CHILE RELISH

Makes about ½ cup

2 tablespoons minced garlic

2 tablespoons minced fresh bird's eye chiles, or to taste

1 tablespoon distilled white vinegar

1 teaspoon sugar

½ teaspoon kosher salt (see → 26)

In a small bowl, stir together the garlic, chile, vinegar, sugar, and salt.

La Pause, Laurent Saillard, Loire, France

Gamay is one of my all-around, go-to wines. I tend to think of Gamay as clean and bright, or wild and earthy-funky. Laurent Saillard's Gamay is definitely in the former camp—it's pure juicy fruit—but it has just enough unruliness to keep it interesting. It's light and nimble, and I often describe it as minimalist in all the right ways. The coolest things about wines like these is how much each producer and bottle can vary—although they're essentially using the same grapes and the same basic methods, environmental differences like ambient yeast have a huge impact on the final product. That's what gives these wines their particular sense of place.

LEMONGRASS HOT AND SOUR SOUPS

The first time I ever met Andy Ricker, he wanted soup. It was a few years ago, and the founder of Portland's Pok Pok and I had signed on for a collaborative dinner that Singha Beer had sponsored for Songkran (Thai New Year). The idea was for him to fly down to Night + Market and cook a rough menu we had mapped out via e-mail, then fly back up to Portland. The dinner event felt like a blind date. I had no idea if hosting the most acclaimed Thai chef in America at my restaurant was a brilliant idea or a terrible one. I had no idea if we'd bond over our love of *khao soi* and *nam prik*, or if it would just be . . . awkward. But when he showed up at the restaurant the night before the dinner, it was almost closing time and he looked weary after what I imagine was a long day of travel. I was ready to fire the whole menu and roll out the red carpet, but all he asked for was a bowl of *tom khar*—chicken soup—and maybe a beer, I think. After that night we became fast friends, and I've since referred to him as my white Thai brother, a guy who is as in love with, and dedicated to, Thai cooking as anyone I've ever met.

But back to soup: In Thailand—as with pretty much everywhere in the world—chicken soup is synonymous with the comforts of home, or the healing power of a mother's love, etc. A good tom khar can bring you back to life, as anyone who has used Thai takeout to sweat out a cold can tell you. There's not only the soothing effect that any chicken soup has, but also the herbal aromas of galangal, lemongrass, and kaffir lime, the richness of coconut milk, and the brightness of lime and cilantro. At the restaurant we make our chicken or shrimp stock with scraps and then season it with bouillon cubes for extra oomph. The soups come in large flaming tureens for the table, usually at the start or end of the meal, but assuming you don't have those in your cupboard, it's best to serve yours in communal pots for guests to ladle out themselves. Following are two essential soup recipes— twin pillars of the Thai-American soup game—that can easily be scaled up to feed a crowd or create an oil drum's worth of leftovers. One is for *tom khar gai*, the classic aromatic chicken soup, and the other is for *tom yum goong*, a proto-variation made with coconut milk and shrimp.

COCONUT LEMONGRASS CHICKEN HOT AND SOUR SOUP
TOM KHAR GAI

Serves 4

1 stalk lemongrass, dry outer leaves removed and root trimmed

3 cups chicken broth

4 kaffir lime leaves, torn

1-inch piece of galangal, cut into thin coins

2 chicken bouillon cubes

2 (13½-ounce) cans coconut milk

1½ tablespoons sugar

1½ tablespoons fish sauce

1 cup fresh oyster mushrooms, torn into large pieces

¾ pound Brined Chicken thighs → 313, cut into bite-size slices

4 tablespoons Chile Jam → 304

2 teaspoons Chile Oil → 303, or to taste

2 teaspoons minced fresh bird's eye chiles, or to taste

4 tablespoons lime juice

1 cup thinly sliced green onion

1 cup roughly chopped cilantro, with stems

1. Cut the tips off the lemongrass, leaving about three-fourths of the stalk remaining. Wrap it in a paper towel and pound it with a heavy object to bruise, then slice the entire stalk crosswise at an angle into 2-inch lengths.

2. In a large saucepan, bring 3 cups water and the chicken broth to a boil. Add the lemongrass, lime leaves, galangal, and bouillon cubes, stirring until dissolved. Reduce the heat and simmer for 15 minutes.

3. Stir in the coconut milk, sugar, fish sauce, mushrooms, and chicken and bring to a boil over medium-high heat, then reduce the heat to a simmer. Cook until the mushrooms are soft and the chicken is cooked, 3 to 4 minutes. Remove from the heat.

4. Transfer to a large serving vessel with a ladle. Even though they're not eaten, we leave in the lemongrass, galangal, and lime leaves at the restaurant. You can strain them out before serving, if desired.

5. Into each of four individual bowls, portion out 1 tablespoon chile jam, ½ teaspoon chile oil, ½ teaspoon minced chile, and 1 tablespoon lime juice. Have guests ladle the soup into their bowls and garnish with some green onion and cilantro. Stir to combine and consume immediately.

SHRIMP HOT AND SOUR SOUP
TOM YUM GOONG

Serves 4

1. Cut the tips off the lemongrass, leaving about three-fourths of the stalk remaining. Wrap it in a paper towel and pound it with a heavy object to bruise, then slice the entire stalk crosswise at an angle into 2-inch lengths.

2. Peel the shrimp, reserve the heads, and discard the shells. In a large saucepan, bring 2 quarts water to a boil. Add the shrimp heads, lemongrass, galangal, lime leaves, and bouillon cubes, stirring until dissolved. Reduce the heat and simmer for 15 minutes.

3. Remove the shrimp heads and discard, then add the sugar and fish sauce and bring to a boil over medium-high heat. Add the mushrooms and cook for about a minute, then add the shrimp and cook until they turn opaque, about 2 minutes. Remove from the heat.

4. Transfer to a large serving vessel with a ladle. Even though they're not eaten, we leave in the lemongrass, galangal, and lime leaves at the restaurant. You can strain them out before serving, if desired.

5. Into each of four individual bowls, portion out 1 tablespoon chile jam, ½ teaspoon chile oil, ½ teaspoon minced chile, and 1 tablespoon lime juice. Have guests ladle soup into their bowls and garnish with some green onion and cilantro. Stir to combine and consume immediately.

1 stalk lemongrass, dry outer leaves removed and root trimmed

12 head-on, shell-on large shrimp

1-inch piece of galangal, cut into thin coins

4 kaffir lime leaves, torn

2 chicken bouillon cubes

1 tablespoon sugar

2 tablespoons fish sauce

1 cup fresh oyster mushrooms, torn into large pieces

4 tablespoons Chile Jam → 304

½ teaspoon Chile Oil → 303, or to taste

2 teaspoons minced fresh bird's eye chiles, or to taste

4 tablespoons lime juice

1 cup thinly sliced green onion

1 cup roughly chopped cilantro, with stems

GREEN PAPAYA SALAD
SOM TUM

Serves 2 to 4

5 tablespoons fish sauce

5 tablespoons coconut or palm sugar

4 garlic cloves, peeled but kept whole

3 fresh bird's eye chiles, or to taste, stemmed

16 green beans, cut into 3-inch lengths

½ cup shredded carrot

3 cups shredded green papaya (about one-third of a 1½-pound papaya)

3 tablespoons lime juice

½ cup Seasoned Fried Peanuts → 309

4 small Roma (plum) tomatoes, cut into wedges

Serve with Sticky Rice → 296–299.

POTENTIAL PAPAYA SALAD BOOSTERS:

Avocado chunks

Crushed pork rinds

Sliced boiled eggs

Corn kernels

Dried shrimp

Shredded beef jerky

If Thai food were laid out as one of those nutritional pyramids they showed you in health class, green papaya salad would be at the bottom, right above rice. In other words: It is fundamental. You can eat it by itself, or with rolled-up balls of sticky rice, or with barbecued meats like they do in the Isaan region of Thailand. As with fried rice → 205, it's an infinitely riffable blank slate, and almost every cook in every region has a way to customize it. You can trick out *som tum* with fermented fish sauce, raw blue crabs, salted rice paddy crabs, waterbugs, hog plums, and a wide array of other Thai ingredients (see a few suggestions you probably have on hand below). But all those things start with the essential balancing act of lime, sugar, fish sauce, and chiles that make som tum what it is.

Ideally, you'll want a mortar and pestle when you make papaya salad. Find a lightweight version made out of clay or plastic—the heavy-duty granite versions are used for curry pastes. Much like sushi chefs or bartenders who slap herbs before serving them, your goal should be to bruise the ingredients to release their essence without destroying them in the process.

If for some reason you're unable to get hold of a mortar and pestle, you will still be able to make a killer papaya salad. You'll build the dressing in a food processor or blender first, then transfer it to a large bowl where you'll do the "bruising" part.

1. In a saucepan, combine the fish sauce and coconut sugar and cook over low heat, stirring, until the sugar is melted and the sauce begins to thicken slightly. Remove from the heat and let the fish sauce syrup cool.

MORTAR AND PESTLE METHOD:

1. Before you start throwing things in the mortar, arrange your *mise en place* in this order: garlic, chiles, green beans, carrot, green papaya, fish sauce syrup, lime juice, peanuts, and tomatoes. Hold the pestle in your dominant hand and a spoon in the other. Rather than pounding straight down, you're going to push the pestle down the sides of the mortar.

recipe continues

2.   Throw in the garlic and pound until it becomes a rough, pulpy mash. Add the chiles—pound them heavily if you prefer it spicy, or gently if you want it less spicy. Add the green beans, carrots, and green papaya, bruising lightly with the pestle and mixing with the spoon for about 10 seconds between each addition. Add the lime juice and fish sauce syrup, pound, and mix for another 10 seconds. Add the peanuts and tomatoes and repeat. Everything in the mortar other than the chiles and garlic should be bruised but intact. Don't overpound. If you want to mix a handful of other ingredients → 84 you can stir them in at this point, adjusting the seasoning as needed.

BOWL METHOD:

1.   Combine the fish sauce syrup, lime juice, garlic, and chiles in a blender or food processor and blend until the garlic and chiles are totally pulverized. This is your som tum dressing and it can be refrigerated until you're ready to make the salad.

2.   In a mixing bowl, combine the papaya, carrots, and dressing. Using your hands, stir, mix, and squeeze the shredded salad to infuse the dressing and mimic the bruising of the mortar and pestle. Lightly crush the peanuts and toss in, along with the tomatoes.

3.   Transfer the salad to a plate and serve with sticky rice.

THE SEARCH FOR GREEN PAPAYA (AND WHEN TO CALL IT OFF)
When picking out a green (unripe) papaya, you'll want to find one that sounds like knocking on a wooden table. It should be rock hard and not give at all. Most are between 1 and 2 pounds, and you can usually find them in the produce section of Asian markets (where they'll be marketed specifically as green papaya). Sometimes at markets like Whole Foods, you might come upon unripe smaller papayas (the ones you normally eat ripe), which you can use, as long as they're not soft or yellowish—they should be rock hard. Occasionally you might even come upon pre-shredded green papaya, which will save you some time. If you do get the whole one, peel the skin like you would a potato. Halve it, scoop out the seeds, quarter it, then use a mandoline or vegetable spiralizer to shave off long, narrow ribbons— about the dimensions of linguine. You can also sometimes find nifty hand shredders specifically meant for green papaya at Asian markets. When you're grating, don't act like a wood chipper; take it soft and slow. You don't want shards; you want long strands. If you're unable to find green papaya, don't worry too much. The basic appeal of this recipe is less the papaya and more the dressing, so feel free to experiment with shredded green cabbage, shaved radish, peeled cucumber, or unpeeled green apple (soak the latter in water and a little lime juice after julienning so it doesn't turn brown). Or leave out the green papaya part altogether and increase the amounts of green beans, tomatoes, and carrots.

BANANA BLOSSOM SALAD
YUM HUA PLEE

Serves 4

This salad can be traced back to Thailand's old capital, Ayutthaya, just north of Bangkok. Unlike *som tum*, it's not meant to be spicy—the flavors tend toward creamy and sweet. In and of themselves, banana blossoms aren't crazy flavorful (they fall somewhere between jicama and endive, the latter of which works well as a substitute) but have a brilliant crunch and a slight bitterness that make them an ideal vehicle for this salad's sweet and pungent dressing. I differ a bit in how I make it versus how my grandma makes it—I toast the shredded coconut until it's amber-colored and drizzle on coconut milk before serving to turn up the addictiveness factor—but the result is mostly the same: crunchy, sweet, tangy, and crowd-pleasing, like a vastly brighter and more flavorful version of coleslaw. If you're planning out a full meal, eat this as a precursor to a spicy curry dish; the crunch and sweetness acts as a nice contrast.

1. In a small dry saucepan, toast the coconut over medium-high heat, stirring occasionally, until golden brown, about 4 minutes. Remove from the pan and set aside.

2. In the same saucepan, combine the coconut sugar and fish sauce and stir over low heat until dissolved. Remove from the heat and stir in the garlic and minced chile, then set the dressing aside to cool.

3. Cut and peel the tough exterior of the banana blossoms until you get to the soft white core (think of it like a big artichoke). Cut ½ to 1 inch off the bottom stump and halve the blossom lengthwise. Lay each half on a cutting board and slice into ⅛-inch-wide slivers; you should have about 2½ cups sliced. (If you're using endive, skip the peeling part but otherwise cut them in the same way.) Submerge the sliced blossoms or endive in cold water along with 2 teaspoons of the lime juice to keep from browning while you assemble the salad. Massage the banana blossoms with your hands to remove any residual stickiness.

1½ cups sweetened shredded coconut

2 tablespoons coconut or palm sugar

½ cup fish sauce

2 teaspoons minced garlic

1 teaspoon minced fresh bird's eye chiles, or to taste

2 banana blossoms, or 6 small red endives

¼ cup plus 2 teaspoons lime juice

2 tablespoons Chile Jam → 304

2 cups thinly sliced (root to stem) red onion or shallot

8 large poached shrimp, peeled and deveined and halved lengthwise

1½ cups roughly chopped cilantro, with stems

¾ cup Seasoned Fried Peanuts → 309

⅓ cup coconut milk

You can also make this salad vegan by leaving out the shrimp and replacing the fish sauce with thin soy sauce.

recipe continues

4. In a large bowl, stir together the chile jam and dressing until combined. Add the red onion and well-drained banana blossoms or endive and toss to coat. Add the shrimp, cilantro, toasted coconut, peanuts, and the remaining lime juice. Toss again until combined. Transfer to a plate and drizzle with the coconut milk before serving.

We are cruising up a winding two-lane highway that stretches from Chiang Mai to Chiang Rai in a rented hatchback. As we pass the steep hillsides covered in dense green forest, my wife, Sarah, sits shotgun, using her phone to navigate despite the agonizingly slow cell service. We might be hunting for a good *khao soi* spot that someone's second cousin recommended, or maybe we're seeking out a *larb* shack that a security guard at our hotel tipped us off to. The itinerary for each travel day is loose at best. The two weeks or so I spend in Thailand each year are less about intensive research and more about wandering around, an ambling collection of visits to relatives and long conversations about cooking, eating, and other things that the older generation expects the younger generations not to care about.

In culinary terms, each trip puts me in a new headspace. I've been comfortable cooking the regional Thai food I grew up with and, in some cases, took for granted. Now when I travel, it's as an observant chef, breaking down the permutations of overlooked dishes, figuring out how I can hone my skills and tuck away that insight for later. I've visited Thailand every year since I was three years old and spent a large portion of my teenage years going to school in Bangkok, but there is still a sense of cognitive dissonance when I arrive. I am home, but I'm still a tourist.

This chapter is meant to illuminate the Night + Market dishes that can be traced back to a particular place—the ones that are inspired by, or are a

tribute to, three parts of Thailand that have the most influence over the type of food we serve. There's the spicy-sour-pungent cooking that dominates the rural countryside of Isaan, like grilled pork salad and marinated prawns. Then there's the fragrant, earthy, and more nuanced cooking found on the mountainous northern border, close to where my family lives in the town of Mae Chan. Finally, there's Bangkok, a sweltering and hectic megacity that has some of the greatest street food in the world and a strangely fascinating mixture of Western and international influences.

These dishes aren't always exact copies of what you'd find in those specific places, but that's kind of the point. For me, it's about capturing the sensibility and translating it into the context of Los Angeles, having it make sense even if you hadn't traveled to the point of origin. If I can pull that off, then all those hours spent driving the back roads were worth it.

AN ISAAN STATE OF MIND

There's a good chance you've heard of Isaan, the northeastern region of Thailand tucked up against the border with Laos. Its cuisine has something of a cult following, but the region itself is the poorest and, until recently, the most isolated part of Thailand. It's intensely rural, a vast, flat expanse of lush green fields cut by murky rivers. In the dry season it gets baked by the harsh sun,

and in the wet season it's drenched by monsoons—imagine the Everglades, but with rice paddies. The food of Isaan, which might be its biggest cultural export, is what you could label "peasant cooking" in the most affectionate terms: aggressively seasoned with searing-hot chiles, tart limes, and a swampy, chunkier variety of fish sauce called *pla raa*. The strong seasonings help stretch a meager portion of protein to flavor a larger portion of sticky rice, which is the most filling part of the meal.

Even before I set foot in Isaan, I was obsessed with the food. It started in Bangkok, where my parents and I moved when I was a preteen so that I could attend a private school for international students. A year earlier, my dad, burned out by the restaurant business, had moved back from LA to Thailand to work with my uncle. The move was temporary, but that didn't mean it was any easier for my mom— she had to look after me (the only child) and manage the restaurant. Out of boredom and curiosity, I developed a mild case of kleptomania, though I wasn't very good at it. I was like a clumsy, pimply adolescent Thomas Crown who had yet to shed his baby fat. Over the summer, one of my friends and I went to Disneyland and stuffed our cargo pockets with probably the dumbest thing to steal—about $100 worth of those polished rocks they sell by the pound. A "cast member" confronted us—Disneyland has cameras everywhere—and we ended up in Disneyland jail for shoplifting until my friend's mom picked us up. That was part of the reason my parents decided it was time for me to move to Thailand, to keep me from turning into a professional criminal by high school, at least in their minds. My uncle paid the tuition for the international school, which was attended mostly by wealthy kids from all over the world. I was one of maybe five Thai kids in my class, but at the same time I was surrounded by and inundated with more Thai culture than ever before.

School was a weird transition. For the private school kids, being prep was cool; driving a Benz was cool. The stuff I knew from my suburban middle-class life in LA—skate shoes and Snoop Dogg—hadn't made it across the Pacific quite yet. Two of my favorite pastimes were sagging my pants and flirting with girls. In my free time I would hang out at basement swap meets and dig out pairs of Airwalks, a Morrissey shirt, or a Tupac cassette tape. Unlike most of my classmates, I was one of the few people interested in working-class culture. Thai culture can be classist, and for the wealthy Thai kids, the idea of willing association with blue-collar types seemed bizarre. The rich kids at the school went to the cafeteria to eat at the sushi station or the hamburger bar. I came from LA. I had enough burgers. I wanted real Thai food. So I ended up befriending a lot of the maintenance staff at the school. When I hung around with them long enough, they'd open their lunch boxes to this privileged but curious kid, and their food blew open my mind. I was the one wondering, *Who's that guy on the corner selling papaya salad? Who's the security*

guard? Who's the janitor? What are they eating for lunch? I was fascinated by working people because that's what I had seen back home; my parents and grandma (and everyone else at Talésai) broke their backs working, so that was my normal. As for the people I met in Bangkok, I'm not sure if I was more interested in the people and used the food as an excuse to break the ice—or vice versa—but that was part of how I realized for the first time that this place was where I belonged. This was my country, and food was a tangible way of diving into that identity.

I was fascinated with language, so I'd talk to strangers on the street to pick up on accents and dialects in Thai. On the bus, or at a strip club, or at a food court, I would ask someone where they're from, or where they liked to eat, and the conversation would expand from there. As it turns out, a lot of those people I talked with were from Isaan, or were eating Isaan food. Since the Northeast is the main supply line for manual labor in the city, the cooking of Isaan had permeated Bangkok in so many ways, and the same people I was chatting up at lunch had fond memories of the intensely seasoned food they used to eat in the countryside. That was how—before I had even begun to think about cooking as a profession— the Bangkok-Isaan connection had me gravitating toward the bombastic, raunchy, and stinky that permeate so much of Thai country cooking. That was where the excitement was.

When I first started outlining a rough menu for Night + Market, the

dishes that first jumped to mind were from Isaan—sour sausages, spicy salads, and grilled meats. It's food that sticks in your brain long after you've finished. The flavors are crass and unpolished, and nothing about the preparation or presentation is at all precious. More important, perhaps, is the context you're eating it in, which is to say around a big table with cold booze. Even now when I visit Bangkok, I spend a lot of my time hanging out with those same types of people, in the same types of places. What I've realized in the years since, I think, is that Isaan is less a place than a state of mind.

STARTLED PIG
MOO SADOONG

Serves 4

1 pound pork shoulder steak (about ½ inch thick)

¼ cup black soy sauce

¼ cup Thai seasoning sauce

2 tablespoons vegetable oil

2 teaspoons ground white pepper

1 tablespoon Chile Jam → 304

3 tablespoons fish sauce

1 teaspoon sugar

1½ tablespoons Roasted Chile Powder → 304

2 tablespoons thinly sliced lemongrass (see → 25)

½ cup torn Thai basil leaves

½ cup roughly chopped cilantro, with stems

2 tablespoons minced garlic

1 tablespoon minced fresh bird's eye chiles, or to taste

2 tablespoons lime juice

1 tablespoon Toasted Rice Powder → 299

Serve with Coconut Sticky Rice → 299 or Sticky Rice → 296–299.

The roughly translated name for this grilled pork salad comes from the idea that you are heaping so many aggressive flavors onto a burnt hunk of meat, you're "startling" the pig. It packs pretty much everything that makes Isaan food so addictive and intense into a single plate—spicy, sour, pungent, smoky. It was one of the original Night + Market dishes and has remained a perennial favorite ever since. The key to this dish is to get a very aggressive char on your pork in order to maximize flavor. Don't even think of using tenderloin or any lean cut—I use a thick steak of pork shoulder, which is well marbled and easy to find. Once the grilled meat has cooled, cut it into long thin slices so it can soak up the seasoning, and if there are extra fatty bits of the meat, mince those up so they disperse evenly throughout.

This is traditionally eaten with plain sticky rice, but I find startled pig also goes well with Coconut Sticky Rice → 299. The sweet creaminess balances out the spicy-sour flavors without making the whole thing any less startling.

1. Preheat a well-oiled grill or grill pan over very high heat. In a shallow bowl or dish, rub the meat with the black soy, seasoning sauce, oil, and white pepper to form a thin glaze. Once the grill is as hot as possible, cook the pork until well charred but slightly pink inside, about 2 minutes per side. Set the pork aside and let it cool.

2. In a large bowl, stir together the chile jam, fish sauce, and sugar until the mixture is smooth. Add the chile powder, lemongrass, basil, cilantro, garlic, and minced chile, but don't mix them together into the sauce just yet. Slice the pork into thin strips and drape over the top of the herbs, and then cover with the lime juice and rice powder. Once everything is added, use your hands to thoroughly mix it all together—be sure to massage the pork slices, as the lime will help cure the meat, like a ceviche. Plate and serve with sticky rice or coconut sticky rice.

SPICY GARLIC PRAWN SASHIMI
GOONG CHAE NAM PLA

Serves 2 to 4

In Isaan, a plate of raw marinated shrimp means it's time to drink. That's true in Bangkok too, where you'll find Isaan-style beer gardens that often cater to blue-collar workers, low-level bureaucrats, cabdrivers, or really anyone with a sense of nostalgia for country life. These democratizing establishments function kind of like honky-tonk bars—no matter what your social status, you're there to dance, eat, drink beer and whiskey, and watch performers in bedazzled outfits singing ballads about unrequited love and rural courtship.

To make this classic beer garden dish, go find the highest-quality prawns you can get your hands on. Fresh is always preferred, but there are also some really nice frozen ones—if you have a Japanese market nearby, that's a pretty good place to look. Make sure they're "head-on, shell-on." If you're not averse to ripping the head off a squirming crustacean (I find it gnarly), I'd even suggest buying live spot prawns if they're in season.

Unlike, say, Mexican ceviche, you won't be "cooking" the prawns in lime juice but quickly curing them in fish sauce, which preserves their silky raw texture. The result is gooey, creamy, and kind of lush, with a tangy raw pungency added by the lime, garlic, and chile. Garnish with a dab of chile jam and fresh mint, which is a traditional accompaniment to raw Thai dishes like *larb* and *koi*.

12 head-on, shell-on prawns, thawed if frozen

3 tablespoons fish sauce

2 teaspoons sugar

1 tablespoon minced fresh bird's eye chiles, or to taste

1½ tablespoons minced garlic

2½ tablespoons lime juice

¼ cup thinly sliced green cabbage

1 tablespoon Chile Jam → 304

2 or 3 springs mint, plucked

1. Butterfly and devein each prawn by cutting along its back with a sharp knife, leaving the head intact but removing the tail and the rest of the shell. Make sure to spread each butterflied prawn apart for maximum marinade absorption. Place the peeled prawns on a bed of ice to keep them cold while you work.

2. In a medium bowl, stir together the fish sauce, sugar, chile, and garlic. Add the prawns and massage with the marinade. Refrigerate for about 2 minutes, then stir in the lime juice.

3. To serve, spread the green cabbage onto a large plate. Lay out the prawns on the plate (so they have elbow room) and top with the remaining marinade. Dab each prawn with chile jam and eat with mint leaves. Enjoy with cold beer.

ISAAN SALMON CEVICHE
KOI SALMON

Serves 2 to 4

1 pound sushi-grade salmon, cut into ½-inch cubes

1½ tablespoons fish sauce

½ cup thinly sliced (root to stem) red onion or shallot

1 teaspoon sugar

1 tablespoon Roasted Chile Powder → 304

½ cup roughly chopped cilantro, with stems

12 mint leaves, torn

2 tablespoons thinly sliced lemongrass (see → 25)

1½ tablespoons lime juice

2 tablespoons Toasted Rice Powder → 299

5 or 6 whole dried chiles (optional), roasted (see → 304)

Serve with shrimp chips or Sticky Rice → 296–299 and cold beer.

Northern Thai raw *larb* → 152 fits into a genre of drinking foods often preferred by truckers, gamblers, and other degenerate old dudes. In Isaan, the equivalent is more or less *koi*, a term that means "chopped up into pinky-size morsels." Koi is sometimes made from raw beef, raw liver, or tiny freshwater shrimp that look like sea-monkeys. As with Northern larb, the uncut version isn't for the faint of heart.

At Night + Market we make koi as a kind of flash-marinated salmon ceviche that can be prepared in a matter of minutes. The slight fattiness of raw salmon is a nice fit in this case, but tuna works well too. The raw fish should be pristine sushi quality—something most people don't always have the luxury of accessing in rural Isaan—but the pungent salty/sour/spicy backwoods seasoning is intended to be the same as in the original. It's ridiculously addictive. Traditionally you would eat this dish on its own (the beer you're drinking alongside koi functions as liquid rice), but that directive is flexible. My alternative recommendation would be to pick up a bag of puffy shrimp chips and use them as scoops in a seafood-y riff on chips and dip. Of course, sticky rice works nicely as well.

In a large bowl, stir together the salmon, fish sauce, red onion, sugar, chile powder, cilantro, mint, and lemongrass. Add the lime juice and rice powder last, and stir again. Transfer to a plate and, if desired, garnish with roasted chiles broken in half. Serve immediately.

CRISPY RICE SALAD
NAM KHAO TOD

Serves 4

What is the most popular dish at Night + Market? The crispy rice salad wins by a mile. The popularity isn't exactly surprising, and not just because people in LA love salad: The charm of this dish is the freshness and vibrancy—the crunch of the rice, the snap of the raw ginger, and the tension between the salty/tart dressing and fresh herbs.

The original inspiration for the crispy rice salad comes from Isaan, where it's known as "sour pork with deep-fried rice." The emphasis there is on the little nubs of crumbled pork, which ferment in the open air for a few days until they turn sour; the rice, which gets rolled into balls and fried until barely crisp, acts as filler. In our version, the perspective gets flipped. The crispy rice is separated into individual grains to enhance the crunch; and the sour pork is more of a bonus than a necessity. So that's why we don't call it by its Thai name very often—it has mutated and evolved into its own thing, more Isaan by way of LA than anything else. At the restaurant, this is the dish I tell people to order first, because the combination of flavors foreshadows everything that will come later in the meal.

In a big bowl, stir together the chile jam, fish sauce, sugar, and chile powder until they form a sauce. Add the minced chile, red onion, green onions, cilantro, sour pork, and lime juice. Toss until coated. Fold in the ginger, peanuts, and crispy rice and quickly toss once more before plating. Garnish with a little more cilantro and serve immediately.

2 teaspoons Chile Jam → 304

¼ cup fish sauce

1 teaspoon sugar

1 tablespoon Roasted Chile Powder → 304

1 tablespoons minced fresh bird's eye chiles, or to taste

1 cup thinly sliced (root to stem) red onion or shallot

½ cup thinly sliced green onions

½ cup roughly chopped cilantro, with stems, plus more for garnish

¼ cup crumbled Sour Pork Bundles → 170 or diced Spam (either is optional)

2 tablespoons lime juice

3 tablespoons peeled and julienned fresh ginger (soaked in cold water for 10 minutes, then shaken dry)

¼ cup Seasoned Fried Peanuts → 309

2 cups Crispy Rice → 301

KRISPIE RICE SALAD, IF YOU MUST If you don't have time to make the crispy rice, you can try what is probably the most bootleg hack in this book—substitute Rice Krispies. The crunchy texture isn't going to be exactly the same as using our crispy rice, but you'll still experience the intense seasoning that makes this dish so addictive. If using Rice Krispies, increase the amount of rice in the recipe above to 3 cups total. Also be aware that Krispies tend to get soggier faster (you'll hear them snap, crackle, pop as you toss), so try to serve the salad as immediately as possible.

AT HOME IN THE UPCOUNTRY

The house my mom grew up in is on the main drag in Mae Chan, a town of around 10,000 people just south of the Burmese border and just north of Chiang Rai. The house is an old two-story wooden building that my grandfather built from scratch, and it's where my aunt and uncle have lived for as long as I can remember. They live on the second floor, actually; on the first floor they run a shop that sells offerings for Buddhist monks and supplies for religious ceremonies. Behind the house there is a big outdoor kitchen, jerry-rigged together by my uncle using scrap parts. He's in his seventies, and up until a few years ago he would run five kilometers every morning, wearing a pair of threadbare running sneakers that I gave him years ago, held together with duct tape. He's a Thai Jack LaLanne, basically, and I'm sure he could still kick my ass if he wasn't the most kind-hearted person alive.

Life in Mae Chan is slow, at least when I visit. Instead of late nights drinking at beer gardens, I'll fall asleep early so I can wake up at six a.m. and greet the monks as they pass by the shop for a morning blessing. (My aunt has a saying, "If you don't make the morning offering, then you haven't been to Mae Chan.") A few days of that routine and the stresses of normal life have faded away. Lunch might involve driving out toward the lush green mountains on the horizon to hunt down a *larb* spot. Dinner might be a haul from the outdoor market in the center of town, rows upon rows of tables crammed together along the sidewalks where you can cobble together a meal of grilled sausage, fried chicken, and dips made from roasted chiles and mashed waterbugs. I could eat that simple meal over and over again, on repeat, forever.

But there is business too. I head over to the small market stall where my mom's cousin, Jay Pawn, sells homemade spice blends, coconut milk, and curry pastes, and pick up as many kilos' worth of her *hanglay* powder and larb spice as I can cram into my suitcase to use at the restaurant. I smuggle it back in newspaper-wrapped bundles, but not before it gets a blessing from the monks to help it avoid US Customs. The next stop is esteemed local artist Meiji, a barrel of a man in weathered flip-flops who screen-prints our aprons and makes plastic signs for the restaurant in bright Day-Glo colors. If there's time,

PA LEE, LOONG SONG, MEIJI

I'll swing by the restaurant supply store, where I pick out as many tin platters and decorations for the restaurant as we can carry, and sometimes even more than that.

The highlight of any trip up north for me, however, is dabbling in the larb lifestyle. Outside the city limits, halfway to the Burmese border, is Larb Jah Jit, one of my all-time favorite larb restaurants. The owner is a retired border patrol agent turned cook. There's a big red chest fridge out back that's filled with various animal parts—meat, fat, blood, bile, etc.—and a rotating chopping block with mechanized cleavers that are used to pound tough cuts of meat into minced oblivion. Near the entrance, chunks of grilled pork teat are slowly smoking over a fire barrel and lines of moonshine bottles run along the counter. This is not a place to hang out with the young and hip. This is where you nurse a Singha over ice until your wife yells at you to come home. This is the place where you day-drink and shoot the shit when it's too hot to do anything else.

Although I literally try to carry as much of Mae Chan back with me to Los Angeles as I can, to a certain extent there's only so much you can physically do to capture that essence of a place. Since it shares a border with Myanmar (Burma), Northern Thai food tends to use a lot more of the fragrant, earthy dried spices that you see in Burmese food, more so than other regions of Thailand.

That's why I buy the spice mixtures and haul them back—the stuff smells hauntingly of Mae Chan, and if you somehow had the recipe written down (most people there don't), re-creating it somewhere else wouldn't be quite the same. But as a chef trying to capture those dishes back in LA, those limitations can actually work as an advantage. Rather than obsessing over exact recipes, I try to focus on the sensations burned into my memories, or the context of where I was and what stood out the most. It's easier for me to cook something that evokes the same feelings, rather than worrying about creating an exact duplicate. Ideally, even if it sounds like sacrilege, you end up with something that actually tastes better than the original.

CHIANG RAI FRIED CHICKEN
GAI TOD NAENG NOI

Serves 2 to 4

4 (6-ounce) skin-on, boneless Brined Chicken thighs → 313

1¼ cups tempura flour or tempura batter mix

⅓ cup tapioca flour

⅓ cup white rice flour

1 teaspoon kosher salt (see → 26)

1 teaspoon ground white pepper

3 cups club soda

Vegetable oil, for deep-frying

Good fried chicken is even better with a dipping sauce. Serve this with either *nam prik noom* (Roasted Green Chile Dip, → 191) or Ranch Dressing → 262, or both.

I think a lot about the great fried chickens of the world: Southern pan-fried chicken, Japanese *karaage*, Korean double-fried chicken, Popeyes, etc. In Northern Thailand, the gold standard of fried chicken is the kind you'll find at market stalls, where vendors sell crispy chicken quarters bundled up in banana leaves. The skin actually gets crunchier the longer you let it sit, which is partly why you can roll it up to go, drive it home on your motorbike, and it will still be crunchy hours later.

I procured my fried chicken recipe from a family who I feel makes the best fried chicken in Chiang Rai, and although they wouldn't give me their entire recipe, they let me know enough to put the puzzle pieces together.

The secret is a mixture of different flours and club soda, a watery batter that produces a super-crunchy crust without soaking up too much oil. The soda water is technically a substitute for hydrolyzed limewater, which is called *nam poon sai* in Thai, but the two are interchangeable in my experience. The batter itself isn't heavily seasoned—instead you'll be relying on brining the chicken beforehand, which will give it a garlicky flavor and ensure it stays indecently juicy.

At the restaurant I use boneless chicken thighs because they're easier and more enjoyable to eat. If you prefer to use bone-in chicken, that's fine too. Let your raw chicken come to room temperature before frying, and once you've taken the thighs out of the oil and drained them on paper towels for a few minutes, use a knife to make a small incision under the non-skin side to see if it's done to your liking. If not, put it back in the fryer for another minute, and then check again before slicing into strips.

1. Remove the chicken from the refrigerator, drain, and let come to room temperature, about 30 minutes. Use a paring knife to score the non-skin side of the thighs to help them cook faster and more evenly.

2. In a medium bowl, stir together the tempura, tapioca, and rice flours, and the salt and pepper. Pour in the soda water. Use your hands to mix thoroughly until no lumps are left. The batter should be thinner than pancake batter.

3. Pour 3 inches of oil into a wok, Dutch oven, or heavy-bottomed pan with several inches of clearance and heat over high heat to 350°F. (Throw in a grain of uncooked rice or a fleck of batter; if it pops up and starts sizzling right away, the oil is ready. Or use a thermometer.) Dunk each thigh in the batter until coated, then quickly transfer to the hot oil. Working in batches if necessary, fry the thighs until the crust turns a deep amber color, 6 to 7 minutes, flipping once halfway through. Remove the chicken and let cool on a wire rack or paper towels. (You can make a small cut on the non-skin side to make sure it is cooked through if you want.) Slice each thigh into ½-inch-wide strips and serve with ranch dressing or *nam prik noom*.

CHIANG MAI CURRY NOODLES
KHAO SOI

Serves 4

Khao soi—the famed Burmese-Thai coconut curry soup with its own cult following—goes by many names. The way it's referred to changes in the region. In Mae Chan, most people refer to it as Muslim khao soi and if you ask for straight up khao soi, you'll be handed *nam ngiew*, which is the recipe *right after this one.* The semantics can be confusing. My dad, in his entrepreneurial wisdom, once dubbed the version our family cooked as C.C.C., or "Chiang Mai coconut curry," as a sort of branding mechanism (it has yet to catch on, but I'm hopeful).

When I opened the restaurant, khao soi wasn't on the menu. People would come into the restaurant and ask for it, like *How can you serve Northern food and not have khao soi?* The problem was Night + Market was never intended to be a compendium of Northern Thai greatest hits, like some authenticity-obsessives wanted it to be. It was just the things with which I was personally captivated, so not having khao soi wasn't something I lost sleep over.

Yet the more I ate it in Thailand, the more I understood the obsession with it. The heart of the dish is the curry paste, which is beautiful when done right: earthy, smoky, fragrant, and surprisingly lacking in heat. Then you hit it with a splash of coconut milk, which lends richness. There are chewy egg noodles and a mound of crisp toppings, which turn it into a one-bowl meal.

Most of the labor involved in khao soi goes into making the curry paste, which you can prepare in large batches and keep in the fridge for weeks. Once that step is done, you're assembling a simple curry. Remember that the broth should be *slurpable*—khao soi is technically a curry, but it should be thinner in consistency than most, more like a soup. In this recipe, we're using hanger steak, but you could also substitute brined chicken or pork. We even offer a vegan version at the restaurant, which is made with tofu and oyster mushrooms and uses thin soy sauce instead of fish sauce.

1. For the curry: In a large pot, combine the steak, salt, fish sauce, coconut sugar, and coconut milk. Bring to a simmer over medium heat and cook for 20 minutes.

CURRY:

1 pound chuck steak or shoulder steak, sliced against the grain into ¼-inch-thick strips (see Note)

1 teaspoon kosher salt (see → 26)

2 tablespoons fish sauce

2 tablespoons coconut or palm sugar

2½ cups coconut milk

3 tablespoons Khao Soi Paste (recipe follows)

1 teaspoon ground turmeric

1 teaspoon mild curry powder

NOODLES AND VEGETABLES:

10 to 12 ounces fresh wide egg noodles (see Note)

Vegetable oil, for deep-frying

1 cup bean sprouts

1 cup thinly sliced (root to stem) shallots

1 cup roughly chopped cilantro, with stems

1 cup store-bought Chinese pickled mustard greens, rinsed and roughly chopped

4 teaspoons Chile Oil → 303

4 lime wedges

recipe continues

Just about any cut of beef works well for curry, as long as it isn't too lean or hasn't been completely trimmed of its fat and connective tissue, which help keep the meat tender as it simmers.

If you don't want to deep-fry the noodles, just use 1 cup store-bought crunchy chow mein noodles instead, and omit the deep-frying step and the extra 2 ounces of noodles.

2. Skim off any beef gunk that has floated to the top. Stir in the khao soi paste, turmeric, and curry powder and simmer until the meat is tender, 40 minutes to 1 hour. Thin out the curry with 1¾ cups water, which should bring the consistency to something slightly thicker than a bisque or chowder (tweak the amount of water as needed). Bring the pot to a boil once more, then remove from the heat.

3. Meanwhile, for the noodles: Measure out about 2 ounces of the noodles and set the remainder aside.

4. Pour 3 inches of oil into a wok or large saucepan with several inches of clearance and heat over medium-high heat to 350°F. (Throw in a small bit of noodle; if it pops up and starts sizzling right away, the oil is ready. Or use a thermometer.) Fry the 2 ounces of noodles until crispy. Drain on paper towels.

5. Boil the rest of the noodles until just cooked, according to the package directions. Drain and cool.

6. Into four serving bowls, portion out the cooked noodles and top with the meat and curry. Dividing them evenly, top each bowl with fried noodles, bean sprouts, shallots, green onions, cilantro, and mustard greens. Drizzle the chile oil on top and serve with a lime wedge on the side. As you eat, try to get a little bit of each topping with every bite.

RAQUEL

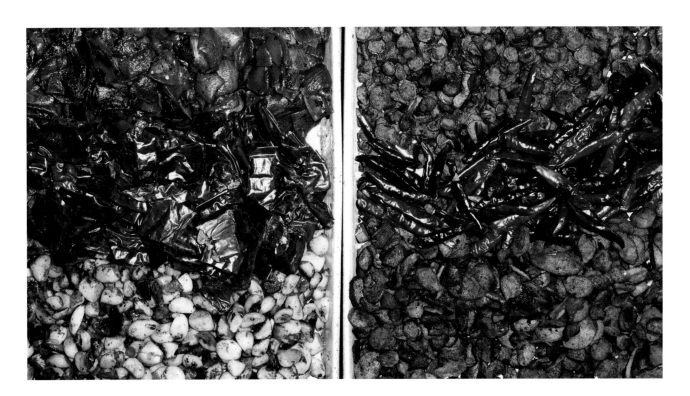

KHAO SOI PASTE

Makes about 1¾ cups

1. In a dry wok over medium heat, toast the turmeric, garlic, ginger, shallots, and chile segments separately, until blackened and slightly soft. This should take 5 to 10 minutes each, with the wetter ingredients taking longer to blacken.

2. Transfer the blackened aromatics to a food processor, blender, or mortar and pestle along with the chile powder, cardamom, salt, and oil and blend until a thick paste forms. Store the paste in a sealed container in the fridge and use as needed—the paste will keep for several weeks.

¼ cup sliced
fresh turmeric

¼ cup sliced garlic

⅓ cup sliced
fresh ginger

⅓ cup sliced shallots

3 large dried New
Mexico chiles, seeded
and cut into segments

1 tablespoon Roasted
Chile Powder → 304

1½ teaspoons ground
cardamom

1 teaspoon kosher salt
(see → 26)

2 tablespoons
vegetable oil

PORK RAGU NOODLE SOUP
NAM NGIEW

Serves 4

This is what many people refer to as the "other *khao soi*" in Northern Thailand, despite it being vastly different in taste and preparation from the creamy coconut stuff (the name *ngiew* itself is a derogatory term that refers to the Shan people of Myanmar, from whom the dish originated). It's arguably less famous than the creamy version, but growing up this was my perception of "real" khao soi, and because of that, it has become much more near and dear to my heart.

At its base, this soup is a simple pork broth with rice noodles (you can use whatever noodles you'd like). From there you heap on different flavors and textures: a salty and sour tomato-pork ragu, crunchy bean sprouts and pickled greens, fresh herbs, and crispy fried garlic. In some ways it's not dissimilar to ramen or Mexican pozole, and equally capable of curing a hangover, in my experience.

In Thailand, the mild pork broth that you see on almost every stovetop is made from boiled pork bones, MSG, and salt. The MSG is optional for our purposes. When making nam ngiew, some cooks like to simmer the broth and tomato dip together as one thing, but I prefer the method where they're kept separate until you mix them together tableside. In this case, I'm repurposing the recipe for *nam prik ong* (Chiang Rai Pork Chile Dip, → 198) as a component in the dish.

Once you've assembled everything together, stir the whole thing up and dive in.

1. In a big pot, bring 3 quarts water to a boil. Add the riblets, tomatoes, and salt and simmer over low heat, uncovered, until the water has reduced by roughly a third and the meat is tender, about 1 hour. Skim if desired. (You can also use a pressure cooker for this step to speed up the process.) At this point, you've made a simple pork broth, which you can use for other dishes by straining out the pork ribs and tomato skins and reserving the liquid.

2. Meanwhile, if you haven't already, make the pork chile dip.

3. Into four serving bowls, portion out the noodles and top with the riblets and pork broth. Dividing them evenly, top with the pork chile dip, bean sprouts, green onions, cilantro, mustard greens, and fried garlic. Serve with lime wedges and a side of pork rinds.

---

1 pound pork riblets (pork ribs cut into 2½-inch sections; ask your butcher)

1 cup cherry tomatoes

1 tablespoon kosher salt (see → 26)

2 cups Chiang Rai Pork Chile Dip → 198

10 ounces wide rice noodles, cooked according to package directions

1 cup bean sprouts

¼ cup thinly sliced green onions

¼ cup roughly chopped cilantro, with stems

¼ cup store-bought Chinese pickled mustard greens, rinsed and roughly chopped

¼ cup Fried Garlic → 311

4 lime wedges

Serve with pork rinds.

DRUNKARDS, GAMBLERS, AND BLOOD SOUP

To a certain subset of people, Night + Market will forever be known as "that Thai place that serves blood soup." And I have to admit, when I first put it on the menu, I knew it was going to be one of those things that polarized people.

In his review of Night + Market Song, the great restaurant critic Jonathan Gold labeled it as part of an "aesthetic of culinary transgression" (intended as a compliment, I think) and noted, "I have been eating with Ruth Reichl for more than 25 years, and this is the one dish I have ever seen her refuse to touch." There were diners who assumed that I was serving it merely for the shock value—like the culinary equivalent of jumping the Grand Canyon. There were "adventurous foodie" types who saw the dish as a challenge, like something they could impress their friends with by claiming it was "authentic." The truth was something more complicated.

Luu is a dish found in parts of Northern Thailand. Even up there, it's pretty niche—a majority of Thai people don't really eat it, or if they do, then very rarely (you can die from eating raw blood, and a few of my countrymen do each year as a result of enjoying this delicacy). The main component is fresh liquid blood, which is then seasoned with what I think of as an all-purpose "Northern

Thai spice trifecta" consisting of *makwaen*, *malaep*, and *deeplee* (three types of peppercorns, basically). Mixed in different proportions, these are the same spices that would season, say, Northern-style *larb*. So you massage the blood with lemongrass leaves to "purify" it, add a pinch of salt and MSG (Thais love MSG), then top it with some rough chopped raw herbs, crispy noodles, and pork skin cracklings. It is often served with a sweet sauce on the side, which some (myself included) tend to ignore. Though it is served in a bowl large enough to pick up and slurp like miso soup, the way I consume it is by using a ball of sticky rice to soak up the blood, then scooping up herbs and crispy stuff like deep-fried intestines served on the side (our version cuts back on the blood, and instead of having the herbs and noodles on the side, they're piled on top).

The most important ingredient, however, isn't even mixed into the dish—it's the alcohol that you are undoubtedly consuming if you're eating luu. You see, luu is really only eaten by derelict, sometimes alcoholic, fun-loving, old-timey Northern guys—guys like Loong Laa, my uncle who runs a small lottery ticket kiosk in front of my family's house in Mae Chan (by the way, this guy is not even my uncle; he's my mom's elementary school friend, but he's become like extended family). The nickname Laa is sort of like saying "a guy who ducks out." *Laa*

pai, laa ma is a phrase that translates to something like "you're here, you're there, but you're never where you need to be." This is the type of lovable no-goodnik who eats luu from time to time, the erstwhile drunk uncle. When we opened Night + Market Song, I told people I wanted to be a sort of neighborhood diner, where instead of a club sandwich, you could drop in and have some luu, a cold beer, and maybe some fried chicken. The tricky thing was, I obviously couldn't serve raw blood. So I had to invent something. I had to dream up a way to create the same sensation you get when you're eating raw blood, only with cooked blood. When you serve something cooked, in Thai you call it "*suk*," thus it became *luu suk.* It was a workaround; something that didn't exist in Thailand.

To me, the heart of the experience revolved around that awesome spice mix, which tastes and smells uniquely of Northern Thailand like the way gingerbread smells like Christmas. It's something that I literally hauled back to the United States in suitcases and found a way to approximate for this cookbook. Luu, for me, is a way to experience the act of dipping and sharing the same plate of food among friends. It was never a gross-out item or an exoticism thing. It was something with which I had a personal connection. On a good night we would sell maybe three or four, and even though my servers hated it, and the cooks thought it was a pain in the ass

to make, it made me feel good to serve something that I associated with my friends and family.

The irony was that a year or two after we introduced it, this new Thai restaurant in Hollywood began serving something called "cooked blood soup with herbs" that was listed as *lue sook*, which of course was not an actual Thai dish but something I had made up. The restaurant in question is closed now, but at the time I was more confused than offended. Why would they rip off my worst-selling dish? Why not take the chicken wings instead? So after that minor fiasco I decided to hang up the jersey on blood soup.

But the larger lesson, or at least what I got out of it, was when you serve something like blood soup, people will extract different meanings from it. There are those who wrongly assume because it's the most squeamish dish on the menu, it *must* be the most "authentic." It's that thinking that turns the perception of authentic "ethnic" food into an arms race to the bottom, as if the entire point of cooking any regional cuisine is to seek out the most outlandish and obscure dishes, like some sort of culture vulture. The truth behind the blood soup is nuanced, and sometimes nuance can be hard to express with large groups of people. It's natural that we want food to represent something, to make a deeper comment about culture and all that, but sometimes that comment is simply *Here's this unique and interesting thing I enjoyed in Thailand, I kind of messed with it, try it with alcohol.*

BLOOD DIPPING SOUP
LUU SUK

Serves 2 to 4

SOUP:

½ pound fresh coagulated pork blood

Kosher salt (see → 26)

1 stalk lemongrass

¼ cup pork bone broth → 111 or chicken broth

1 instant ramen seasoning packet (pork flavor)

½ teaspoon Larb Spice → 157

ACCOMPANIMENTS:

Handful of cilantro sprigs

¼ cup thinly sliced scallions

Handful of sawtooth (culantro) sprigs

Handful of *rau ram* leaves

Handful of mind sprigs

1 tablespoon thinly sliced lemongrass (see → 25)

2 or 3 dried chiles, roasted (see → 304) and broken in half

4 or 5 kaffir lime leaves, deep-fried at 355°F for 20 seconds, until crispy

Handful of kaffir lime leaves

Bag of pork rinds

2 ounces uncooked rice vermicelli noodles, deep-fried at 355°F for 20 seconds, until crispy

2 tablespoons Thai sweet chile sauce (optional)

There's a specific way to eat Northern blood dipping soup: Roll gumball-size wads of sticky rice between your fingers, dip them in one or two of the herb piles, then drag the rice through the blood dip. The sweet chile sauce is optional but you can dip into that too. Crumble more noodles into the blood as needed and use the pork rinds as alternative dipping vehicles. Consume with some type of chilled alcohol (mandatory).

1. For the soup: Put the blood in a large bowl and season with a pinch of salt. Peel off 4 or 5 outer layers from the lemongrass stalk. Use your hands to knead/crush/massage the peeled lemongrass fronds into the blood—gloves aren't a bad idea here—which will help the blood liquefy. Knead for 3 to 4 minutes, then strain out the liquid pooling at the bottom of the bowl. Repeat the process until you've yielded about ⅓ cup of strained, liquefied blood, then discard the lemongrass fronds and any leftover blood chunks.

2. In a small saucepan, heat the bone broth over high heat until it reaches a very strong boil for 30 seconds. Reduce the heat to as low as possible and slowly pour in the blood with one hand while stirring with the other. Remove the pan from the heat and continue to stir for another 30 seconds. The blood will be cooked at this point, but it will still have the slick texture of raw blood.

3. Sprinkle the seasoning packet and *larb* spice into a wide shallow dish and pour the blood soup over the top. Arrange the accompaniments in small piles around the edge of the plate. Heap a handful of pork rinds and fried noodles in the middle. Set a small dish of the sweet chile sauce (if desired) next to it. Serve with sticky rice.

Serve with Sticky Rice → 296–299 and some kind of alcohol.

STEAMED BLOOD RICE TAMALE
KHAO GAN CHIN

Serves 4

2 tablespoons oyster sauce

¼ cup Thai seasoning sauce

1 teaspoon sugar

1 teaspoon kosher salt
(see → 26)

½ teaspoon ground
white pepper

4 cups Steamed Jasmine
Rice → 296

1 cup liquid pork blood,
thawed if frozen

¾ cup ½-inch diced pork
jowl or pork back fat,
quick-cured (see → 178)

8 kaffir lime leaves

ACCOMPANIMENTS:

2 tablespoons Garlic
Oil → 311

2 tablespoons Fried
Garlic → 311

4 to 6 pulla or árbol chiles,
roasted (see → 304), or
2 teaspoons Roasted Chile
Powder → 304 (optional)

½ cucumber, cut crosswise
into ¼-inch-thick
half-moons

½ cup thinly sliced (root to
stem) shallots

Handful cilantro

4 green onions

Lime wedges

Khao gan chin—jasmine rice mixed with a bit of pig blood and steamed in a banana leaf pouch—is a pure example of "upcountry food" in that it's rustic and turns modest ingredients into something transcendent. In the Northern dialect, the word *gan* roughly means "to squeeze liquid from one thing into another," so in essence you're squeezing pork blood (*chin*) into rice (*khao*). As with most Northern dishes, the fresh herbs and toppings are essential to balance the rich earthiness of the blood and fatty pork. It's a fantastic combination, and if the idea of blood in rice freaks you out slightly, this is the dish that can convert anyone.

In Mae Chan, the sole purveyor of blood rice I knew has actually moved on to hawking iced lattes. It was at a shophouse around the corner from my family's home; the son made money with the coffee while his mother, probably in her eighties, had a steamer out front stacked with these little rice-stuffed banana leaf pouches. I'm guessing she sold fewer than two dozen daily. That's how a lot of these traditions get lost. It's not that the parents think their kids aren't interested, it's just not that economically viable. They'd prefer them to be doctors and lawyers (or sell cappuccinos, at least). But for a chef, these recipes are diamonds in the rough.

When I started selling the blood rice at Night + Market, I tweaked the traditional recipe by bulking it up with diced Pork Toro → 178 and serving it with a lime wedge (limes are more commonly used in Isaan cooking to temper the richness). You can use parchment paper instead of banana leaves, or just spoon the rice mixture into a shallow bowl covered with plastic wrap and steam it in that.

Equipment: 8 banana leaves (or parchment paper), toothpicks

1. In a mixing bowl, stir together the oyster sauce, seasoning sauce, sugar, salt, and white pepper. Then add the rice and mix. Taste it at this point (before the blood has been added) so you can adjust the seasoning if necessary. Add the raw blood and diced jowl and stir with a spoon or spatula until everything is completely incorporated.

2.   Wash the banana leaves, pat them dry, then double layer them dull side to dull side with their horizontal grooves slightly offset from one another. If you're using parchment paper, tear off four 18-inch lengths (you don't need to double wrap) and lay them out. Spoon one-fourth of the rice mixture into the center of each banana leaf, top each with 2 lime leaves, then fold the banana leaves inward widthwise and then lengthwise, folding over the extra wrapping on top like a hem. Pin each package closed with a toothpick.

3.   Set up a steamer rack in a pot with a few inches of water at the bottom. Bring the water to a boil over high heat, then reduce to a simmer. Place the bundles in the steamer basket, cover, and steam until the blood has turned dark brown, about 10 minutes.

4.   Serve unwrapped. Spoon the garlic oil, fried garlic, and roasted chiles over the rice. Arrange the rest of the accompaniments around the edges. Mix it up with a spoon before eating.

Serve this as is, or with a green onion and cilantro-topped bowl of the pork broth (from Pork Ragu Noodle Soup → 111) for sipping on the side.

"JELL-O" CURRY
GAENG GRADANG

Serves 4 to 6

½ cup kosher salt
(see → 26)

¼ cup plus 1 tablespoon
sugar

2 teaspoons ground
white pepper

2 pig's feet or trotters
(20 ounces total) sliced
into ½-inch discs (ask
your butcher)

1 pound pork butt, cut into
¾-inch cubes

¼ cup All-Purpose Curry
Paste → 303

¼ cup fish sauce

½ cup thinly sliced
green onions

½ cup roughly chopped
cilantro, with stems

½ cup Fried Garlic → 311

Serve with freshly made
Sticky Rice → 296–299
or warm bread.

The first time I encountered *gaeng gradang* in Chiang Rai it was six or seven years ago, when I was visiting my family in December. It gets cool in the North that time of year—not freezing, but cold enough. It's also the time when gaeng gradang shows up at the markets, where it's sold out of aluminum cake pans and cut into thick squares. This stuff is essentially Thai head cheese: It's a curry that turns solid after being exposed to the chill winter air, with little chewy bits of pork suspended in curry-flavored gelatin. You lay a block atop a mound of warm sticky rice and it starts to melt slightly. It's a surprisingly nuanced combination of textures.

Even before I tried it in Thailand, I'd read about the rough concept of what I had dubbed "Jell-O curry," and had been tinkering around with my own version with mixed success. Even though it's traditionally a winter dish, I would serve it at Night + Market Song in the dog days of summer when cold jiggly things make the most sense. The secret is to use quick-cured trotters (pig's feet), which contain a lot of natural gelatin but are more manageable to work with than a whole pig's head, which is traditionally used. Also, keep in mind a lesson I think I learned after reading either *Ma Gastronomie* or a Michael Ruhlman book: Cold dishes need a higher level of seasoning so they don't taste bland once they're chilled.

1. Combine the salt, ¼ cup of the sugar, and white pepper in a large bowl, then add the sliced pig's feet and coat evenly. Let them cure in the fridge for at least 30 minutes and up to 1 hour. Rinse them in fresh water.

2. In a large pot, bring 2 quarts water to a boil and add the pig's feet and cubed pork butt. Simmer, partially covered, over low heat until the feet are tender and begin to break down, about 2 hours, removing the cover and skimming off the foam occasionally. Remove the pig's feet from the broth and let them cool.

3. Using a paring knife and your hands, dig out the meat/skin/cartilage from the bone. Cut the meat into small chunks, like carnitas, and then return to the still-simmering broth, discarding the leftover bones. The broth-to-meat ratio should be around 2:1, so add more water or reduce further if needed.

4. Add the curry paste, fish sauce, and the remaining 1 tablespoon sugar and stir over low heat until combined and heated through. Pour the curry mixture into a 9 x 11-inch casserole dish and let cool. Once cooled, cover and refrigerate for a few hours until set.

5. When you're ready to serve, pull the curry out of the fridge and let it return to room temperature for 15 to 20 minutes. Cut out squares and garnish with the green onions, cilantro, and fried garlic. Serve over warm sticky rice or, in a non-Thai twist, with warm bread.

MANEE, ZEFERINO, NENG

BURMESE PORK BELLY CURRY
GAENG HANGLAY

Serves 4

2½ pounds pork belly or pork shoulder, cut into 1½-inch cubes

2 tablespoons All-Purpose Curry Paste → 303

¾ cup black soy sauce

1 tablespoon kosher salt (see → 26)

3 tablespoons Hanglay Powder (recipe follows)

⅓ cup coconut or palm sugar

3 tablespoons fish sauce

3 bulbs store-bought Thai pickled garlic

3 tablespoons julienned fresh ginger, soaked in cold water for 10 minutes, then drained

½ cup Tamarind Water → 313

Serve with Sticky Rice → 296–299.

There's no Northern Thai dish that reminds me of growing up more than *gaeng hanglay*, an earthy/tart/spicy pork belly soup that some Thais refer to as "Burmese curry" because of its superfragrant spices that originate from the spice trading routes of Burma. My mom would make it when I was a kid, and I remember being obsessed with the smell that fills the room when it's on the stove. That scent is almost reminiscent of mole—deep, dark, musty—probably because they share similar ingredients like mace, cardamom, coriander seed, turmeric, and black pepper. For the restaurant I usually buy the *hanglay* powder from my mom's cousin in Mae Chan and haul it home, but after years of buying out her entire inventory, I was able to coax the secret recipe from her and share it with you here.

The proper way to make hanglay is to massage the spices into the pork and let it marinate for at least an hour (overnight is better), which ensures that the meat soaks up the flavors and becomes tender when you simmer it. The beauty of the dish is that although it uses rich cuts of meat, the tamarind and ginger brighten up the final product and make it seem lighter than anything loaded with pork belly has any right to be.

1. In a large pot, combine the cubed pork belly, curry paste, black soy, salt, and 2 tablespoons of the hanglay powder. Use your hands to mix and massage the paste into the pork belly cubes (plastic gloves are a good idea to avoid stains) and let marinate in the fridge, covered, for at least 2 hours and up to 12 hours.

2. Once the meat is marinated, add enough water to cover by a ¼ inch and bring to a boil over high heat. Stir in the coconut sugar, fish sauce, pickled garlic, 2 tablespoons of the ginger, and the remaining 1 tablespoon hanglay powder. Reduce the heat and simmer until the pork is soft and jiggly but not falling apart, 1½ to 2 hours, adding water as necessary to keep the pork submerged. Remove from the heat and stir in the tamarind water.

3. Pour the curry into a large communal bowl and garnish with the remaining ginger for extra brightness. Serve with sticky rice.

LEFT TO RIGHT: LARB LANNA, HANGLAY, NORTHERN FRIED CHICKEN

HANGLAY POWDER

Makes about 1 cup

½ cup coriander seeds

6 tablespoons cumin seeds

2 teaspoons whole cloves

1½ teaspoons black peppercorns

3 (3-inch) cinnamon sticks

6 tablespoons ground turmeric

1 tablespoon ground cardamom

1¼ teaspoons freshly grated nutmeg

¾ teaspoon ground mace

1.   In a large dry skillet, toast the coriander seeds, cumin seeds, cloves, black peppercorns, and cinnamon sticks over low heat until fragrant, 4 to 5 minutes, shaking and stirring often. Be careful not to let any of the spices burn, or it will taint the whole curry. Remove the whole spices from the pan. Add the turmeric, cardamom, and mace and toast over lower heat, stirring and shaking, until fragrant, 2 to 3 minutes.

2.   Working in batches if necessary, transfer everything to a spice grinder, coffee grinder, or mortar and pestle and pulverize until fine. Store in a cool, dry place.

TING, "THE BOSS" OF NIGHT + MARKET WEHO

MEATBALL CURRY
GAENG JIN NOONG

Serves 6 to 8

I originally learned this dish from my mom's first cousin who lives in Mae Chan. She's a fantastic cook and before she went into semiretirement she would sell a handful of dishes out of a makeshift kitchen-slash-dining-room in the front of her house.

Northern Thai meatball curry falls into the same rustic, soul-satisfying category as *hanglay*, but it is somewhat simpler to make. The hypnotizing earthy flavor comes from dark soy sauce and the hanglay powder, which you mix both into the meatballs and the broth. In the northern dialect, *jin noong* is a term for a loose meatball, and the technique for making them is to pinch off little rounds of meat and toss them into the broth. If you want to turn this curry into a balanced meal, I'd suggest pairing it with any type of *larb* and Chiang Rai Fried Chicken → 104.

I find that this tastes better with jasmine rice, but you could also eat it with sticky rice, which is typical in the North.

1. Pierce the tomatoes with a paring knife or fork and add to a large saucepan along with 1½ quarts water and 2 teaspoons of the salt. Bring to a boil over high heat.

2. Meanwhile, in a medium bowl, combine the pork, the remaining ½ teaspoon salt, half of the hanglay powder, and 2 tablespoons of the black soy sauce. Mix with your hands until combined and set aside.

3. Once the water is boiling, reduce the heat to a simmer. Add the curry paste, fish sauce, coconut sugar, the remaining hanglay powder, and the remaining soy sauce. Stir until combined and simmer for 5 minutes.

4. Pinch off gumball-size portions of the pork mixture and loosely shape them into lumpy meatballs with your fingers. Add them to the broth as you shape them (add the cooked blood cubes now too, if you're using them). Let all the meatballs simmer until cooked, about 5 minutes. Stir in the tamarind water, simmer for 1 to 2 more minutes, then remove from the heat.

5. Portion the curry into individual bowls and serve with rice.

2 cups cherry tomatoes

2½ teaspoons kosher salt (see → 26)

2 pounds ground pork

⅓ cup Hanglay Powder → 124

¾ cup black soy sauce

2½ tablespoons All-Purpose Curry Paste → 303

3 tablespoons fish sauce

1½ tablespoons coconut or palm sugar

½ pound cooked pork blood (optional), cut into 1-inch cubes

⅓ cup Tamarind Water → 313

Serve with Steamed Jasmine Rice → 296, which I like better with this, or Sticky Rice → 296–299, which is traditional.

GRILLED CATFISH TAMALE
HOR AB

Serves 2 to 4 (makes 2 large tamales)

Hor ab started off as a rudimentary thing in Northern Thailand. It's upcountry food that's been prepared for generations, something you could wrap up in a banana leaf and grill over a fire and bring with you for lunch after a day of working the fields. A loose analogy is that it's like an exceptionally moist and flavorful Mexican tamale; instead of using corn masa and meat, you're wrapping leaves around catfish, pork fat, chiles, and bright aromatics and cooking the entire bundle. Normally, this is one of those dishes where I don't try to mess with tradition too much—it's hard to improve on something that's been honed over generations to the point where it's infallible—but at the restaurant we save time by parbaking the packets in the oven and finishing them on the grill, which lends a trace amount of smoke flavor. If you have the time to cook them fully on a grill, you'll get a much smokier flavor; but if you use an oven that's fine too. If you can't find banana leaves, use a dual layer of parchment paper and foil.

Equipment: 4 banana leaves (or parchment paper and foil), toothpicks

1. In a blender or food processor, puree the chiles, bell pepper, shallots, garlic, oil, and 1 teaspoon salt until a chunky salsa-like paste forms. Remove and set aside. Add the fresh turmeric, seasoning sauce, fish sauce, sugar, and a pinch of salt to the blender/food processor. Puree until liquefied.

2. In a bowl, combine the catfish, pork fat, lemongrass, cilantro, sawtooth, turmeric mixture, and ½ cup of the chile paste (you may end up with some left over). Mix until combined.

3. Preheat the oven to 375°F or preheat a well-oiled grill to medium heat.

4 fresh bird's eye chiles, or to taste, stemmed

1 habanero chile, stemmed (optional)

4 jalapeño peppers, roughly sliced

½ green bell pepper, roughly sliced

2 cups thinly sliced (root to stem) shallots

8 cloves garlic, peeled but kept whole

¼ cup vegetable oil

Kosher salt (see → 26)

2 (1-inch) nubs of fresh turmeric

¼ cup Thai seasoning sauce

2 tablespoons fish sauce

1 tablespoon sugar

½ pound catfish fillets, cut into 1 × 2-inch chunks

¼ pound pork fat, ground or roughly chopped

2 tablespoons thinly sliced lemongrass (see → 25)

½ cup roughly chopped cilantro, with stems

½ cup roughly chopped sawtooth (culantro)

recipe continues

Serve with Sticky Rice
→ **296–299** or Coconut
Sticky Rice → **299**.

Bonus: A common post-shift meal for me involves a leftover tamale heated up in the microwave and served with sticky rice, a fried egg, cilantro, and sliced avocado. Occasionally I'll swap out the rice for tortillas and make catfish tamales tacos topped with Salsa Roja → **285**.

4. Wash the banana leaves, pat them dry, then double layer them dull side to dull side with their horizontal grooves slightly offset. If you're using parchment paper, tear off four 18-inch lengths and lay them on top of each other. Spoon about half of the filling into the center of the banana leaf, fold inward widthwise and then lengthwise, folding the extra wrapping on top like a hem. Pin each package closed with a toothpick (or wrap each parchment bundle with foil to bind).

5. Transfer the tamales to a baking sheet and bake for 25 minutes, flipping once. Or cook on the grill for 10 to 15 minutes on each side; the tamale will start to seep out liquid as it cooks. Once slightly cooled, unwrap and serve with sticky rice.

BOON

CHIANG RAI CHICKEN STEW
OB GAI

Serves 4

Northern curries are almost elemental in their simplicity. In the strictest terms, a curry paste in the north would be made from pulverized chiles, garlic, and shallots—that's it. But rather than make a different curry paste for each specific curry, I find it makes more sense to use a more all-purpose Central Thai curry paste → 303.

With *ob gai*, a classic, comforting Northern stew that's like a red curry without the coconut milk, you're using the curry paste as a base and amping it up with extra lemongrass, lime leaves, and baby dill, which gives the broth its characteristic fragrance. Salty, tangy, oily, and strongly herbaceous, this is a stew you can smell simmering from down the hallway.

1. In a large saucepan, combine the chicken with 1 quart water and bring to a boil over high heat. Add the lemongrass, lime leaves, and salt. Reduce to a simmer and cook for 10 minutes. Stir in the curry paste, fish sauce, and sugar and simmer for another 10 minutes. Add the dill last, stir for a few seconds, then remove from the heat.

2. Divide the soup among four bowls, removing the lemongrass pieces, if desired (they're not meant to be eaten). Garnish with equal amounts of the green onions, the sawtooth, and cilantro. Serve the lime wedges on the side. Serve with sticky rice or coconut rice and roll into little balls for dipping.

12 chicken drumettes or wing flats (wingettes)

1 stalk lemongrass, trimmed (see → 25) and cut crosswise on an angle into 2-inch lengths

4 or 5 kaffir lime leaves, torn

1 teaspoon kosher salt (see → 26)

¼ cup All-Purpose Curry Paste → 303

¼ cup fish sauce

1 tablespoon sugar

4 or 5 dill fronds, stems removed

GARNISHES:

½ cup thinly sliced green onions

½ cup roughly chopped sawtooth (culantro)

½ cup roughly chopped cilantro, with stems

Lime wedges

Serve with Sticky Rice → 296–299 or Coconut Sticky Rice → 299.

THE GREAT MALL(S) OF BANGKOK

No one does shopping malls better than Bangkok. The city is a sprawling, multilayered metropolis of endless energy, with skyscrapers slapped on top of old shophouses and small alleyways that weave through the city blocks like sidewalk cracks. Yet even with all the stark differences that the city highlights, there is something universally Thai about heading to the mall.

Part of that might be because it's humid enough to soak your shirt most of the year, and the big malls always have incredibly powerful, freezing-cold A/C—pumping out borderline-illegal-levels-of-Freon air-conditioning. It also might be that since the Thai economy boomed in the '90s, modern consumerism has given to endless locations of Gucci, Louis Vuitton, and Prada (Thai people love name brands). These shopping megaplexes usually have grand titles like Central Plaza, EmQuartier, Gaysorn Plaza, Central Embassy, Platinum Fashion World, Siam Paragon, or Central World (formerly known as the World Trade Center, but that was changed for obvious reasons). I remember as a kid going to one that had an outdoor water park on the roof. Others have built-in aquariums, wax museums, video arcades, or ice skating rinks. If you were a junior high kid in the '90s, the malls were where you spent all your free time.

Yet the nerve center of any Thai shopping mall is the food court. And while I'm sure there are people who will disagree with me, it turns out a lot of the mall food in Thailand is legitimately good, far better than the Sbarro and Hot Dog on a Stick you might find in America. You can pick anything from boat noodles and sukiyaki to chile-spiked spaghetti and deep-fried steak cutlets, all crammed together and accessible via escalator.

Don't get me wrong, there is a lot of Bangkok street food worth seeking out—like the places that serve fried oyster omelets in Chinatown, the noodle vendors who cook pad Thai over coal-powered wok stations in Old Bangkok, or the gentleman who has been hawking late-night grilled pork skewers in the go-go bar–filled Patpong district for two decades plus. (Whenever I ask him what his secret recipe is, he just points to his chest with a sly look and says, *Mak duay jai rak*, "It's been marinated with a loving heart.")

As a Thai-American private school punk, those were my first loves, but I learned that even street food has limits. If you want to see how a majority of Bangkok's citizens eat, go to a food court. Thai society is notoriously self-aware of social class—everything from clothes to restaurants to shopping habits are categorized as either *hiso* (high society) or *loso* (low society)—but the food court is the place where you'll see a construction worker eating from the same kiosk as a business tycoon. The reason for this is actually pretty straightforward: Imagine you were a vendor who made spectacular seafood curry and sold it from a street cart daily. Maybe you hustle hard and at some point earn enough money to

สปาเก็ตตี้ขี้เมาทะเล
Stir-fried Spaghetti with Spicy Herbs and Seafood

สปาเก็ตตี้กุ้งผัดซอสมะเขือเทศ
Spaghetti in Tomato Sauce with Shrimp

upgrade your operation. You pay the token rent at one of the smaller malls out in the outer boroughs of the city, and maybe accumulate enough name recognition to expand into another slightly larger mall down the road. Soon enough you're expanding across the city. That's the Thai dream right there.

What I'm saying is that the biggest limitation in associating Thai food with street food is that you relegate it to something that belongs in the street. When I opened Night + Market, I kind of adopted the label of street food, whether I was conscious of it or not. The more I spend time in Bangkok, I realize that I'm fascinated by the tension between the food we deem commercialized and that which we deem authentic. The *larb*-flavored potato chips, the curry-topped pizzas, and the hot dogs flavored with chile paste—which category do these fall under? Does it even matter? If you're going to portray real Thai food, I think you have to embrace all of it, even the stuff that might be written off as unworthy or bastardized.

BANGKOK MALL PASTA
SAPA-GET-EE PLA KHEM

Serves 2

This dish is more or less a riff on spaghetti *kee mao*, and I started calling it mall pasta because it reminded me of these '90s-era vaguely Italian restaurants you'd occasionally find in Bangkok shopping plazas—places where you could find this type of spicy stir-fried spaghetti on the menu. As far as noodles go, this is like a really good *cacio e pepe*. It's simple enough to make as a snack but sophisticated enough to pair with a nice bottle of wine and a hot date. At Night + Market we use Barilla thick spaghetti, the stuff you find on almost every bodega or supermarket shelf. Whatever brand you have on hand is fine. Using dried pasta is crucial, though, as delicate fresh pasta won't hold up to the rigors of a hot wok.

    The holy trinity behind this dish is fried garlic, anchovies, and chile. Stir-fry them together in oil and you'll get this aromatic salty-pungent base that permeates the noodles. At the restaurant we toss the cooked pasta with fresh basil, raw garlic, and brined green peppercorns, but I really enjoy the sharp fruitiness that pink peppercorns bring too.

1. In a large pot of salted boiling water, cook the pasta until al dente. Reserving ¼ cup of the pasta water, drain.

2. Heat an empty wok over high heat until it begins to smoke, then swirl in the olive oil. Once the oil is shimmering, add the anchovies, anchovy oil, minced garlic, chile, and bell pepper and stir-fry until the bell pepper is softened, 2 to 3 minutes. Add the pasta, reserved pasta water, oyster sauce, seasoning sauce, and sugar and cook, tossing, until the sauce is slightly thickened, about 2 minutes. Add the sliced garlic, green peppercorns, white pepper, and torn basil leaves and toss. Top with the whole basil leaves and serve.

6 ounces dried thick spaghetti

2½ tablespoons extra-virgin olive oil

1 (2-ounce) tin oil-packed anchovy fillets, drained, finely chopped, and oil reserved

1 tablespoon minced garlic plus 1 tablespoon thinly sliced garlic

1 teaspoon minced fresh bird's eye chiles, or to taste

½ red bell pepper, thinly sliced

1 tablespoon oyster sauce

2 tablespoons Thai seasoning sauce

1½ teaspoons sugar

1 tablespoon brined green peppercorns or dried pink peppercorns (or to taste)

Pinch of ground white pepper

¼ cup torn Thai basil leaves, plus small whole leaves for garnish

STRIP CLUB FRIED RICE
KHAO PAD AMERICAN

Serves 2

SAUCE PRIK:

¼ cup ketchup

¼ cup Sriracha sauce

1 teaspoon distilled
white vinegar

WIENER BLOSSOMS:

2 hot dogs (pork/
chicken wieners)

Vegetable oil, for deep-frying

RICE:

1 egg

2 slices lunchmeat ham

2 cups cooked jasmine rice,
preferably day-old

½ cup frozen peas
and carrots

½ teaspoon sugar

1½ tablespoons Stir-Fry
Sauce → 306

2 tablespoons ketchup

¼ cup raisins

Ground white pepper

2 or 4 fried chicken wings
(see Note)

The best way I can describe *khao pad American* (American fried rice) is "strip club food." You'd order it in the same places you'd see your expat biology teacher getting a lap dance. As deplorable as the Thai sex trade is, growing up around it introduced me to the actual workers behind it, real people who found a way to get by making money off sleazy foreigners. American fried rice is a cultural relic from a time before Western chain saturation, where nonperishable staples like supermarket wieners, canned ham, peas and carrots, ketchup, and raisins could be turned into something intended to please white tourists. Even the presentation is distinctly American—it looks like a Swanson TV dinner.

Of all the dishes I've ever served at Night + Market, this is the most conceptual in a sort of Andy Warhol way. For better or worse, this is part of Thai food culture too. That said, wiener blossoms with fried rice are pretty delicious. I can eat about fifty blossoms in a single sitting (I'm vile). They can be made with any type of hot dog, but the recipe works best with crappy wieners. You want to taste the sodium and nitrates.

Sauce *prik*, which is what you serve on the side, is a generic term for any sauce that is kind of spicy, bottled, and sold next to ketchup in a Thai supermarket. It goes well with greasy foods. I find a mixture of ketchup, vinegar, and Sriracha to be a good approximation.

1.   For the sauce *prik:* Stir together the ketchup, Sriracha, and vinegar until combined.

2.   To make the wiener blossoms: Halve each hot dog crosswise. Starting on the rounded end, slice each wiener a bit more than halfway down the middle, toward the round end. Rotate the wiener 90 degrees and make the same cut. Do that two more times—four cuts per half wiener. The idea is to score each wiener with an "asterisk," so it creates curled-up petals when fried → 139.

recipe continues

Serve with a soggy piece of lettuce and a few underripe tomato slices.

Make the Hey-Ha Party Wings → 252 without sauce or buy wings from Popeyes.

3. Pour 2 to 3 inches of vegetable oil into a wok and heat over medium-high to 350°F. (Throw in a grain of uncooked rice; if it pops up and starts sizzling right away, the oil is ready. Or use a thermometer.) Working in batches, fry the wieners until the petals bloom outward, about 30 seconds. Drain on a paper towel.

4. For the rice: Splash a few teaspoons of the frying oil into a skillet and heat over medium-low heat. Crack the egg into the center. Use a spatula to trim away any unruly strands while the egg fries: You want this egg to look like it was cooked in a factory. After a few minutes—once the white is set—remove the egg along with any excess oil. Add the 2 slices of ham to the same pan and cook over medium heat to warm through.

5. Pour the frying oil from the wok into a heatproof container. Heat the empty wok over high heat until it begins to smoke, then swirl in about 3 tablespoons of the frying oil. Once the oil is shimmering, add the rice, peas and carrots, sugar, and stir-fry sauce. Stir-fry for a few minutes until the sauce has been absorbed, the peas and carrots have "steamed," and the rice has taken on a little color. Squeeze in the ketchup and toss until everything is incorporated. Throw in the raisins last so they don't get soggy, then remove from the heat.

6. To plate, fill a small bowl with the rice, then invert it onto a plate to form a dome. Place the egg over the fried rice and garnish with a few shakes of finely ground white pepper. Roll the slices of ham into cones and place beside the rice. Arrange the wiener blossoms next to the ham, and place the fried chicken wing wherever there's room. Feel free to get creative with the plating here—the sky's the limit. Serve with a bit of the sauce prik, and, if available, a soggy leaf of lettuce and a few underripe tomato slices.

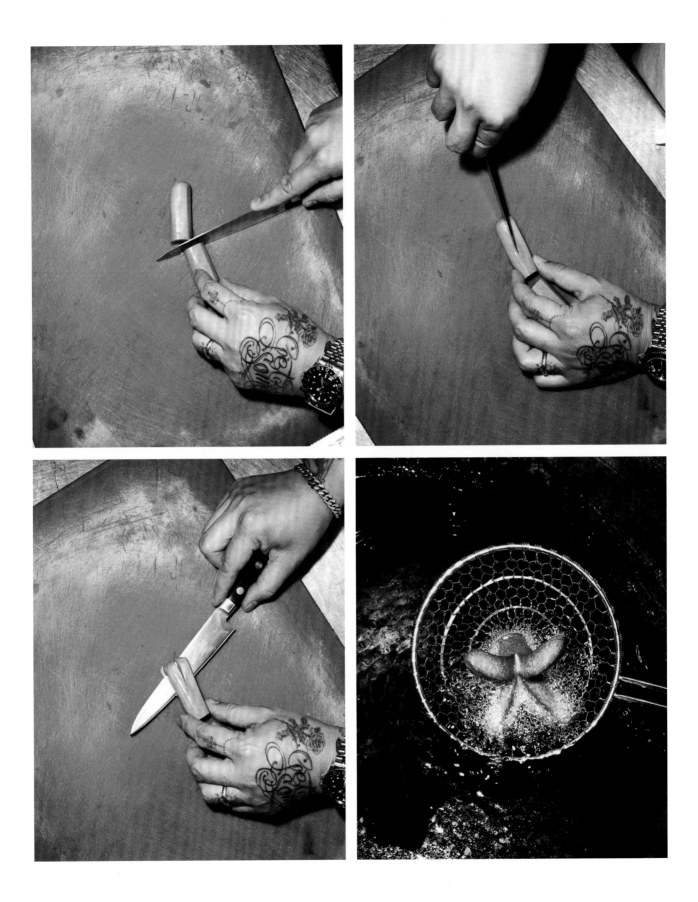

THAI BOXING CHICKEN
GAI YANG SANAM MUAY

Serves 2 to 4

Muay Thai is big business in Thailand. In Bangkok, there are stadiums all over the city, but the oldest and most venerated is Ratchadamnoen Stadium, even though its glory days are mostly in the past. When you go to see a boxing match, the other tradition is to stroll around the corner pre- or post-fight and hit up one of the BBQ chicken vendors that are rife throughout the neighborhood. The streets reek with smoke in the best way. I've never been super into Thai boxing, but I do appreciate the chicken at Likhit Gai Yang, a vendor that I always make a pilgrimage to when I'm town. I've tweaked together my own version of their salty/sweet/garlicky marinade, using thighs for ease of use, but you could also do this with a half chicken like they do. Usually the vendors would sell you the chicken à la carte, but at our restaurant, we pair it with papaya salad and sticky rice to transform it into a heavy hitting, all-in-one lunch plate.

⅓ cup coconut or palm sugar

1½ cups coconut milk

⅓ cup Thai seasoning sauce

⅓ cup Garlic-Cilantro Paste
→ 308

1½ teaspoons kosher salt
(see → 26)

4 boneless, skin-on chicken thighs (around 6 ounces each), not brined

Serve with Green Papaya Salad → 84, Sticky Rice → 296–299, Jaew → 172, and store-bought Thai sweet chile sauce.

1. In a small saucepan, combine the coconut sugar, coconut milk, seasoning sauce, garlic-cilantro paste, and salt and stir over low heat until combined. Remove from the heat and let the marinade cool.

2. Place the chicken in a plastic bag or shallow dish and cover with the marinade. Refrigerate and marinate for 3 hours, or overnight for a stronger flavor.

3. Preheat a well-oiled grill to high heat.

4. Remove the chicken from the marinade and grill for 4 to 5 minutes on each side, brushing the chicken with extra marinade as it cooks. Once cooked through and slightly charred, slice each thigh crosswise into strips and serve with sticky rice, papaya salad, *jaew,* and sweet chile sauce.

SCORCHING SOUTHERN DRY CURRY
KHUA KLING

Serves 4

1 pound beef tenderloin or sirloin, sliced across the grain into thin bite-size strips

½ cup All-Purpose Curry Paste → 303 (see Note)

10 to 15 fresh bird's eye chiles, or to taste, stemmed

3 (1-inch) nubs of fresh turmeric, roughly sliced

3 tablespoons vegetable oil

1½ tablespoons coconut or palm sugar

3 tablespoons fish sauce

10 to 12 kaffir lime leaves, deveined and finely julienned

Since curry paste is difficult to prepare in small batches with a food processor, you're going to end up with roughly double the amount of curry paste needed for one batch. This is fine—the *khua kling* paste can also be used as a substitute for the paste in Jungle Curry Clams → 75 to create an alternative Southern doppelganger of the dish. If you have a mortar and pestle, you can halve the curry paste recipe → 303 to make enough for one batch, mashing together the curry paste, chiles, turmeric, and oil until combined.

Even though there aren't many Southern Thai dishes on the Night + Market menu, my Southern-born dad has always had a soft spot for the chile-intensive food you find in the South and in many parts of Bangkok. After he cooked me his version of *khua kling*, essentially an extra-spicy beef dry curry stir-fried in the wok, I ended up getting into it. In my opinion, the baseline for this dish should be searing hot. Traditionally you would make a curry paste especially for this dish, but I hack it by taking our all-purpose curry paste and blending in raw bird's eye chiles and turmeric to make it fit the Southern flavor profile.

You'll be quickly searing the beef in the wok, so I would recommend using a nicer, more tender cut if possible, like tenderloin. This dish isn't limited to just beef, though, and you could also use pork, chicken, or any type of ground meat. Even mushrooms could work. This dish is about showcasing the spicy curry paste rather than the protein.

1. Remove the beef from the fridge and let it come to room temperature. Meanwhile, in a blender or food processor, combine the curry paste, bird's eye chiles, and turmeric and blend to a paste. Remove the curry mixture and set aside.

2. Heat an empty wok over high heat until it begins to smoke, then swirl in the oil. Once the oil is shimmering, add about ¼ cup of the prepared curry paste and stir-fry until fragrant, 20 to 30 seconds. Add the beef, stir-frying until it's opaque and halfway cooked. Add the coconut sugar and fish sauce and stir-fry until the meat is cooked and the sauce is slightly thickened. Transfer the khua kling to a plate and top with the lime leaves. Serve with jasmine rice.

Serve with Steamed Jasmine Rice → 296 or Coconut Sticky Rice → 299 and a Crispy Fried Egg → 244, and maybe a sliced avocado to cool this tongue-scorcher.

PRIK KING VARIATION

If you aren't into cooking things that are extremely spicy, you can try another variation of dry curry called *prik king,* which you can make by omitting the bird's eye chiles and turmeric, and throwing ¼ cup julienned fresh ginger (soaked in cold water for 10 minutes) into the stir-fry. You could use beef, but prik king also lends itself well to Brined Chicken → 313, shrimp, tofu, pork, or battered-fried fish.

FOR TRUE LARB,
I WILL SACRIFICE

Larb (noun, verb) / laap / : a spicy minced meat salad meant to be eaten with your hands along with herbs, sticky rice, and various vegetables.

A year or so ago, I was in Isaan hanging out at a house owned by the sister of my friend Ah Pong. I met Ah Pong several years ago because he worked under my uncle Vilas (the one who was a general) as a sergeant in the Thai army. He is from Udon Thani, the largest city in Isaan, and his real name is Pongkham, but I call him Ah Pong—*ah* being a way of calling someone *uncle* when they're not necessarily related to you. Occasionally we'd take trips to Isaan together. On one of those trips, I ended up talking to Ah Pong's sister's husband about *larb*, and somehow the subject of turkey larb came up—a dish that I had heard about but had never tried before. *Oh, let's make some right now,* came the immediate response from the husband. So we crowded into a pickup truck, drove out to the boonies at dusk, and hiked to a mosquito-infested "ranch" run by a former high school teacher who had gotten into the turkey-raising business after retirement. He told us the turkeys were too scrawny to sell—they had some fattening up to do before the end of summer—but after

some coaxing he sold us the largest bird of the flock, which weighed in around 12 pounds.

So after bagging that turkey inside an old rice sack, we hauled it home and got to work on the larb. Someone sliced the turkey's throat while I held it by the legs upside down, the blood sputtering into a metal bowl as it drained from its body. As someone who had never slaughtered a live animal before, it was borderline traumatizing to feel an animal fight for its life (I could see the imprint of its feet in my hands afterward). And I realize I say this as a chef who serves and consumes a lot of meat, but it's not the best feeling to kill an animal. There's a certain mixture of apprehension and adrenaline that hits right before as you realize you're going to be eating that same bird in a short span of time. After doing it once, I'm good on slaughtering for a while.

We plucked the feathers, butchered the bird into fat cuts of pale pink meat, then took turns chopping the meat on a wide tree stump until it became a fine turkey mince. The whole ordeal took two to three hours, lubricated by copious amounts of icy beer and pork rinds. Making larb from scratch can be an intensive process, but it's also a communal thing, like a clambake or a tri-tip barbecue. When you butcher a whole animal for larb, everyone pitches in to prepare some element. One person is making stock from the bones, another person is straining and

cleaning the blood, and someone else is frying up the skin to make cracklings to crumble on top. Somebody takes their turn on meat mincing duty (*thwack! thwack!*) while the little kids are in the corner chopping up fresh herbs. There's a remarkable efficiency to the whole thing. And of course there are the older guests on the sidelines nursing beers, watching and occasionally acting as sort of cheerleaders while the larb takes shape. By the time you're actually ready to eat, you realize that the social context in which you're making it matters as much as the food itself.

The word *larb* is a loaded concept. Almost everyone in Thailand knows its meaning, but for each person it can signify something totally different. It can be used as a verb, as in, I'm going to larb the hell out of this turkey, or that slab of pork, or this catfish I pulled out of the lake. In the most literal terms it means you're going to chop to some degree of fineness, possibly until your hands ache, then season it with a variety of herbs and spices; but in a larger sense it represents this folksy idea of cooking, like how the term "barbecue" conjures specific images with deep emotional resonance in parts of the United States. When it comes to the world of larb, the two basic, extremely broad schools of seasoning are the Lao-style in Isaan (lime, spicy, fish sauce, rice powder) and the Lanna-style in Northern Thailand (earthy, salty, bitter herbs). Both are really good drinking foods; in fact, they sort of demand alcohol.

The idea is to make little bites by scooping up a bit of the larb with sticky rice, then alternating with some raw vegetables. I've even seen people use cabbage leaves to make tiny larb tacos. It's not quite an appetizer, not quite a main dish, but something you can keep coming back to throughout the meal.

My own personal obsession with larb runs deep. When you walk into any of the Night + Market dining rooms, just off to the side of the doorway, you'll see a bright neon sign that reads "Larb King." I think of Larb King as my fantasy alter ego, a larger-than-life persona. As Liam Neeson says in *Batman Begins*, "If you make yourself more than just a man, if you devote yourself to an ideal, you become something else entirely." I think about iconic LA spots like King Taco and Original Tommy's Hamburgers, both specialists that have an instant association with their names. What if larb could be on *that* level?

My goal is that someday larb goes mainstream—that it becomes its own *thing*, like pad Thai, rather than something food nerds debate over. Even among Thai people, there are more hot dog stands than larb vendors. If we don't turn it into a pop sensation, who will?

The reason why I find larb so important in particular is because I have this dream that five years from now, it won't be considered exotic. It will be normalized. It won't be something to be gawked at. It's so particularly Thai that, if anything, I want to pull the focus *off* the food, not because the taste isn't important but because I want people

to enjoy sitting there and socializing around it. That's when the idea of larb comes full circle from what it is in Thailand. After all, you and your friends probably don't spend a lot of time talking about how blown away you are by In-N-Out every time you eat one of their burgers—you know it's delicious, they know it's delicious, and everyone moves forward with their lives.

The good news is that larb, despite a funny name and a particular way of being consumed, doesn't exactly need a PR team. It represents the way people like to eat now. It has bold flavors, it's

veggie-heavy, it's quick to prepare, it's customizable, it's refreshing, and it works well with alcohol.

The next seven recipes are all variations on the larb we serve at Night + Market and, for the most part, they increase in difficulty as you advance. If you haven't already, I'd recommend heading to the Basics section of this book and preparing the Roasted Chile Powder → **304** and Toasted Rice Powder → **299** before you start, which will allow you to make a basic larb in under 10 minutes.

CHICKEN LARB
LARB GAI

Serves 2 to 4

¾ pound ground chicken

3 tablespoons fish sauce

1 teaspoon sugar

1½ tablespoons Roasted Chile Powder → 304

½ cup thinly sliced (root to stem) red onion or shallots

¼ cup thinly sliced green onions

12 mint leaves, torn

½ cup roughly chopped cilantro, with stems

2 tablespoons lime juice

1 tablespoon Toasted Rice Powder → 299

SERVE WITH:

2 small wedges fresh green cabbage

½ cucumber, peeled lengthwise in striped segments and cut crosswise into ½-inch slices

16 green beans, trimmed

Sticky Rice → 296–299

This is what I call "gateway *larb*." That's partly because it's the restaurant's biggest seller in the larb genre, but also because it's extremely straightforward to prepare—there's no *oh wow, that's how you make it* revelation to be had. By the strictest definition, larb equals meat that is chopped, cooked, and seasoned. From there, a million spin-off variations are possible. Do you cook the meat in oil? Do you drain it or leave it wet? Do you add in chopped offal?

But before your head starts swimming with infinite possibilities, this Isaan-style chicken larb is the one you want to master first. An essential larb-making skill is seasoning the meat in the correct order, i.e., don't throw in everything at once and mush it all together. Ideally you'll dress your larb in the moment—*à la minute*, in chef speak—and then serve it immediately.

1. Put the chicken in a small saucepan and cover with water, stirring over medium heat until the chicken is opaque but still soft. Use a spatula or spoon to break the meat up into small clumps. Drain off the water, then stir in the fish sauce and sugar until they're completely dissolved. Remove from the heat and let it cool.

2. Once the chicken is cool, add the seasonings, in this order, giving a quick toss after each addition: the chile powder, red onion, green onions, mint, cilantro, and lime juice. Once you're ready to serve, add the rice powder at the last moment, then plate. Serve with green cabbage, sliced cucumber, raw green beans, and sticky rice on the side.

TOFU LARB VARIATION
Yes, vegan larb is a thing (not in Thailand, per se, but at Night + Market at least). The key with this variation is to deep-fry the tofu first for textural contrast; otherwise it turns into mush once you mix in the rest of the seasonings.

For the ground chicken, substitute an equal amount of firm tofu cut into 1-inch cubes. Heat a few inches of vegetable oil in a wok or deep fryer to 350°F. (Throw in a grain of uncooked rice; if it pops up and starts sizzling right away, the oil is ready. Or use a thermometer.) Pat the tofu very dry with paper towels, then fry just to the point where the cubes are developing a golden-brown hue on the outside, 45 seconds to 1 minute. Remove the tofu from the oil, transfer to a large bowl, and use a spoon to mash each cube into small pebble-size chunks. Follow the method for chicken larb, substituting thin soy sauce for the fish sauce.

ISAAN CATFISH LARB
LARB PLA DUK

Serves 2 to 4

2½- to 3-pound
whole catfish

¼ cup finely minced
fresh galangal

1 teaspoon sugar

2 tablespoons fish sauce

2 tablespoons Roasted
Chile Powder → 304

2 tablespoons thinly sliced
lemongrass (see → 25)

½ cup thinly sliced (root to
stem) red onion or shallots

½ cup roughly chopped
cilantro, with stems

12 mint leaves, torn

½ cup thinly sliced
green onions

½ cup chopped
sawtooth (culantro)

2 tablespoons *nam pla ra*
(or fish sauce if unavailable)

¼ cup lime juice

1½ tablespoons Toasted Rice
Powder → 299

SERVE WITH:

2 small wedges fresh
green cabbage

½ cucumber, peeled
lengthwise in striped
segments and cut into
½-inch slices

16 green beans, trimmed

Sticky Rice → 296–299

If it moves, you can *larb* it. For instance: a whole fish. In Isaan, it starts with grilling a fresh catfish over slow-burning embers, scraping the flesh off the bones, then chopping it up into larb. You can basically do the same thing at home over a gas or charcoal grill, using the flames to introduce a subtle smoky flavor into the fish. Once you've scraped the fish skeleton clean, use a large cleaver to chop the meat together.

1. Preheat a grill to medium heat.

2. Remove the head and tail from the catfish and wrap the fish in foil. Grill, flipping occasionally, until cooked through, about 30 minutes. When the fish is cool enough to handle, use a fork or your hands to remove the flesh from the bones until you have about 2 cups of meat (preferably with a little skin mixed in). If you have some left over, you can eat it however you want.

3. Place the catfish in the center of a large cutting board and top with the minced galangal. Use a meat cleaver to chop the fish and galangal until it begins to resemble a rough paste, 1 to 2 minutes.

4. Transfer the fish mixture to a saucepan, stir in the sugar and fish sauce and cook over low heat until dissolved. Once the liquid reduces slightly, remove from the heat and let it cool. Once the fish is cool, add the seasonings, in this order, giving a quick toss after each addition: chile powder, lemongrass, red onion, cilantro, mint, green onions, sawtooth, *nam pla ra*, lime juice, and toasted rice powder. Serve with a wedge of green cabbage, sliced cucumber, raw green beans, and sticky rice.

This recipe calls for *nam pla ra*, which is another type of fish sauce used in Isaan cooking that's chunkier and swampier than the regular stuff. If you can't find it in a Thai market or online, you can just substitute fish sauce.

DUCK LARB IN THE STYLE OF PHEN ADMINISTRATIVE DISTRICT
LARB PED UMPHOE PHEN

Serves 2 to 4

2 (10- to 12-ounce) bone-in, skin-on duck leg quarters

¼ cup finely minced fresh galangal

1 teaspoon sugar

2 tablespoons fish sauce

3 tablespoons Roasted Chile Powder → 304

¼ cup thinly sliced lemongrass (see → 25)

½ cup thinly sliced (root to stem) red onion or shallots

½ cup roughly chopped cilantro, with stems

12 mint leaves, torn

½ cup thinly sliced green onions

½ cup chopped sawtooth (culantro)

2 tablespoons *nam pla ra* (or fish sauce if unavailable)

¼ cup lime juice

1½ tablespoons Toasted Rice Powder → 299

This recipe is loosely inspired by a version of *larb* that I encountered at a roadside restaurant in Isaan that specializes in all things duck—duck hot pots, fried duck heads, duck stir-fry, etc. Besides the usual combo punch of chile/lime/fish sauce, what makes this larb stand out is that you're imparting concentrated duck meat essences by including the rendered fat and the crispy bits of skin.

1. Using a paring knife, remove all the meat from the thighs and drumsticks, scraping the bones clean and picking out the sinewy bits. Separate the duck skin from the meat. Slice the skin into thin strips and set aside. On a large cutting board, sprinkle the meat with the galangal and chop vigorously with a large cleaver, folding the meat back over itself, until a rough paste forms, about 5 minutes.

2. In a saucepan, cook the duck skin over medium heat until crispy, 5 to 7 minutes; the fat will render out as well. Remove the skin and drain on a paper towel. Pour off all but about 3 tablespoons of the rendered fat. Add the chopped meat, sugar, and fish sauce to the pan and stir-fry until cooked through but soft, about 3 to 4 minutes. Remove from the heat and let the duck cool. Once cooled, add the seasonings, in this order, giving a quick toss after each addition: chile powder, lemongrass, red onion, cilantro, mint, green onions, sawtooth, *nam pla ra*, lime juice, and toasted rice powder. Top with the crispy skin and serve with a wedge of green cabbage, sliced cucumber, raw green beans, and sticky rice.

SERVE WITH:
2 small wedges green cabbage
½ cucumber, peeled lengthwise in striped segments and cut into ½-inch slices
16 green beans, trimmed
Sticky Rice → 296–299 or Coconut Sticky Rice → 299

NORTHERN-STYLE PORK LARB
LARB LANNA

Of all the foods I've cooked at Night + Market, few if any have pulled me down the rabbit hole like Northern *larb*, a thing of elegant and restrained beauty. The whole dish is powered by dark, earthy spices—the twang of lime and the grainy crunch of rice powder you'd find in Isaan larb are gone. If you're a student of *lanna* cuisine, the term for the old Northern Thai kingdom from which the culture is descended, then *larb lanna* is heavy-artillery stuff, as much a ritual as it is a dish. The pork is hand-chopped until it becomes a slick meat paste, seasoned with blood and liver and occasionally bile, which makes for a bitter version, something locals find extremely appealing, then paired with whatever herbs are growing on the mountainous hillsides. Like most great foodways in the world, it's a dying art form. All of this is to say, there are no shortcuts or substitutions when making this stuff. But while this might be the most labor-intensive recipe in the book, it's also one of the most life changing.

The three recipes that follow are essentially different forms of the same thing, larb lanna. The most common version, more or less, is the cooked version, *larb suk*, which is made from hand-chopped meat that has been heavily seasoned, flash-sautéed with oil so it stays soft and tender, tossed with pungent herbs, and garnished with crispy fried garlic to form a sort of meaty salad. Then there is *larb dip*, a raw meat dish that you can imagine as the rustic sibling of steak tartare, or as sausage stuffing that hasn't been cooked yet. The seasonings are similar, but the herbs are showered on top rather than mixed in. And last is *larb tod*, which turns the seasoned larb paste into flat little fried patties. Traditionally, all these styles are made by chopping pork for the better part of an hour, but we start with ground pork to lessen the cleaver workload. The ground pork is fattier, but I find the added lushness is more delicious even if it's not entirely traditional (I also add fish sauce, which you won't find in most Northern larbs, for similar reasons). Each version is garnished with the same herbs and eaten the same way, with fingerfuls of Sticky Rice → **296 and 299** and bites of raw veggies. Think of them as the Holy Trinity of Northern larb.

RAW LARB TARTARE

LARB DIP VARIATIONS

To make the raw larb, follow the first four steps of the Larb Suk, omitting the liver. Spread the raw meat mixture onto a plate and top with a small handful each of chopped green onion, cilantro, mint, sawtooth, *rau ram*, and Fried Garlic → 311. Serve with pork rinds, raw vegetables (cucumber, cabbage, green beans), and Sticky Rice → 296–299.

Note: Since this version is served raw, instead of regular ground pork use lean ground pork loin, or lean ground beef sirloin if you'd prefer. If you're not down with eating raw blood, which I'd understand, cook the blood using the same hot broth technique as the *luu suk* (Blood Dipping Soup, → 114), or omit it altogether.

FRIED LARB PATTIES

LARB SUK

Serves 4

4 ounces pork liver (or calf's liver if unavailable)

Kosher salt (see → 26)

¾ pound ground pork

1 pound fresh coagulated pork blood

1 stalk lemongrass, whole

3 tablespoons Larb Spice → 157

1½ tablespoons Roasted Chile Powder → 304

1½ tablespoons shrimp paste

2 teaspoons sugar

2 tablespoons fish sauce

2 tablespoons vegetable oil

1½ tablespoons minced garlic

¼ cup chicken broth

½ cup roughly chopped cilantro, with stems

12 mint leaves, torn

½ cup chopped sawtooth (culantro)

½ cup chopped *rau ram*

2 heaping tablespoons Fried Garlic → 311

1. Slice the liver into ⅛-inch slivers, using the tip of the knife to remove any veins or connective tissue. Place the sliced liver in a small bowl and cover with a few tablespoons of salt. Let the liver cure in the fridge for 10 minutes.

2. While the liver is curing, place the ground pork in the center of a large cutting board. Using two large knives or meat cleavers, chop the meat vigorously for 10 minutes until it resembles a rough paste, folding the meat pile over itself every so often using the flat part of the knife (your arm might get sore, but push through the pain).

3.   Remove the liver from the fridge, rinse off the salt, and set aside. Add the coagulated blood to a large bowl and season with a pinch of salt. Remove 4 to 5 outer layers from the lemongrass stalk, then use your hands to knead/crush/massage the lemongrass stalks into the blood. Knead for 3 to 4 minutes, then strain out the liquid at the bottom of the bowl, keeping the liquid. Repeat the process until you've produced about ½ cup of liquid blood, then dispose of the leftover blood and lemongrass.

4.   In a bowl, stir together the strained blood, larb spice, chile powder, shrimp paste, sugar, and fish sauce. Fold in the chopped pork and liver and mix with your hands until something resembling sausage filling forms.

5.   In a saucepan, heat the oil over high heat until shimmering. Add the minced garlic and stir-fry until fragrant. Reduce the heat to low, stir in the ground pork mixture and chicken broth, breaking up the meat with a spatula until it's cooked through but still soft—there should be a little liquid left—moist but not soupy, 4 to 5 minutes. Remove the pan from the heat and let the meat mixture cool. Once cooled, toss in the cilantro, mint, sawtooth, and *rau ram*.

6.   Plate and top with fried garlic. Serve with cabbage, green beans, cucumbers, and sticky rice.

LARB TOD

Follow the first four steps of the Larb Suk, then roll the raw larb mixture into meatballs roughly the size of a Ping-Pong ball and set aside. In a large skillet or wok, heat ¼ cup vegetable oil over medium-high heat until shimmering. Add the meatballs, flattening them with a spatula, and cook until browned outside but still slightly soft inside, 2 to 3 minutes on each side. Serve over a bed of sliced raw cabbage and garnish with small handfuls of chopped green onion, cilantro, mint, sawtooth, *rau ram*, and Fried Garlic → 311. Serve with a wedge of lime and Sticky Rice → 296–299.

SERVE WITH:

2 small wedges green cabbage

½ cucumber, peeled lengthwise in striped segments and cut into ½-inch slices

16 green beans, trimmed

Sticky Rice → 296–299

LARB SPICE

Makes about 3 tablespoons

My mom's cousin Jay Pawn dries the ingredients for her *larb* spice mixture in her backyard. But if you don't want to rely on the power of the sun, then you can speed up the process with a food dehydrator or an oven on its lowest temperature setting. Traditionally a cone-shaped spice called long pepper would be used here, but the closest common approximation I've found is black peppercorns.

This makes enough for one batch of Larb Suk, but you can easily double or triple the recipe to have the mixture on hand. It keeps for months in an airtight container in the fridge.

2 tablespoons finely minced fresh galangal

2 tablespoons thinly sliced lemongrass (see → 25)

1 tablespoon crumbled shrimp paste

1 teaspoon Sichuan peppercorns

1 teaspoon prickly ash bark (or an equal amount of Sichuan peppercorns if unavailable)

1 teaspoon coriander seeds

½ teaspoon black peppercorns

1. Spread the galangal, lemongrass, and shrimp paste onto a sheet of parchment paper or foil and place in a food dehydrator or an oven on the lowest setting with the door slightly ajar until they're dry and crumbly, which should take about 1 hour, depending on your equipment.

2. In a large skillet, toast the Sichuan peppercorns over low heat until fragrant, 3 to 4 minutes. Remove from the skillet. Repeat with the prickly ash bark, coriander, and then the black peppercorns.

3. Working in batches if necessary, in a spice grinder, coffee grinder, or mortar and pestle, pulverize the toasted spices and dried aromatics until fine. Store in a cool, dry place.

CHAPTER 3
THE MAGNETIC EFFECT OF
MEATS AND DIPS

In the year or so before the idea for Night + Market was conceived, I took a trip to France to check out Loire Valley wine country. Even though I was supposed to be running Talésai at the time, I was managing the restaurant so poorly that my dad basically nudged me to take off, thinking that he would be able to right the ship to a degree while I was gone. In hasty preparation I had scrawled down various winery addresses pulled from the bottle labels I had been pouring at Talésai with plans to talk my way into tastings with winemakers I had come to revere.

After landing in Paris, the trip quickly devolved into a comedy of errors, like a scene out of a Mr. Bean movie. My friend and I had planned to rent a car, but when we showed up at the rental kiosk, the compact Peugeot I had reserved turned out to have a manual transmission. I had driven a bit of stick in Thailand, so I figured I could handle it. But after struggling for an hour to get the jerking car out of the lot, I went back to the smug clerk to ask, defeated and emasculated, if there was anything available in an automatic. He informed me, with all the iciness of a host at the hot restaurant who lets you know that your table will be a 2½-hour wait, that since it was Sunday the only car left was a luxury BMW that would cost an extra 300 euros per day.

More determined than ever, I hit the road that much poorer. At some point I realized that since it was Sunday, most of the wineries were closed, and since it was right after harvest season (when winemakers are busy putting wine into production), the ones that *were* open were too busy to deal with an American kid who showed at up their doorstep speaking very rusty French. By design I had decided I was going to visit these wineries unannounced, since calling on the phone likely meant being told no—these aren't places where you can just show up. At that point, though, I was feeling ballsy (and desperate) enough to try anything.

After getting soundly rejected by several winemakers, I ended up at the legendary domaine Clos Roche Blanche, only to be told that the owners were leaving for New York in thirty-six hours and didn't have time to entertain me. As a conciliatory gesture, they sent me to this gal down the road, Noëlla Moratin, a winemaker who was renting out a parcel of their land.

After getting lost and having to call her for directions, I cruised in over a half hour late to meet Noëlla and learned that she was flying to New York in thirty-six hours too (they were all headed to a trade tasting). Somehow I convinced her to let me do a quick tasting, and after whisking me through the *chai* (production facility), she told me she had twenty minutes to spend with me and proceeded to guide me through their wines with the studied efficiency of someone without plans to linger.

At this point, a cherubic farmhand peeked his head into the room while we were tasting and said hello, then asked if we were from Brooklyn. It turned out that this French guy was Noëlla's partner, and he used to be the proprietor at what was one of my favorite restaurants when I lived in New York, iCi, a place that happened to serve the sort of brilliant wines I had come to the Loire to sample. What was supposed to be a twenty-minute tasting soon turned into dinner, which then turned into bottles being pulled from the cellar, which became a long night of drinking and eating that stretched past midnight.

The food seemed to appear out of nowhere: charcuterie like *saucisson sec*, head cheese, and rillettes all made from a farm pig named Copain, some local cheese from the fridge, a crust of bread, and a salad thrown together with vegetables from their backyard garden. It was the platonic ideal of country life made real. Many of the wines we drank would later make up the first list at Night + Market, and it was the first time I drank what quickly became my true love, *pét-nat* (naturally sparkling wines, see → **22**). And more important, that night served as the seedling for what would become Night + Market once I started hosting dinner parties in the empty space next to Talésai.

To me, that entire experience in France captured the best aspects of the rural lifestyle, the idea that at any moment you could conjure up a good time by gathering people around a few simple foodstuffs and something to drink. It was at that point that I started to draw connections in my mind between rural Thailand and rural France, not so much in the tastes, but in the way that food and alcohol had the magnetic effect of bringing people together. In Thailand, instead of cured meats you're probably eating something grilled, and you're probably drinking watery beer, but the combined effect is the same.

At the core of Thai social eating are grilled meats and chile dips—they are, at minimum, the basic foods you'd put out when hosting a get-together. It's a communal thing, and like throwing a neighborhood BBQ it has the power to draw people out of the woodwork in odd ways, especially when combined with alcohol. It reminds me of something Jonathan Gold once told me, which was that food is interesting, but *eating* is fascinating. The spread—specifically drinks, meat, and stuff to dip it in—offers an excuse to get together, but it's everything else going on around it that's more important. That night in the Loire was basically the same thing I would aim for at my restaurant, but with Thai flavors, the spirit of good wine, and sausage that crosses cultures.

My sincere hope is that when you cook the recipes in this chapter, they provide the same function to you as they did to me when I started serving them. They should be an excuse to invite some people over, open up a few beers or a bottle of wine, and kick back in an apartment, a backyard, an empty parking lot, wherever. You might end up debating the meaning of life or the merits of the latest Bourne movie, but you will leave fat, dumb, and happy. That, really, is always the goal.

SAUSAGE PARTY

There are many types of sausage in Thailand—sweet Chinese-style sausage, noodle-stuffed sausages, blood sausage. But out of all the different variations, there are two that I think yield the most reward in terms of effort for the home cook: Northern herb sausage (*sai uah*) and Isaan sour sausage (*sai krok Isaan*).

If you don't have a meat grinder with a sausage attachment, that's fine. For almost a year, before I bought a legit hunting-grade stuffer, we stuffed every sausage at Night + Market by hand with a Chinese soup spoon. We stuffed a lot of sausage that way, and it probably gave me carpal tunnel. Thankfully, you won't ever have to make these recipes in that quantity.

NORTHERN-STYLE HERB SAUSAGE
SAI UAH

Makes about six 6-inch links

2 pounds ground pork (80% lean)

½ pound pork fat or pork belly, cut into ¼-inch cubes

¾ cup thinly sliced lemongrass (see → 25)

1 cup roughly chopped cilantro, with stems

¼ cup deveined and slivered kaffir lime leaves

2 tablespoons grated key lime zest

2 tablespoons grated fresh turmeric

2 tablespoons fish sauce

2 tablespoons All-Purpose Curry Paste → 303

2 tablespoons Roasted Chile Powder → 304

1½ tablespoons sugar

¼ cup Thai seasoning sauce

¼ cup coconut milk

Serve with Sticky Rice → 296–299, Roasted Green Chile Dip → 191, and sliced cucumbers or a few cilantro stems on the side.

The name *sai uah* comes from the Northern Thai dialect. It can refer to lots of things beside sausage—guts, intestine, the filling that goes inside dumplings—but most people associate it with a specific pork-and-herb sausage you find in Chiang Mai, Chiang Rai, and all the Northern towns in between. You'll see market vendors, street carts, and small restaurants grilling it over smoldering charcoal (almost smoking it, really) and selling hacked-off segments to eat as a snack or to take home for later. I've been eating this stuff since I could chew solid food—there is never a bad time for Northern sausage.

The most defining aspect of sai uah is its depth of seasoning. There are a lot of fragrant and herbaceous dimensions to it—lemongrass, lime, curry paste, cilantro, turmeric, roasted chiles, coconut milk—that all meld together to produce a maximalist sausage experience. In some ways, it's the antithesis of *sai krok* (Isaan Sour Sausage → 165), which is seasoned only minimally and develops its complex flavors through fermentation.

The most obvious application for this sausage is to stuff it into casings, but you could also cook it in the same way you would chorizo or any other seasoned ground meat. Shape it into flat patties and fry in a skillet to eat with fried eggs for breakfast. Cook it with tomato sauce to make a face-melting spaghetti. Stuff it into some big mild green peppers with sticky rice and bake it in the oven. Or sauté it with onions and garlic to make Sai Uah Tacos → 287.

Equipment: 4 feet or so of natural hog casings; Chinese soup spoon or meat grinder with sausage attachment; cotton twine, cut into 2-inch lengths

1.   If the hog casings come packed in salt or brine, which most do, remove them from the packaging and rinse them thoroughly, then run water through the insides. If there are any holes or leaks, cut out those sections. I like to soak the casings in a bowl of room-temperature water with 1 tablespoon distilled white vinegar, which helps them loosen up a bit.

recipe continues

**Bovin, Hervé Villemade,
Loire, France**

Wine names in the Loire
Valley are often cheeky
and fun, which, I think, is
an indication not to take
them too seriously. Hervé
Villemade's Bovin is a perfect
example. The bottle has
a picture of a cow on it. It
comes in a big liter bottle,
which is an encouragement
to drink it freely and
copiously, and perhaps
more importantly, it's priced
as something you can
consume daily or bring to
any backyard party (slightly
chilled). It's dependable and
simple, but still very special.
In wine terms, it's not a
completely wild and unruly
Gamay, but it does have a
certain barnyard character
that makes it go well with
the gaminess of grilled pork.

2. In a large bowl, use your hands to thoroughly mix together all the ingredients until everything is evenly combined.

3. Cut off about 4 feet of casing and tie a knot at one end—a simple overhand knot or a length of twine will do fine. If you have a meat grinder with a sausage attachment, you can stuff the filling according to your machine's instructions. But if not, here's a low-tech hack for stuffing the sausage: Take a Chinese soup spoon, the kind with a little valley along its handle, and slip the first 6 inches of the casing onto the handle of the spoon like you are putting on a condom in the exact wrong way, the way they taught you not to do it in sex ed class. Then place a 1-inch ball of filling into the bowl of the spoon and use your thumb to push it into the casing while cradling the spoon with your other hand. Carefully inch the lump of stuffing down the casing with your thumb and fingers, pushing it along like a mouse inside a boa constrictor until it reaches the end.

4. Once you've stuffed about 6 inches of sausage, tie it off with 2 lengths of string back-to-back. Tying two knots close together about ⅛ inch apart will ensure that you can cut each link apart without severing the string. Once you've stuffed the entire casing, segmented into 6-inch lengths, tie off the other end and wind the finished sausages into a big meaty spiral.

5. To bake: Preheat the oven to 350°F. Poke the sausage skin a few times with a toothpick to let steam escape, and bake for 30 minutes. After they've baked, brown them in a lightly oiled skillet over medium-high heat, 3 to 4 minutes per side. Let cook for 10 minutes before slicing.

   To grill: Set up a grill for indirect heat and preheat to medium-low. Place the sausages on a sheet of foil on the cool side of the grill, close the lid, and cook until they reach an internal temperature of 150°F (use a thermometer), 30 to 40 minutes. Then move them off the foil onto the grill and char them over high direct heat for 3 to 4 minutes to add some color. Let cool for 10 minutes before slicing.

6. Serve with sticky rice and *nam prik noom* (Roasted Green Chile Dip), which are traditional accompaniments.

ISAAN SOUR SAUSAGE
SAI KROK ISAAN

Makes twenty-five 1½-inch balls

One of Isaan's most famous culinary exports is sour sausage, which you'll find all over Bangkok as well—on nearly every corner you'll see two types of sausage stands: one selling American-style hot dogs and the other hawking deep-fried sour sausage shoved onto a wooden skewer. In Isaan, the preparation is a little more varied and intensive. You'll often find it slow-grilled over charcoal, and it's not uncommon for the sausage guy to ask your sourness preference—do you want the stuff that's been curing for two days or four days?

Each link of sour sausage is like a little essay on the beautiful, lightly gamy undertones of fermented meat. Most people who try sour sausage for the first time swear it's made with lime juice, but the mild pucker is actually subtler and more fragrant. As the sausage ages, the raw garlic softens and deepens in flavor and, together with the natural, fermented sourness, balances out the fatty richness of the ground pork. It seems almost impossible that something so complex could come out of just eight ingredients.

I'd imagine that the technique developed as a rustic preservation method that evolved into a specific taste people craved. It's a folk tradition that's been going on for a very long time. I'm no biochemist, but from what I understand this type of fermentation is pretty basic. In the span of a couple days, the bacteria reacts with the starch and sugar mixed into the meat and produces lactic acid, which tastes sour.

Unlike *sai uah* → 162, which is heavily seasoned from the start, the flavor in *sai krok* develops as it sits, which means you'll have to account for that missing element by slightly overseasoning when adding the garlic, salt, and sugar in the unfermented stage. Once the sourness kicks in, the sausage will be balanced.

Okay, so here is where it seems to get weird: To make this, you have to hang the seasoned, raw sausages in a warm place for a couple days. (Or use *naem* powder as a shortcut; see → 170). As with any type of bacterial fermentation, there are things that can go wrong, but I've been eating homemade sour sausage for most of my life and have never gotten sick, which I realize is not an airtight argument,

2 pounds fatty ground pork (80% lean)

1 cup cooked Sticky Rice → 296–299, at room temperature

¾ cup Steamed Jasmine Rice → 296, at room temperature

1 tablespoon sugar

2½ tablespoons kosher salt (see → 26)

2 teaspoons ground white pepper

¾ cup minced garlic

1 (2.4-ounce) package *naem* powder (optional; I like Lobo brand)

recipe continues

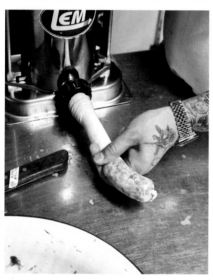

SERVE WITH:

Sticky Rice → 296–299

Fresh ginger, peeled and cut into matchsticks, soaked in cold water for 10 minutes, then shaken dry

Fresh bird's eye chiles

Cilantro sprigs

Seasoned Fried Peanuts → 309

Green cabbage, cut into wedges

but I think it emphasizes how commonplace this method is in Thai households.

If the idea of hanging raw sausages in a pantry doesn't sound like your thing, or you live in an area where the climate is too cold to allow for fermentation, you can also use 1 package naem powder, which is sort of a Thai housewife kitchen helper. It not only speeds up the souring process to less than a day, but it lets you sour the meat in the fridge, too.

Traditionally sour sausage is eaten on its own with sticky rice, ginger, peanuts, and chiles. If you want to mess around with putting sour sausage into fried rice or egg omelets, that's fine too, but that category of stuff is more commonly done with *naem* (Sour Pork Bundles → 170), which is like a cousin of sai krok without a casing.

Equipment: About 4 feet of natural hog casings; Chinese soup spoon or meat grinder with a sausage attachment; cotton twine, cut into 2-inch lengths

1. If the hog casings comes packed in salt or brine, which most do, remove them from the packaging and rinse them thoroughly, then run water through the insides. If there are any holes or leaks, throw those ones out. I like to soak the casings in a bowl of warm water with 1 tablespoon distilled white vinegar, which helps them loosen up a bit. (See photo → 166.)

2. In a large bowl, combine the pork, sticky rice, jasmine rice, sugar, salt, white pepper, garlic, and naem powder (if using to boost the souring process) and mix with your hands until everything is evenly dispersed and no clumps of rice remain. This process will take some time, but it's essential to make sure your sausage ferments properly. Don't worry about overmixing. Once mixed, you can cook pinches of filling in the microwave for 10 seconds to test for seasoning, which should be robust but not overpowering. Adjust as necessary.

3. When you're ready, cut off about 4 feet of casing and tie a knot at one end—a simple overhand knot or a length of twine will do fine. If you have a meat grinder with a sausage attachment, you can stuff the filling according to your machine's instructions. But if not, here's a low-tech hack for stuffing the sausage: Take a Chinese soup spoon, the kind with a little valley along its handle, and slip the first 6 inches of the casing onto the handle of the spoon like you are putting on a condom in the exact wrong way, the way they

taught you not to do it in sex ed class. Then place a 1-inch ball of filling into the bowl of the spoon and use your thumb to push it into the casing while cradling the spoon with your other hand. Carefully inch the lump of stuffing down the casing with your thumb and fingers, pushing it along like a mouse inside a boa constrictor until it reaches the end. (See photos on the previous pages.)

4.   As you stuff, tie 2 lengths of string back-to-back every 1½ inches to form oblong balls. Tying two knots close together about ⅛ inch apart will ensure that you can cut each ball apart without severing the string. Once the casing is full, tie off the other end of the casing.

5.   Now comes the fermentation. Hang the sausages from a length of string with a sheet of cardboard below to act as a drip tray (they will weep). The key is to place them in an area with a relatively constant room temperature (mid-70s) and low humidity (<50%). A pantry or garage works great. The sausage can take anywhere from 2 to 4 days to ferment. After 2 days, cut off a link, cook it, and sample it for sourness—you can keep checking every 12 hours or so until it reaches your preferred level of sour, ranging from a mild balanced tanginess to a sharp acidic quality (beyond 4 days the sausage won't really increase in sourness, but turn more gamy and musky). Once done, throw it in the fridge to stop the fermentation and the sausage will keep, uncooked, for a little over a week.

6.   Cook on a well-oiled preheated grill over medium heat until browned but still a little pink inside, 6 to 8 minutes. If the sausages have been sitting in the fridge, they may need to warm up for 2 to 3 minutes on indirect heat before grilling.

TIPS:

Just as you should any time you're dealing with raw meat, do your best to work clean. Wash your hands, cutting boards, etc.

When you make your filling, mix in the rice well enough so that it has a uniform texture. This will help the fermentation occur more evenly.

Check the sausage fairly often, since temperature, humidity, and the microbes in the air will vary the process for everyone. Ours usually takes two to three days, but there's a certain wild-card element involved— you're searching for what fermentation experts call "the sweet spot between rancid and sublime."

If there are any bad rancid smells, bad colors, things that are clearly off—pitch it. (Obviously a sour smell is normal, and what you want.)

Ideally, once you cook the fermented sausage it will still be a little pink inside, almost like semi-dry charcuterie. If desired, though, you can cook it longer until no pink-ness remains.

SOUR PORK BUNDLES
NAEM

Makes about 2 pounds

1 (2.4-ounce) package *naem powder* (look for Lobo brand)

1 tablespoon sugar

2½ tablespoons kosher salt (see → 26)

2 teaspoons ground white pepper

¾ cup minced garlic

2 pounds pork tenderloin, chopped into ¼-inch chunks

10 fresh bird's eye chiles, or to taste, stemmed and slightly bruised

There are two main differences between *naem* and *sai krok* → 165. The first and most obvious is that naem doesn't have a casing. It's usually portioned out and wrapped in banana leaves, but you could just as well use plastic sandwich bags. The second difference is that it uses lean pork rather than fatty pork, which gives it a firmer texture.

Although you could ferment this in the same way as sai krok, I use naem powder as a shortcut, since loose packets of fermenting meat look sketchier to health inspectors than hanging sausages. Naem powder is a handy acidity regulator/souring agent, marketed to Thai housewives, that helps the meat sour in a shorter amount of time *and* in the fridge rather than in a laundry room—which is partly why we use it at the restaurant. You can buy packets online for a few dollars.

Naem is pretty versatile as an ingredient. You can cook it multiple ways—steam, stir-fry, grill—then toss in with salads like Crispy Rice Salad → 101, fried rice, or omelets. Basically use it as you would regular ground pork, but when an extra punch of flavor is welcome.

Equipment: 8 plastic zip-top sandwich bags

1. In a large bowl, combine the naem powder, sugar, salt, white pepper, and garlic. Mix with your hands until the seasonings are evenly dispersed. Fold in the chopped pork and bruised chiles (the chiles impart flavor, but can be removed before eating). Divide into 8 portions and scoop into the plastic sandwich bags, pressing out the air and sealing. Let the packets cure at room temperature overnight, or in the fridge for slightly longer—about 24 hours. After that the souring process should be done, so you can store it in the fridge, but for best results use it within a week. Beyond that it will start to go from smelling tangy to smelling rancid, and you won't want to use it.

2. To prepare, use in the way you would normal ground pork. It's already cured, so you are basically heating it up rather than cooking it all the way through. You'll still want it to be a little pink in the middle.

GRILLED WINGS WITH JAEW

Serves 4

Think of *jaew* as the ultimate dipping sauce for grilled meats. It's a Northeastern Thai staple and despite being relatively simple to make, it has all the right elements—salty, sour, spicy, a little bitter— to elevate smoky charred protein into something spectacular. The predominant flavor comes from a balance of fish sauce and lime, amped up with chile powder, and a faint bitter nuttiness that comes from the toasted rice powder or sesame seeds (which also help to thicken the sauce slightly).

At Night + Market, jaew is probably best known as what comes with the fatty, decadent Pork Toro → 178, but it does just as well with leaner stuff like grilled rib eye or chicken too.

In the summer, I like to mess around with grilled wings quickly soaked in a basic Thai marinade. Add a few ears of coconut-glazed Grilled Sweet Corn → 231 and you have all the makings of a classic backyard barbecue.

1 cup Stir-Fry Sauce → 306, or ½ cup thin soy sauce plus ½ cup oyster sauce

2 tablespoons sugar

2 tablespoons vegetable oil, plus more for the grill

2 teaspoons ground white pepper

24 chicken drumettes and/or wing flats (wingettes)

Jaew → 172, for dipping

Equipment: 12 (8-inch) bamboo skewers soaked in water for at least 1 hour

1. In a large bowl, whisk together the stir-fry sauce, sugar, oil, and white pepper. Add the wings and toss to coat with your hands. Marinate for 20 to 30 minutes (if allowed to sit for much longer, they'll be too salty).

2. Preheat a well-oiled grill to high heat.

3. Thread 2 flat wing pieces onto each skewer on a diagonal, spacing them about ½ inch apart. Grill along with the drumettes, turning occasionally, until lightly charred and cooked through, 15 to 20 minutes. Serve with the jaew for dipping.

NORTHEASTERN CHILE DIP
JAEW

Makes about ¾ cup

¼ cup fish sauce

¼ cup lime juice

1 tablespoon sugar

1 tablespoon Roasted Chile Powder → 304

1 tablespoon toasted sesame seeds (optional)

2 tablespoons Toasted Rice Powder → 299 (optional)

In a medium bowl, whisk together the fish sauce, lime juice, sugar, and roasted chile powder until the sugar is dissolved. Tweak with more sugar or lime juice to taste. Just before serving, stir in the sesame seeds or rice powder (if desired). Eat with your favorite grilled meat as a dipping sauce.

LEK, MY GURU. ASIDE FROM MY GRANDMA PROBABLY THE MOST SKILLED OLD-SCHOOL THAI CHEF I KNOW

PRAWNS TWO WAYS
WITH NAM JIM SEAFOOD

You can never have enough *nam jim* seafood in the fridge. Although "seafood" is in the name, the stuff is far more multipurpose than that. It's a quintessential beer garden dip in Thailand, great with deep-fried foods, but especially common at seaside restaurants that specialize in charcoal-grilled or baked prawns, squid, fish, etc. I use boatloads of it both at home and at the restaurant.

Because of its ubiquity, it's also kind of an imprecise thing. There is always fish sauce, lime juice, sugar, chiles, and garlic, but every cook has their preferred ratios. As with most Thai sauces, you can tweak the seasoning of nam jim seafood to suit your own tastes. It's hard to mess up.

I've provided instructions for making it two ways. One is a more simplified, on-the-fly method with sugar. This is the stuff my parents would whip up at home and bring with them in a little plastic container whenever they would go out to eat Japanese *shabu-shabu* to use as an all-purpose flavor booster. Generally I favor a blender method, which is only slightly more involved and yields a product that is more incorporated.

One of the greatest things to eat with nam jim seafood, in my opinion, are big fat prawns. Go find a couple dozen of the highest-quality prawns or shrimp you can get your hands on. Live or fresh are always preferred, but there are also some really nice frozen ones found at Japanese markets that sell sashimi—12/14, which means there are between 12 and 14 prawns per pound, is a good size. The most important part is that you get them "head-on, shell-on," which means they are fully intact instead of prepeeled.

My preferred shrimp cooking methods are grilling or boiling. If you're grilling—and the recipe opposite is almost like prawn satay— larger prawns are ideal because they will remain juicier. Smaller prawns have a higher chance of overcooking. If you're boiling them, it's even simpler. The goal is to let the pristine flavor of the seafood shine through—as with grilling, just don't overcook them.

GRILLED PRAWNS

Serves 4 to 8

Equipment: 24 (8-inch) bamboo skewers soaked in water for at least 1 hour

1. In a large bowl, whisk together the fish sauce, sugar, and white pepper. Add the prawns and toss to coat. Marinate for 10 minutes. Make sure to do this while the shell is on, so the prawns absorb a little extra flavor without being overpowered by the marinade.

2. Meanwhile, preheat a well-oiled grill to medium heat.

3. Remove the prawns from the marinade but don't toss the liquid; you'll want to brush it on while grilling. Peel the prawns by inserting a small knife along the center of the back ridge, between where the head shell meets the body shell. Insert the knife deep enough so that you can butterfly the prawn, but not so deep that you end up with two separate segments. Clean any intestinal gunk out of the prawn with your knife. Discard the shell and tail but keep the head intact. Wiggle the prawns onto the end of the skewers, starting at the tail so the skewer tip ends up lodged in the head. Set aside until ready to grill.

4. Getting the right heat on the grill for seafood can be a little tricky. You want it hot enough to lend some smoky flavor, but mild enough that the prawns cook evenly. Start with medium heat and adjust after cooking the first one; undercooked prawns are preferable to overcooked. When the grill is hot, whisk the oil into the remaining marinade. Throw the prawns on the grill, turning every so often and brushing with the marinade to keep them juicy. Grill them to your desired doneness. I like them slightly translucent on the inside, which should take no more than 1 to 2 minutes on each side. Serve with nam jim and garnish with cilantro. Be sure to suck the juices from the heads.

½ cup fish sauce

1½ teaspoons sugar

1 teaspoon ground white pepper

2 dozen head-on, shell-on jumbo prawns

¼ cup vegetable oil

Nam Jim Seafood → 177, for serving

Finely chopped cilantro, with stems, for garnish

PEEL-AND-EAT PRAWNS

Serves 4

In a large pot, bring about 4 quarts well-salted water to a boil over high heat. Use a small knife to split the outer shell of the prawns along the back. Remove any intestinal gunk, but leave the tail, shell, and head intact. Once the water is boiling, add the prawns and cook until opaque, 3 to 4 minutes. Scoop out the prawns with a strainer and transfer them to a bowl. (You can check the prawns for doneness and give it another minute in the water if you like.) Serve with nam jim and garnish with cilantro.

Kosher salt (see → 26)

2 dozen head-on, shell-on jumbo prawns

Nam Jim Seafood (recipe follows), for serving

Finely chopped cilantro, with stems, for garnish (optional)

NAM JIM SEAFOOD

Makes about 2 cups

The blender method will give you a sauce that's more like salsa verde, while the unblended version will have larger flecks of garlic and chile. Either way, the sauce will keep in the fridge for weeks.

1 cup fish sauce

¼ cup coconut sugar or granulated sugar

6 large garlic cloves, peeled but kept whole

12 fresh bird's eye chiles, or to taste, stemmed

½ cup lime juice

1. In a saucepan, combine the fish sauce and sugar and heat over medium heat until the sugar is dissolved. Remove from the heat and let cool until just warm.

2. Pour the sauce into a blender, add the garlic and chiles, and puree until smooth. Remove from the blender and stir in the lime juice.

    Quick non-blender method: Whisk together the fish sauce and sugar (use granulated sugar for this method) in a small bowl until dissolved. Finely mince the garlic and chiles, or crush them in a mortar with a pinch of salt, transfer to the bowl, and stir in the lime juice.

PORK TORO
KOR MOO YANG

Serves 4 to 6

1½ pounds pork jowl or neck (trimmed of skin), sliced ¼-inch thick

½ cup kosher salt (see → 26)

¼ cup sugar

1 tablespoon ground white pepper

¼ cup black soy sauce

2 tablespoons Thai seasoning sauce

Handful of roughly chopped cilantro, with stems (optional)

⅔ cup Jaew → 172

Typically pork toro is eaten by itself as a drinking snack— no rice needed—but it also works as an appetizer as part of a larger spread, or serve it with Coconut Sticky Rice → 299 to create an addictive sweet-salty flavor combo.

When we first opened the doors at Night + Market, there was a very specific Thai dish that I wanted people to experience while they were drinking: superfatty, luscious slices of pork jowl glazed in a salty-sweet sauce and charred over an open flame. It's one of my favorite things to both eat and cook. Imagine the candied bacon of the Thai world, but far superior.

I could have simply labeled it "grilled pork" on the menu—or kor moo yang in Thai—but that didn't seem to do it justice, and I really wanted people to try it. So I started calling it toro, because it reminded me of the rich decadence that you get from a slab of seared tuna belly at a sushi restaurant.

Technically the jowl cut of the pig encompasses a large swath of the neck area, so you might also see it labeled "pork neck" or "collar," all of which offer the same marbled texture you're looking for. In Thailand, you'll usually find the whole jowl grilled as one thing, then sliced up to order. I prefer it sliced and then grilled, since you get that charred and caramelized fat on all sides instead of just two.

To make sure the fat develops that snappy bacon-like texture when it cooks, cure the jowl in salt and sugar for about 20 minutes before grilling. If you can't find any pork jowl cuts at the butcher, you can also use pork belly or pork shoulder steaks that have a good amount of marbling—just make sure to cure those cuts as well.

1. In a bowl, combine the pork, salt, sugar, and white pepper. Let the mixture sit for 20 minutes at room temperature. Rinse off the seasoning and pat the pork dry. In another bowl, whisk together the black soy and seasoning sauces.

2. Meanwhile, preheat a well-oiled grill to very high heat. You'll want the grill as hot as possible so the soy glaze will char and caramelize.

3. Thoroughly dip each strip of jowl in the sauce mixture before throwing it on the grill, then use a brush to liberally glaze each piece as it cooks. Grill until charred on both sides, 6 to 8 minutes total. Transfer to a plate, garnish with cilantro, and serve *jaew* on the side.

CONDENSED MILK PORK WITH CUCUMBER SALAD
MOO YANG NOM KHON

Serves 4 to 6

1½ pounds pork jowl (neck) or fatty pork shoulder, cut into ½-inch steaks

½ cup plus 1 tablespoon kosher salt (see → 26)

¼ cup sugar

1 (13½-ounce) can coconut milk

½ (14-ounce) can sweetened condensed milk

3 tablespoons coconut or palm sugar

3 tablespoons thin soy sauce

1½ teaspoons ground turmeric

1½ teaspoons mild curry powder

Dash of ground white pepper

Cucumber Salad (recipe follows)

The idea for this dish came about at Night + Market when I was trying to think of a way to make pork satay without threading hundreds of meat chunks onto skewers every night. This is a reformatted version that offers the same decadent, sweet-salty, coconut, and charred sugar flavor you get from satay sticks at the best street vendors—but instead of meat chunks, you're grilling marinated pork steaks and slicing them afterward. Instead of the shallot and cucumber slices that usually come on the side with satay, the meat is draped over a super-simple, sweet, and tangy cucumber and onion salad.

1. At the restaurant, we quick-cure any fattier cuts of pork intended for grilling. You can do this by rubbing the meat with the ½ cup kosher salt and the sugar. Let sit for 20 minutes, rinse, then it's ready to use.

2. In a large bowl or plastic bag, combine the coconut milk, condensed milk, coconut sugar, soy sauce, turmeric, curry powder, and 1 tablespoon salt. Mix until dissolved. Add the cured pork and marinate for 1 to 2 hours at room temperature or overnight in the fridge.

3. Preheat a well-oiled grill to very high heat. You'll want the grill as hot as possible.

4. Grill the marinated meat until the exterior begins to caramelize and char, 4 to 5 minutes on each side. Let rest for 5 minutes, then cut into strips. Arrange over a plate of the sweet-sour cucumber salad and serve.

CUCUMBER SALAD

¼ cup distilled white vinegar

¼ cup sugar

½ teaspoon kosher salt (see → 26)

1 medium cucumber, peeled lengthwise in striped segments
and cut crosswise into ⅛-inch-thick half-moons

½ cup shredded carrot

½ cup thinly sliced (root to stem) red onion or shallot

¼ cup roughly chopped cilantro, with stems

Dash of paprika

In a small saucepan, stir together the sugar, vinegar,
and salt over medium-low heat. Bring to a boil, stirring
often, until the sauce is slightly thinner than maple
syrup. Remove from the heat and let cool. Toss with the
cucumber, carrot, and red onion and transfer to a plate.
Garnish with the cilantro and paprika.

FRANCISCO, TYLER, KAYSIE

CRISPY PIG TAILS

Serves 2 to 4

Flashback to the earlier months of Night + Market: We'd been open less than a year and business was decent but flat. We had some good press here and there, but nothing seemed to stick. In a shameless move, I went to a panel where the restaurant critic Jonathan Gold was speaking. I bum-rushed him after he spoke, handed him my business card, and sputtered out an invite to come try our food. What did I have to lose? He gave this kind of knowing half smirk he does and said something like, "*Oh, I've heard about you,*" and left it at that. I had no idea if he was coming.

A week goes by and I'm taking a math test at UCLA night school. Around this time I was looking into business school as a backup plan if Night + Market went down in flames, so the precious waking hours I wasn't at the restaurant were spent studying remedial math. Of course, the one night I'm not in the kitchen I get a text saying, "J Gold is here." I freak out. Screw the test, I'm running down the halls, trying to call one of the servers. But by the time I get out of the parking garage, he's already left the restaurant.

The next day, my phone starts buzzing with congratulations texts from other chefs. Someone explains that I should check Twitter. I see a tweet from Jonathan. *Oct. 6, 2011:* "Fried pigtail, braised pig ear, fermented ribs with garlic: Ever get the sense that a restaurant is just waiting for you to stumble into it?" I figured it had to be about us. What other place was serving all three of those dishes? A day later, I get an e-mail from an *LA Weekly* photographer who wants to set up a photo shoot. We're being reviewed.

A month later, Jonathan brought René Redzepi to dinner when the chef was in town from Copenhagen. After that, he brought in Anthony Bourdain. Then David Chang rolled through. They all ate the pig tails—in fact, that's what Bourdain still stops by for when he's staying at the Chateau Marmont.

Unlike most of the dishes at Night + Market back then, the crispy pig tails, for lack of a better term, were something I just came up with. They weren't based on any Thai recipe. I saw that this Asian market in Echo Park had pig tails, so I bought some and figured I would turn it into some hard-core drinking food.

2 pounds pig tails (the big fat stubby kind), cut between the joints into 4-inch sections (your butcher may already have them precut)

1 cup kosher salt (see → 26)

½ cup plus 2 tablespoons sugar

⅓ cup vegetable oil, plus more for deep-frying

¼ large white onion, sliced

1 tablespoon minced garlic

2 tablespoons fish sauce

2 tablespoons distilled white vinegar

1 teaspoon ground white pepper

1½ cups tempura flour

½ cup Nam Jim Seafood → 177

Handful of cilantro, chopped

recipe continues

Braised until soft then deep-fried, pig tails transform into one of the most deliciously crispy and chewy parts of the hog. It's a cut that contains the perfect proportion of skin, fat, tendon, and meat. What you're left with is juicy, decadent, and gelatinous. There is nothing better to gnaw on with a cold beer.

1.   Coat the pig tails in a mixture of the salt and ½ cup of the sugar and let cure in the fridge for 30 minutes to 1 hour. Rinse and pat dry.

2.   In a wok or Dutch oven, heat ⅓ cup of the oil over medium-high heat until shimmering. Add the onion and cook until softened and fragrant. Add the garlic and cook until fragrant. Throw in 1 tablespoon of the sugar and the pig tails and toss to coat. Season with the fish sauce, vinegar, and white pepper, then continue to stir-fry until the pig tails begin to turn golden brown, 5 to 6 minutes.

3.   Once the pig tails are browned on all sides, cover with hot water, bring to a simmer, and cook uncovered until they're soft, gooey, and on the verge of collapsing, about 1½ hours (adding more hot water as needed to keep the pig tails submerged, but check after 1 hour). Remove the tails from the wok and let them cool on paper towels to drain off the excess liquid. When cool to the touch, completely pat dry (this part is very important to avoid oil splatter when they're fried).

4.   Meanwhile, discard the contents of the pan and wipe it out. Add a few inches of oil—enough to submerge the tails while keeping a few inches of clearance in the pan—and heat over medium-high heat until the oil reaches 350°F. (Throw in a grain of uncooked rice; if it pops up and starts sizzling right away, the oil is ready. Or use a thermometer.)

5.   Roll the pig tails in tempura flour until evenly coated. Working in batches, carefully slide them into the oil and fry until the fatty skin is rendered crispy and golden brown, 3 to 5 minutes, then transfer to paper towels to drain.

6.   Toss the fried pig tails with the *nam jim* seafood, serving any unabsorbed sauce on the side for dipping. Garnish with cilantro.

Cheverny Blanc Frileuse
Qvevri, Clos du Tue-Boeuf
(Thierry Puzelat),
Loire, France

One of my all-time favorite winemakers, Thierry Puzelat, is as prolific as he is talented. For example, he bottles many different versions of a wine he calls Cheverny Blanc, a blend of mostly Sauvignon Blanc and Chardonnay but with a few other grapes tossed in on occasion. With this version, however, he ages the wine in Georgian clay eggs called *qvevri* (for many years Puzelat was the main guy importing Georgian wines into France). The qvevri-aged wine is more mellow and nuanced than its non-qvevri sibling, and what it loses in raciness, it gains in a rich suppleness.

GRILLED SALT-CRUSTED FISH
PLA PAO

Serves 2 to 4

It's something you see all over the streets of Thailand: a whole fish, covered in a shell of salt, spinning on a rotisserie over an open fire. The salt crust keeps the fish juicy and tender—you're really steaming it inside—while a handful of aromatics like lemongrass, cilantro, and galangal stuffed inside the fish's belly give the meat a subtle citrus aroma. It's one of the most brilliantly simple ways to cook a whole fish. I will say, however, that this rustic grilled technique requires you to not be afraid of salt. The idea is to thoroughly coat a rinsed whole fish with kosher salt, using the residual moisture to cause just enough salt to cling to the outside. You won't form an impermeable crust, but what you're looking for is enough coverage to allow the fish to semi-steam rather than just grill. The thin, patchwork salt crust will also allow the skin to get a bit crispy and smoky (once you scrape away the excess salt, those crunchy bits of skin make an excellent drinking snack).

As to which type of fish to use, in Thailand tilapia is the standard—it's everywhere. In the States, however, there is sort of a stigma against tilapia, so at Night + Market I use snapper or branzino. I suppose you could also use any firm-fleshed fish that doesn't have too strong a flavor as well.

1. Preheat a well-oiled grill to medium-low heat.

2. Rinse the fish and shake off excess water but don't dry it. Stuff the cavity with any combination of lemongrass, galangal, cilantro, or lime leaves. Place the fish on a baking sheet and cover it with an ample amount of kosher salt until a thin crust forms (it's okay if a bit of skin peeks through).

3. Grill the fish for 8 to 9 minutes on each side, covering it loosely with a sheet of foil and turning it over only once. The crust should look slightly burnt but intact, like an outer shell of armor. To check for doneness, insert a sharp metal instrument flat against the spine near the middle of the fish. If it's warm against the back of your hand when removed, it's cooked.

Vegetable oil

1 to 1½ pounds head-on fish, scaled and gutted (tilapia, snapper, branzino, or sea bream)

1 stalk lemongrass, tough outer layers removed, cut into 3-inch sections and slightly bruised

1-inch piece of fresh galangal, cut into thin coins

A few sprigs of cilantro

3 or 4 kaffir lime leaves, or 2 teaspoons grated key lime zest

Kosher salt (see → 26)

Serve with a least one kind of dipping sauce, maybe two (one sweet, one salty). Try Nam Jim Seafood → 177, Jaew → 172, or any of the *nam prik* → 191–198 along with their usual accoutrements.

recipe continues

4.	Place the fish on a large platter and serve with salt crust intact. Have your guests peel back the salt crust and pick out the tender meat and crispy skin underneath. Pair with *nam jim* seafood → 177, *jaew* → 172, or *nam prik noom* → 191 for dipping.

THAI BEEF JERKY
NEUA DAT DIEW

Makes about 1 pound

1½ pounds skirt steak (or hanger steak, sirloin flap, boneless short rib)

¼ cup Thai seasoning sauce

2 tablespoons fish sauce

2 tablespoons sugar

1½ teaspoons ground white pepper

½ tablespoon MSG powder (optional)

Vegetable oil, for deep-frying

Serve with Sticky Rice → 296–299 and Red-Eye Chile Dip → 195 or Jaew → 172, or just eat on its own.

When I was a kid, my dad took me on road trips. The destinations were places like Yosemite, the Grand Canyon, Taos—splendor of the American West stuff. We would pack snacks for the drive and certain items were always mandatory: some type of *nam prik*, a huge thermos filled with sticky rice (anyone who grew up in a Thai-American family knows the thermos trick), and beef jerky.

Thai beef jerky is way different from the traditional kind you'd pick up at the liquor store or bodega. Erase that image from your mind. This is far moister, semi-dry rather than completely dry, with a sort of bouncier texture that comes from deep-frying after drying.

The old-school way to make it is to dry it on bamboo mats or on a rooftop, but for our purposes using a food dehydrator or oven on its lowest setting is a more modern method. In Thailand they dry leaner cuts of meat mostly, but I prefer the decadence of fattier cuts like hanger steak. I also like cutting across the grain of the meat rather than the traditional way of cutting it, because it makes for a more pleasurable eating experience.

If you ever wanted to experiment with MSG, this is the time to do it. The stuff really works its magic when seasoning dried meats, similar to how "flavor enhancers" are used to make a Slim Jim taste unnaturally delicious. In Thailand, they would probably use triple the amount of MSG that I do here. You can also customize the marinade with additions like garlic or cilantro stems, or use oyster sauce and reduce the amount of fish sauce and seasoning sauce.

Another application: After the jerky has been dried but before it's been fried, you can throw it into a simmering pot of curry to transform it into a softened, pleasantly chewy cut of meat.

MEAT TAKING IN SOME SUN ON A BANGKOK SIDEWALK

1.   Slice the steak across the grain into strips that are about 1½ × ¼ inch—try not to cut the slices too thin, since they'll shrink as they dry. If you're having a hard time slicing, you can also chill the meat in the freezer for 30 minutes to 1 hour to firm it up.

2.   In a large bowl, whisk together the seasoning sauce, fish sauce, sugar, white pepper, and MSG (if using) until combined. Add the sliced steak to the bowl and mix thoroughly. Cover and marinate at room temperature for 30 minutes to 1 hour—a longer marinade isn't necessarily better in this case.

3.   Meanwhile, set your oven to the lowest temperature, or the "keep warm" setting. You're looking for a temperature around 170°F (crack the oven door open with a wooden spoon if you can't go that low). If you're using a food dehydrator, set it to the same temperature. Space out the marinated meat on the dehydrator rack for maximum airflow, or use the metal racks in the oven with a rimmed baking sheet below to catch the drippings. Let dry for about 1 hour. The texture should be springy, jiggly, and gummy— you want semi-dry, not completely dry.

4.   Pour 2 to 3 inches of oil into a wok or deep saucepan with several inches of clearance and heat over medium-high heat to 350°F. (Throw in a grain of uncooked rice; if it pops up and starts sizzling right away, the oil is ready. Or use a thermometer.)

5.   Working in batches of 2 or 3 strips of jerky, fry until they start to turn a glossy brownish-red, about 30 seconds on each side. Drain on paper towels and pat dry. Once cooled, store the meat in a zip-top plastic bag in the fridge; it should keep for weeks.

Moussamoussettes, Domaine Mosse, Loire, France
When I'm reaching for a bottle of bubbly wine (to eat with fried things), this is what I pull from the fridge. That's especially true if friends are knocking at the door. Moussamoussettes, an unfiltered rosé sparkler that is fruity and earthy and lively, is made by the great Mosse family in Anjou. It's got a touch of sweetness with a perfect amount of balancing funk. There's something invigorating about drinking sparkling wine with things that are fried and well-seasoned.

I DIP, YOU DIP, WE DIP

I could spend hours talking about *nam prik*. It's a tough term to define—it literally means "chile water"—but it ends up somewhere between a relish, a salsa, a salad, and a condiment. The best way to think of nam prik is as a building block around which to assemble a meal. Sticky rice, grilled meats, fried stuff, and seasonal vegetables served either raw or boiled are all fair game. As with many quintessentially Thai foods, there are hundreds (if not thousands) of variations from city to city, household to household. Some have the consistency of fine chile paste, some are watery, some are chunky. They can be super spicy or rather mild, they can involve meat or seafood or neither, depending on what part of Thailand you're in. The unifying element is chiles: fresh, dried, grilled, or deep-fried. Each method brings out a different flavor profile. Fresh chiles provide brighter, sharper flavors, while dried chiles are earthy and fruity; grilled chiles produce smokier nam priks, while deep-fried chiles make for nuttier, roasted flavors.

The reason nam prik plays such a central role in Thai cuisine is that Thai people love to dip things into other things, maybe even more so than Americans do. It's a very specific cultural preference, which also might explain why I love to douse everything in ranch dressing when I'm not eating nam prik. Having the stuff on your table is like having hot sauce around, but better. You can dip whatever you want into it, and you can keep coming back to it throughout the meal.

Traditionally, nam prik is made with a mortar and pestle. If you're making a small amount for two people, then it might be easier to pound the ingredients together, since there is a chance you won't have enough volume to blend it in a food processor without everything running up the sides. But if you're making a decent-size batch—and to be honest, this stuff disappears quickly, so you should—prepare it like we do in the restaurant, using a food processor or blender. Maybe using a mortar and pestle makes it slightly, incrementally better, but in thinking about efficiency and bang for your buck, I'll go with the food processor every time. The essence of nam prik, the soul of it, isn't in the fact that you're sitting there pounding the stuff until your wrist aches. I've talked to my grandma or older cooks back in Thailand, and they were stoked when they first heard about food processors.

Each nam prik recipe that follows has its own suggested list of dippers, but there are really no limits on what you can eat with it. Dip what feels right.

ROASTED GREEN CHILE DIP
NAM PRIK NOOM

Make about 2 cups

This is probably my all-time favorite *nam prik*, or at least the one I've eaten the most. It originates from Thailand's northern regions—Chiang Rai and Chiang Mai. The classic pairing is with *sai uah*, Northern Thai grilled sausage, but its mellow green chile heat works well with lots of things. It's spicy, but not insane, and my version of it highlights the smoky, fruity flavors that come from charred Anaheim or poblano peppers. Its soft, slightly stringy texture is similar to mashed roasted eggplant (at the restaurant it often gets confused with eggplant salad).

Some thoughts on variations: At Night + Market, we serve something called *nam prik maeng da*, which is this popular Northern Thai dip that's essentially *nam prik noom* mixed with mashed waterbugs. It adds a very specific perfume—I've heard it described by some people as overripe bananas. Even though I've developed a taste for it, it's obviously not for everyone. And given that waterbugs are tough to find, outside of Thailand anyway, I've found that adding a couple tablespoons of shredded watermelon radish achieves a similar earthy-pungent effect. You can also riff on nam prik noom by mixing in a few tablespoons of grilled shredded catfish or by substituting the fish sauce for raunchier extra-fermented fish sauce (*nam pla ra*).

Equipment: Wooden skewers soaked in water for 1 hour (if grilling)

1. Preheat a well-oiled grill or dry cast-iron skillet over medium-high heat.

2. Use a fork to poke a few holes in the Anaheim peppers so they'll be able to vent steam. If you're using a grill instead of a skillet, thread the garlic and bird's eye chiles on separate skewers so they don't fall through the grates.

3. Once the grill or skillet is hot, throw all the chiles, the garlic, and the shallots on the grill or skillet and char them on all sides until soft. About three-fourths of the surface of the big chiles should be blackened; the rest of the ingredients slightly less so. Charring

5 large Anaheim or poblano peppers, whole

3 serrano chiles, stemmed

8 fresh bird's eye chiles, or to taste, stemmed

12 garlic cloves, peeled but kept whole

4 large shallots, peeled but kept whole

1½ teaspoons kosher salt (see → 26)

½ teaspoon sugar

1 tablespoon fish sauce

2 lime wedges

Handful of roughly chopped cilantro, with stems

STUFF TO EAT WITH NAM PRIK NOOM:
Sticky Rice → 296–299
Northern-Style Herb Sausage → 162
Pork rinds
Chiang Rai Fried Chicken → 104
Hard-boiled eggs
Steamed vegetables (squash, cauliflower, okra)
Raw vegetables (cabbage, cucumber, green beans, carrots)

recipe continues

time will vary for each, but it should be somewhere between 5 and 10 minutes. Turn as necessary.

4. As each item finishes charring, set aside and let rest until cool enough to handle. For the large chiles, hold the stem as a handle and peel off the charred skin (what you want most is the fleshy part underneath, though I like to leave some of the burnt skin on for that smoky flavor)—ideally you want them about three-fourths peeled. Discard the skin and stems (see Note).

5. In a blender or food processor, pulse the charred garlic until finely minced. You'll want this as close to a paste as possible. Add the shallots next and blend until they are broken down but still have their texture. They should smell sweet and smoky. Finally add the chiles, blending until they become stringy. If you're working with a mortar and pestle, try to achieve the same benchmark with each ingredient before adding the next one.

6. Transfer the nam prik to a bowl. Season with the salt, sugar, and fish sauce (tweak the proportions to taste; it should taste equally sweet and salty with an underlying heat). Mix until totally incorporated. Just before serving, add a squeeze of lime juice. That's not very traditional, but I find that it livens things up. Garnish with cilantro and serve.

As with most chile dishes, you can lower the amount of heat in the final product by removing seeds from the Anaheim or serrano chiles after grilling, and you can omit the bird's eye chiles altogether.

RED-EYE CHILE DIP
NAM PRIK TA DAENG

Makes about 2 cups

This is the first *nam prik* I ever remember eating. I was a kid, and I think we were on a camping trip, and I remember telling a relative of mine who was feeding me "*shiew shiew*," which means to skim or graze. The nam prik was so spicy that I only wanted him to scrape a tiny dollop onto the balls of sticky rice I was eating.

Along with sticky rice and beef jerky, *nam prik ta daeng* is the ideal portable snack because, as I learned, a little goes a long way. The final product looks like an extra-thick hot sauce and basically functions like one: It's great for seasoning rice or any other food that warrants a wallop of heat.

1. Fill a large bowl with warm water and add the árbol chiles. Use a pair of scissors to snip the New Mexico chiles into 1-inch pieces and add those to the water too. Let soak, massaging them with your hands occasionally, until they're soft and flexible, 10 to 15 minutes. Drain and set aside.

2. In a blender or food processor, combine the drained chiles, garlic, shrimp paste, fish sauce, coconut sugar, tamarind paste, and salt and blend until combined. If the mixture seems too thick to blend, thin it out by adding a teaspoon of water at a time. Transfer to a bowl for serving.

2¼ cups dried árbol chiles, stemmed

3 large dried New Mexico chiles, stemmed

16 garlic cloves, peeled but kept whole

¼ cup shrimp paste

¼ cup fish sauce

2 tablespoons coconut or palm sugar

2 tablespoons tamarind paste, seeds removed

½ teaspoon kosher salt (see → 26)

STUFF TO EAT WITH NAM PRIK TA DAENG:

Sticky Rice → 296–299 or Steamed Jasmine Rice → 296

Thai Beef Jerky → 188

Pork rinds

Hard-boiled eggs

Raw veggies (cabbage, green beans, cucumber, carrots)

SHRIMP PASTE CHILE DIP
NAM PRIK GAPI

Makes about 2 cups

This is a classic Central Thai *nam prik* known for being equally stinky and spicy. I find the preparation to be a bit looser than *nam prik noom*, since you can blend it into oblivion without ill effect. The raw eggplant adds an acerbic quality, which is a foil to the pungent umami of the toasted shrimp paste. It's different. And although it's not included in the ingredient list, feel free to blend in a couple boiled shrimp for added body. In particular, this dip is great with anything battered and fried—we've served it with crispy calamari rings and fried eggplant slices to great success.

1. Wrap the shrimp paste in foil and cook in a dry skillet over high heat for about 4 minutes on each side, until the pungent smells hits your nose. This step helps activate the paste's toasty flavors and achieves that sense of *hom*.

2. In a small bowl, microwave the coconut sugar along with 1 teaspoon water for 20 to 30 seconds to soften.

3. In a blender or food processor, blend together the garlic and chiles until a rough paste forms. Add the shrimp paste, coconut sugar, salt, eggplants, lime juice, and fish sauce and continue to blend until combined.

4. Transfer to a small bowl for serving and garnish with whole bird's eye chiles.

STUFF TO EAT WITH NAM PRIK GAPI:

Japanese eggplant, sliced, dunked in beaten eggs, and fried

Fried calamari

Fried lemon wedges

Tempura green beans (the premade frozen variety is great)

Steamed mackerel

Grilled or Peel-and-Eat Prawns → 175 and 177

Egg omelet with bitter greens, cut into squares

Hard-boiled eggs

Steamed Jasmine Rice → 296

Blanched vegetables (okra, cabbage, baby corn, squash)

3½ tablespoons shrimp paste

3 tablespoons coconut or palm sugar

10 garlic cloves, peeled but kept whole

12 fresh bird's eye chiles, or to taste, stemmed

¼ teaspoon kosher salt (see → 26)

4 medium Thai eggplants (apple eggplants), peeled and quartered

½ cup lime juice

2 tablespoons fish sauce

Raw bird's eye chiles, for garnish

If you're into it, save the Thai eggplant peels to toss into Grapow Chicken → 46 at the same time as the green beans. If you're a Thai millionaire, you're probably not saving scraps, but adding eggplant peels to a stir-fry is a rustic cooking technique that adds another layer of texture.

CHIANG RAI PORK CHILE DIP
NAM PRIK ONG

Makes about 3 cups

10 dried árbol or pulla chiles
(or other small hot dried
chiles), stemmed

3 dried California chiles
(or other large mild dried
chiles), stemmed

¼ cup vegetable oil

3 tablespoons minced garlic

1½ tablespoons
shrimp paste

1 cup halved cherry
tomatoes

¾ pound ground pork

½ cup Tamarind Water → 313

1 tablespoon fish sauce

2 teaspoons coconut or
palm sugar

1 teaspoon kosher salt
(see → 26)

Handful of thinly sliced
green onions

Handful of roughly chopped
cilantro, with stems

Another separate
application for *nam prik
ong*, at least for me, involves
scooping it over pork broth
to make a simplified version
of the Northern Thai *nam
ngiew* (Pork Ragu Noodle
Soup, → 111).

Another dip that isn't just about being spicy, *nam prik ong* in its finished form looks a lot like bright red Bolognese sauce, or maybe sloppy joe filling. Made from stir-fried cherry tomatoes, stir-fried ground pork, and dried chiles, it's a milder *nam prik* that you'll find all over Northern Thailand. I have servers at the restaurant who describe it as the perfect introduction to nam prik, since it tends to be mellower and more comforting than most—which isn't to say it doesn't have a decent kick. Since it's made with meat it pairs best with vegetables and herbs, the one notable exception being pork rinds. It's also great over a plate of plain spaghetti.

1. Steep the dried chiles in warm water until softened and flexible, 10 to 15 minutes. Drain the chiles and puree them in a blender or food processor until they form a paste.

2. In a large skillet or wok, heat the oil over high heat until shimmering. Add the garlic and sauté until fragrant. Add the shrimp paste, pureed chiles, and cherry tomatoes and stir-fry until the tomatoes start to wrinkle and brown, 3 to 4 minutes. Add the ground pork and stir-fry until cooked, breaking it apart with a spatula. Stir in the tamarind water, fish sauce, coconut sugar, and salt and simmer until everything is dissolved and incorporated, 3 to 4 minutes. Remove from the heat and let cool before serving. Garnish with green onions and cilantro.

STUFF TO EAT WITH NAM PRIK ONG:
Sticky Rice → 296–299
Pork rinds
Hard-boiled eggs
Raw vegetables (cucumber, cabbage, green beans, broccoli or cauliflower florets, carrots, lettuce, bell pepper, snap peas)
Spaghetti

When our second restaurant, Night + Market Song (song means "two" in Thai) opened in 2014, it was the definition of bare bones. There was no parking, no walk-in fridge, no alcohol, no phone. We'd spent so much of our money building the place out, that after all the delays and setbacks, I didn't even have enough cash on hand to buy a computer to accept credit cards. There was no Dumpster for the first six weeks due to space constraints, so after service I would take all the trash bags—every dirty napkin, green papaya core, and pork scrap—and load them into my Mazda at midnight to toss into unlocked Dumpsters behind construction sites and supermarkets. You don't really realize how much garbage a restaurant produces until you're stuffing bags into the back of an SUV every night.

The way we decorated was purposeful but within our limited means. We laid out oilcloth prints I brought back from Thailand onto tables picked up from the restaurant supply store. We hung up a picture of Al Gore scrawled with a speech bubble that said "Drop LSD," which was left by squatters before we moved in. One critic called it "a high school project titled 'restaurant.'" I like to think we just realized that you have to make something great out of what you have at hand.

I think that same line of thinking applies to the way I cook too. When I was a young kid and my parents were working at the restaurant, my grandpa would babysit me. He didn't really cook, so when he was hungry I did my best to be a good grandson and whip something up for him, like thin-cut pork chops from the supermarket soaked in seasoning sauce then rolled in Italian bread crumbs. I'd fry them up and we'd eat them with leftover rice and maybe a *nam prik* that had been left in the fridge after a family get-together. Times like that were how I learned to open up the fridge and make it happen.

That ability manifests itself in the Thai countryside too, where there's a big tradition of using what is plentiful around you, what you can forage from your neighbor's yard, or honestly, what you can afford. I've been to many a *larb* restaurant where I'll recognize the chopped herbs on the plate as the ones growing on the other side of the driveway. It makes me think of the jerry-rigged outdoor hick kitchen my uncle built on his back patio in Mae Chan, where you'd find a makeshift propane stove, a wall of worn meat cleavers, a few shallots, and a knob of turmeric growing wild in the dirt. When he cooks, dinner might be a combination of whatever is lying around supplemented by a bit of premade meats or curries or dips he picked up from the market that evening. He might buy a Sour Pork Bundle → **170**, use the eggs and fish sauce in his cupboard, and turn it into a sour pork omelet with shallots, chiles, and garlic. As he's gotten older he eats a more vegetable-heavy diet, so he uses a stockpile of sauces to streamline the process of stir-frying whatever greens are available at his homemade wok station. That level of flexibility is helped by the fact that most things in the Thai pantry last forever, basically—fish sauce, garlic, dried chiles. You can always squeeze something out of even the most shriveled lime.

If those things are true for my 75-year-old uncle who is retired and lives in the countryside, they're doubly true for the home cook who probably has a job and whatever else going on. In that sense, the concept of using what you have has a sort of duality to it. On days when you come back from the farmers' market with a giant haul of seasonal whatever, you can make delicious Thai food. On days when your cupboard is all but barren, you can *still* make delicious Thai food.

This chapter is meant to represent recipes that achieve that versatility, and the more often you prepare them, the more you can customize them in ways that fit your life and what's in front of you. That to me is the heart of not just Thai cooking, but all cooking.

This chapter is broken out into broad sections: one about rice and noodles; one about stir-fried, grilled, and curried vegetables; one about salads, and one about eggs. These aren't all necessarily dishes from Night + Market, but more general ideas about offering adaptability and versatility for cooking at home, whether that implies preparing a big satisfying meal for a group of people with wildly different tastes, or throwing together a quick-and-dirty dinner for one on a school night. These methods and flavor combinations will help you think more like a Thai cook, which—like my uncle—means someone who can make the best out of any situation.

RICE AND NOODLES WITH STUFF *206-223*

It's always best to cook rice in big batches, since you can easily stash the leftovers in the fridge to make another quick, delicious meal out of it later. In some cases, as with fried rice, having day-old rice is actually advantageous, since it soaks up the oil and seasoning much better while stir-frying—and fried rice is one of the great vehicles for making a meal out of little bits and pieces of whatever other leftovers you have, so it's like a virtuous leftover-to-meal cycle. Noodles, even though they don't work as well in big batches, are filled with even more potential than rice. Ramen noodles, rice noodles, supermarket pasta—each can offer a potential to expand into a gratifying meal. I'm especially into the idea of preparing a starchy main attraction and serving it with a variety of choose-your-own toppings and sauces, which was the way most staff meals were set up by the Thai staff at Talésai when I was growing up. At home, it means that each person can customize their plate how they want, and you get to skip the task of topping each one individually.

WIDE WORLD OF VEGETABLES *224-235*

The worst feeling is when you finally make time to visit the farmers' market, pick up some pristine produce, and then spend the rest of the week feeling like you're in a race against time before it goes bad. The good news is that Thai cuisine is pretty loose when it comes to vegetables—the Thai cook wouldn't sweat sautéing black kale instead of Chinese broccoli, for instance, or using summer squash instead of bitter melon. So with the recipes in this section, you can always give your greens a fast stir-fry, or fashion a quick curry out of your turnips and that half head of cauliflower you have sitting in the fridge, or grill them with a coconut glaze.

SALAD ANYTHING *236-243*

Thais can make a salad out of anything. It's a cultural gift. In general, most of these salads involve supporting a central ingredient—fruits, vegetables, meats—with a balance of stuff that is sweet, sour, and salty. Achieving that preferred ratio and combination of flavors is up to you on some level, but there are rough frameworks you can follow when designing a salad of your own; you'll get the hang of them through the recipes on pages 236–243. Tasting, adjusting, and seasoning are important in every aspect of Thai cooking, but they're especially crucial in salad construction—since all the ingredients are either cooked or eaten raw, it's helpful to taste the dish each time you add an element.

THAI EGGS THREE WAYS WITH RICE *244-247*

When I cook at home, I'm especially attracted to the bachelorhood aspect of turning a near-empty fridge into a filling meal. Eggs are especially attractive in these situations—you usually have a carton of eggs on hand. The simplest recipes for Thai-style eggs are the most practical, since they only require hot oil and the magic of Thai pantry sauces to become delicious. They're so basic and commonplace I think if you asked a Thai person for these recipes, they would look at you sort of strangely, like you just asked for the recipe for boiled water or something.

The broke way to eat all three of these would be to serve them over steamed jasmine rice, which works for a quick snack or meal in a pinch. The omelet, however, also does well alongside any type of curry, along with maybe some beef jerky, a *nam prik*, and vegetables. The crispy fried egg is a natural topping for anything stir-fried, although its appeal expands well beyond that too. There's a term in Thai, *chu rot*, that essentially means "to boost the flavor," which is what these eggs accomplish when you pair them with other things.

FRIED RICE (KHAO PAD)

I love fried rice because it's a blank slate. It's limited only by your hopes and dreams and what you happen to have in your fridge. If I'm hungover, I throw slices of avocado on top. If I have some leftover barbecue pork or some nice leafy greens from the farmers' market, those go in too. In fact, there's not really a vegetable I can think of that doesn't work well with fried rice. Instead of thinking about fried rice as a side dish—or a slacker meal—I see it as its own technique, a sleight-of-hand maneuver that turns leftover rice and a few staples into something that can satisfy large groups of hungry people. The exact reason fried rice is so delicious is probably obvious—I mean, it's fried, after all—but to examine it more closely is to realize that you're using high heat and oil and seasoning rice with just enough sauce to highlight its addictive starchiness. That is why fried rice is so versatile: Do it right and you've established a base that is delicious on its own; anything beyond that is just bonus points.

As with other wok recipes, having your ingredients laid out beforehand is essential. Try to pare down the *mise en place:* If you've laid out more than six "toppings" for the fried rice, cut out one or two of them.

The old trick of using leftover, day-old cooked rice helps a lot with getting the right texture. If you don't have leftover rice, using fresh rice isn't a deal breaker, but your fried rice can end up clumpier. To avoid that, when you are making the fresh rice in a pot or rice cooker, dial down the amount of water by 10 percent. After cooking, leave it in the fridge, uncovered and preferably spread out on a plate, to cool for an hour or so. Whether you're using fresh or day-old rice, be vigilant in moving your spatula to push the rice around as it cooks. If the rice sticks a little to the pan, that's okay too. Try to scrape it off as it's happening, and don't stress about it too much.

A few things to keep in mind: The order in which you add things to the wok has a huge effect on the end product. Stir-fry the aromatics like garlic first to get their toasty flavor.

Then immediately add proteins like chicken or pork, but add delicate items like cooked shrimp or crab at the end, or else they'll overcook. Here's the order I recommend:

THINGS TO ADD AT THE BEGINNING:
Aromatics (onions, garlic, ginger)
Small-cut vegetables (squash, peppers, tomatoes, greens, peas, diced carrots, etc.)
Proteins (pork, chicken, beef, raw shrimp, firm tofu, etc.)

THINGS TO ADD IN THE MIDDLE:
Cooked meats (leftover barbecue, steak, etc.)
Eggs
Rice
Liquid seasonings

THINGS TO ADD AT THE END:
Delicate cooked proteins (crab, scallops, shrimp, etc.)
Herbs (green onion, cilantro, etc.)
Avocado on top, if you want!

Following are three different takes on fried rice, each of which differs slightly in the ingredients. Beyond these, experiment with anything that sounds good to you.

And although it's not strictly 100 percent essential, I recommend serving fried rice with a small dish of Prik Nam Pla → **306**, a universally beloved Thai condiment made from fish sauce, chile, garlic, and lime.

CHICKEN FRIED RICE

Serves 1 or 2

1. Heat an empty wok over high heat until it begins to smoke, then swirl in the oil. Once the oil is shimmering, add the onion and stir-fry until it's softened and translucent. Add the chicken and stir-fry until opaque but not fully cooked.

2. Crack in the egg and mix with the chicken and onion, forming a single lumpy mass. Once the egg resembles a soft scramble, add the rice, sugar, and stir-fry sauce, working the rice around the wok to distribute the sauce evenly and break up the egg.

3. At this point use your judgment. Continue to stir-fry the rice until the moisture has dried up, but not past the point when the rice begins to stick to the wok. You're looking for a slight toasted color, not full-on browning.

4. Remove from the heat, throw in the green onion and a dash of white pepper, and toss. Transfer to a plate and serve with *prik nam pla*.

3 tablespoons vegetable oil

¼ medium yellow onion, thinly sliced (root to stem)

¼ pound Brined Chicken thigh → 313, cut into bite-size pieces

1 egg

3 cups Steamed Jasmine Rice → 296, preferably day-old

2 teaspoons sugar

2½ tablespoons Stir-Fry Sauce → 306

2 green onions, cut on an angle into 2-inch lengths

Ground white pepper

Prik Nam Pla → 306, for serving

ESTELA

CRAB FRIED RICE

Serves 1 or 2

3 tablespoons vegetable oil

¼ medium yellow onion, thinly sliced (root to stem)

1 tablespoon minced garlic

1 egg

3 cups Steamed Jasmine Rice → 296, preferably day-old

2 teaspoon sugar

1½ tablespoons Stir-Fry Sauce → 306

1½ tablespoons fish sauce

½ cup jumbo lump crabmeat

2 green onions, cut on an angle into 2-inch lengths

Ground white pepper

Prik Nam Pla → 306, for serving

1. Heat an empty wok over high heat until it begins to smoke, then swirl in the oil. Once the oil is shimmering, add the onion and garlic and stir-fry until they're softened and translucent.

2. Crack in the egg and mix with the onion and garlic. Once the egg resembles a soft scramble, add the rice, sugar, and stir-fry sauce, working the rice around the wok to distribute the sauce evenly and break up the egg.

3. At this point use your judgment. Continue to stir-fry the rice until the moisture has dried up, but not to the point when the rice begins to stick to the wok. You're looking for a slight toasted color, not full-on browning.

4. Remove from the heat, throw in the fish sauce, crabmeat, green onion, and a dash of white pepper and toss to combine. Transfer to a plate and serve with *prik nam pla* on the side.

PINEAPPLE SHRIMP FRIED RICE

Serves 1 or 2

3 tablespoons vegetable oil

¼ medium white onion, thinly sliced (root to stem)

1 tablespoon minced garlic

6 ounces peeled and deveined large shrimp

1 egg

3 cups Steamed Jasmine Rice → 296, preferably day-old

2 teaspoons sugar

2½ tablespoons Stir-Fry Sauce → 306

¼ cup drained canned pineapple tidbits or fresh pineapple cut into ¾-inch chunks

¼ cup roasted cashews

2 green onions, cut on an angle into 2-inch lengths

Ground white pepper

Prik Nam Pla → 306, for serving

1. Heat an empty wok over high heat until it begins to smoke, then swirl in the oil. Once the oil is shimmering, add the onion and garlic and stir-fry until they're softened and translucent. Add the shrimp and cook until slightly opaque, 10 to 20 seconds.

2. Crack in the egg and mix with the onion and garlic. Once the egg resembles a soft scramble, add the rice, sugar, and stir-fry sauce, working the rice around the wok to distribute the sauce evenly and break up the egg.

3. At this point use your judgment. Continue to stir-fry the rice until the moisture has dried up, but not past the point when the rice begins to stick to the wok. You're looking for a slight toasted color, not full-on browning.

4. Remove from the heat and immediately throw in the pineapple, cashews, green onion, and a dash of white pepper and toss to combine. Transfer to a plate and serve with *prik nam pla* on the side. Or, if you're feeling ambitious, hollow out the interior of one half of a fresh pineapple and serve the fried rice inside for a dramatic touch. That's how my grandma did it when she worked at Talésai.

SHRIMP PASTE RICE WITH CANDIED PORK AND AN ENDLESS ARRAY OF TOPPINGS
KHAO KLUK GAPI

Serves 4

This is something like Thai Taco Night, where you have toppings spread out on the table and everyone assembles their bowl with whatever they like. Only instead of tortillas, this meal is anchored around shrimp paste (*gapi*) seasoned rice and candied pork—with a buffet's worth of toppings that add heat, texture, and flavor. In this recipe I've included most of the traditional Thai toppings—cilantro, lime, minced chile, cucumber, red onion, sliced egg omelet, and dried shrimp, among other things—but the possibilities are truly endless based on what's in your fridge. Sometimes I like it with sliced avocado (everything I eat late at night gets avocado) or with freshly shucked oysters. If you can't find dried shrimp, use bonito flakes or shredded nori, or just leave out that element altogether. In the restaurant we use shredded green mango, but the tart crunch of a green apple works just as well. The beauty of this dish lies in its flexibility, so exercise creativity as you see fit. The general idea is that you're looking to things that have freshness, crunch, or snappiness to contrast with the tenderness of the pork and rice. Any type of fresh pickle is usually a good call. On the other end of the spectrum, avocado and egg work because they add a sort of lush blandness that mellow out the sweet pork and the salty rice.

As for the two anchors of the dish: When cooking the candied pork, what you're going for is caramelized sweetness with an underlying funky saltiness from the fish sauce and soy sauce. The same goes for the rice. The pungent shrimp paste should be balanced by sugar and white pepper. Taste as you season these items and adjust them according to your palate. That way if you end up with extra pork or rice, you can stash it for later and have something that tastes great eaten on its own.

CANDIED PORK:

1 pound pork shoulder, cut into 1-inch cubes

3 tablespoons fish sauce

¼ cup vegetable oil

½ cup thinly sliced (root to stem) red onion or shallot

2½ tablespoons coconut or palm sugar

¼ cup dark soy sauce

SHRIMP PASTE RICE:

2 tablespoons vegetable oil

2 tablespoons shrimp paste

1 tablespoon sugar

1 tablespoon fish sauce

1 teaspoon ground white pepper

4 cups cooked rice, preferably day-old

recipe continues

OMELET AND OTHER TOPPINGS:

Vegetable oil, as needed

3 eggs

2 teaspoons fish sauce

Ground white pepper

2 tablespoons minced fresh bird's eye chiles, or to taste

½ tart green apple, unpeeled, cut into matchsticks (place in water with a squeeze of lime juice to prevent browning)

½ cup thinly sliced (root to stem) red onion or shallot

½ cucumber, sliced thin

½ cup cut greens beans (¼ inch) (optional)

½ cup roughly chopped cilantro, with stems

½ cup dried shrimp

Lime wedges

1. For the candied pork: Place the pork in a large pot and add the fish sauce and water to cover by ½ inch. Bring to a boil, then reduce to a simmer and cook, uncovered, stirring occasionally, until the liquid is reduced by a little more than half, 15 to 20 minutes. Remove from the heat. Drain the pork well and pat dry with paper towels.

2. In a wok, heat the oil over high heat until shimmering. Add the red onion and stir-fry until softened and fragrant, about 3 minutes. Add the pork and stir-fry until the pork develops a light brown sear. Add the coconut sugar, dark soy sauce, and 2 tablespoons water. Reduce the heat and cook until the sauce reaches the thickness of molasses. Remove from the heat and let cool. Once cooled, the glaze will thicken and the oil will separate—drain off leftover oil, if desired.

3. For the rice: Rinse or wipe out the wok. Heat the empty wok over high heat until it begins to smoke, then swirl in the oil. Once the oil is shimmering, add the shrimp paste and stir until fragrant, then quickly add 2 tablespoons water. Reduce the heat to low and stir in the sugar, fish sauce, and white pepper. Once the sauce resembles dark bubbling hot chocolate—add water if necessary—dump in the rice. Break up the clumps and stir until each grain is coated with the sauce. Transfer the rice to a serving plate.

4. For the omelet: Heat a skillet lightly coated with oil over medium heat until the oil is shimmering. Crack the eggs into a bowl and whisk in the fish sauce and a pinch of white pepper until blended. Pour the egg mixture into the skillet and cook each side for 2 to 3 minutes. You'll want a big flat omelet. If you break it while flipping, no worries. Once the omelet is very lightly browned, remove and let cool on a paper towel. Fold it into thirds, then slice into thin strips.

5. To assemble a plate, scoop 1 cup of the rice into a mound on the center of a plate. Top it with a few tablespoons of candied pork. Form a moat of toppings around the rice: a spoonful of chopped chile, green apple, red onion, cucumber, green beans, cilantro, dried shrimp, and egg strips—or whatever else is in your arsenal. Serve with lime wedges.

THAI RICE PORRIDGE (IN A COUPLE FORMS) WITH TOPPINGS
JOK/KHAO TOM

Serves 4 to 8

If you didn't grow up eating *jok*, it can look like something they'd serve in a Siberian prison. But to Thai people, or really anyone exposed to any type of Asian rice porridge, there is nothing more restorative when you're deathly ill, hungover, or just plain homesick. The idea is that you cook down rice until it softens into something deeply soothing and satisfying, seasoning it with the right amount of salt to keep it interesting (I strongly prefer instant bouillon cubes, because they have that addictive MSG-enhanced quality you don't really get from plain chicken stock). The added beauty of jok is that you can conjure it from leftover rice, which makes it an ideal breakfast/brunch item the morning after you have a big rice-filled party.

The key with jok is to achieve the proper consistency, which to a certain extent is personal preference. There's a late-night (or breakfast, depending on your POV) dish in Thailand called *khao tom* (boiled rice), which is essentially jok in its early stages, before the individual grains have broken down into the hot water. If you want to consume it at that stage, you probably only have to boil the cooked rice for 30 to 45 minutes. Once the grains have all but dissolved so that you can't really tell it's rice anymore—that's jok. Theoretically, as long as you keep adding enough water to keep it from scorching, it's possible to simmer jok forever. Well, not forever. But I find between 1 and 1½ hours is usually the sweet spot.

I almost forgot the biggest appeal of jok: the stuff you put on top. Much like with shrimp paste fried rice, you generally want to include things that contrast against the smooth texture of the porridge, like crunchy fried stuff, pickles, raw aromatics, or fresh herbs (if you want to go deluxe, you can quickly whip up the pickled greens and anchovy relish that follows). Things like soft-boiled eggs and seasoned pork offer richness, but any type of cooked ground meat seasoned with garlic, white pepper, and seasoning sauce works too. Feel free to garnish each bowl with toppings before serving, or lay everything out and allow everyone to top their own bowl.

4 cups Steamed Jasmine Rice → 296 or 1½ cups uncooked rice

3 chicken bouillon cubes

2½ teaspoons kosher salt, or to taste (see → 26)

4 to 8 eggs (1 per person)

¼ cup Fried Garlic → 311

2 (1-inch) nubs fresh ginger, peeled and cut into matchsticks, soaked in cold water for 10 minutes, then shaken dry

½ cup roughly chopped cilantro, sawtooth (culantro), or *rau ram*

½ cup thinly sliced green onions

Thai seasoning sauce or fish sauce

Ground white pepper

Chile Oil → 303 (optional)

recipe continues

If you want to trick out your porridge with something more substantial, top with Mustard Green–Anchovy Relish (recipe follows), or Seasoned Boiled Pork (recipes follows), or eat with a side of Stir-Fried Greens with Mushrooms and Tofu → 227.

1. In a large soup pot, bring 2 quarts water to a boil (if starting with raw rice, make that 3 quarts). Add the rice, bouillon cubes, and salt and simmer over medium heat, stirring occasionally, until the grains have mostly dissolved and the rice has broken down into a porridge, 1 to 1½ hours for already cooked rice, 1½ to 2 hours for raw rice. If you want to make *khao tom*, or boiled rice, cut the simmering time in half. If it seems too thick, thin it out with more water (trust your eyeballs more than a measuring cup in this case). Season to taste with more salt.

2. Meanwhile, bring a medium saucepan of water to a boil over high heat. Boil the eggs for 5 minutes and remove from the pot. Carefully peel once they're cool enough to handle.

3. Once the porridge is done, divide it into serving bowls and garnish each with a soft-boiled egg, fried garlic, ginger, fresh herbs, green onions, and as much seasoning sauce or fish sauce, white pepper, and/or chile oil as you want.

MUSTARD GREEN–ANCHOVY RELISH

Makes about 2 cups

Pickled mustard greens come packed in a salty brine, so I usually rinse them before use. Also, I'd recommend chopping the stems and leaves separately—they have different textures so it's hard to cut them the same way. With the addition of some anchovies, chiles, and sugar, what you end up with is a pungent pickled condiment that adds a needed punch to the relatively bland rice porridge.

2 cups chopped store-bought Chinese pickled mustard greens, rinsed and roughly chopped

16 small anchovy fillets, chopped, or ¼ cup anchovy paste

1 teaspoon minced fresh bird's eye chiles, or to taste

2 teaspoons sugar, or to taste

2 tablespoons sesame oil

In a medium bowl, stir everything together until the sugar is dissolved. Let rest on the counter for 5 minutes before serving. This stuff will keep in the fridge for at least 2 weeks.

SEASONED BOILED PORK

Serves 4 to 8

This dependable recipe isn't exactly a game changer, but it's a genius way to cook tender meat when you already have boiling water on the stove. It's great as a *jok* topping, but you can also use it to make a beloved home-style dish called "Bathing Rama" (Rama is basically the Beowulf of Thai mythology) that consists of equal portions of boiled pork and steamed *gai lan* topped with Peanut Sauce → 308, and Chile Jam → 304 to taste over Steamed Jasmine Rice → 296.

1½ pounds pork shoulder, cut into 2 × 1 × ¼-inch slices

⅓ cup Stir-Fry Sauce → 306

1 teaspoon ground white pepper

2 tablespoons baking soda

1. In a small bowl, combine the pork, stir-fry sauce, white pepper, and baking soda (the latter helps keep the meat moist and tender, a Thai-Chinese restaurant trick). Stir to coat, then let marinate at room temperature for 20 to 30 minutes. Meanwhile, bring a medium pot of water to a boil.

2. Drain the pork mixture and add it to the water. Cook until the pork is just cooked, 1 to 1½ minutes. Use a skimmer or slotted spoon to lift out the pork, then serve over jok or with steamed jasmine rice.

Chinuri, Iago, Georgia

If you ask a Georgian, theirs is the oldest winemaking tradition in the world. And the best producers today are doing it the same way it was done in the Bronze Age. They are the wines in giant clay "eggs" called *qvevri*, which are buried in the ground and provide a natural temperature control system. You can taste the history in these wines. There is an energy and liveliness to them, but they're not zippy Loire wines. The guy who makes this wine, Iago, is a professor turned winemaker, and he works with precision. His orange wines, or skin-contact wine (white wine made in the fashion of red wine production) have texture, chewiness, dryness, and a depth of flavor to them that's staggering.

COLD NOODLES WITH SWEET-SALTY COCONUT SAUCE (AND MANY IDEAS FOR TOPPINGS)
KHANOM JIM SAO NAM

Serves 4

20 ounces uncooked rice vermicelli noodles

1 (13½-ounce) can coconut milk

1 tablespoon granulated sugar

2 teaspoons kosher salt (see → 26)

⅓ cup fish sauce

3 tablespoons coconut or palm sugar

⅓ cup pineapple juice

1 tablespoon minced garlic

3 tablespoons lime juice

GARNISHES:

½ small pineapple, peeled and cut into ¼-inch cubes

¼ cup dried shrimp, pulsed in a spice grinder or food processor until powdery

2 tablespoons thinly sliced fresh bird's eye chiles, or to taste

4 garlic cloves, thinly sliced

4 lime wedges

Other toppings (see Note)

Khanom jim sao nam is an old-school dish once served in the royal Thai court. Since it was usually served either at room temperature or slightly chilled, it's known as a refreshing hot weather dish (and something you could probably slurp all year in LA). The basic components are rice noodles, a salty/sweet sauce made from creamy coconut milk, and a tangier sauce made from fish sauce, pineapple juice, lime, and garlic. There are traditional toppings— diced pineapple, sliced chiles and garlic, dried shrimp powder, and bouncy seafood meatballs—but taken out of its Thai context, this is one of those extremely versatile dishes (like Shrimp Paste Rice, → 213) where you could set up a little buffet station (see below).

1. Cook the vermicelli according to the package directions. Rinse the cooked noodles with cold water, then drain thoroughly. Divide the noodles into 8 portions (about ½ cup each) and coil each handful into a circle, repeating until all the noodles are bundled. Let sit for a few minutes until the noodle bundles are cooled and slightly firm.

2. In a saucepan, combine the coconut milk, granulated sugar, and salt and bring to a boil over high heat. Remove from the heat and let the coconut sauce cool. In a separate saucepan, stir together the fish sauce, coconut sugar, and pineapple juice and bring to a boil over high heat. Once the sauce reduces slightly (a bit thinner than maple syrup), remove from the heat and mix in the minced garlic and lime juice. Let the sauce cool.

3. To plate, place 2 rice noodle bundles on a plate and cover with 2 to 3 tablespoons of the coconut sauce and 1 to 1½ tablespoons of the pineapple–fish sauce mixture. You can adjust to taste, but

recipe continues

Spread out a broad mosaic of toppings and have your dinner guests pick and choose as they like. Since the main draw of the dish involves a balanced tension between sweet/savory and soft/crispy-crunchy, you will have a lot of leeway in choosing toppings, but here are some ideas to get started.

Sweet toppings: slivered unripe mango or green apple, toasted sweetened coconut, shredded ginger, Cucumber Salad → 181, sweet pickled radish, and most things sweet/tart and crunchy.
Savory toppings: Seafood Meatballs (see Variations), poached shrimp, dried shrimp powder, shredded dried seaweed, Fried Garlic → 311, Fried Shallots → 311, bonito flakes, Chinese pickled mustard greens, most things salty/savory and crunchy or tender.

generally you want a 2:1 ratio between the coconut and pineapple-fish sauces.

4.   Garnish with the diced pineapple, shrimp powder, chiles, garlic slices, lime wedges, and other toppings (see → 218) as desired.

VEGAN VARIATION
Substitute shredded nori (dried seaweed) for the dried shrimp powder and thin soy sauce for the fish sauce.

SEAFOOD MEATBALLS VARIATION
Add seafood meatballs as one of the garnishes. Prepare the filling for Golden Triangles → 59. Roll a tablespoon or so of filling into balls and poach in boiling water for 1 to 2 minutes, until cooked through and springy.

STIR-FRIED INSTANT NOODLES WITH BACON (OR WHAT YOU HAVE ON HAND)
MAMA PAD

Serves 2

If you've ever eaten instant ramen, you know the joy that cheap noodles and flavoring packets can provide. If you stick to the package directions, the result is just noodles in broth, which is okay, but instant noodle veterans know the best way to prepare them is to stir-fry rather than boil; you end up with chewy noodles rather than soggy.

In Thailand, the best-known brand is Mama Instant Noodles, which come in a variety of flavors, and is so popular stir-fried that most people refer to it as its own dish, *Mama pad*. Although you can occasionally find Mama pad at working-class diners in Thailand, it's widely seen as a fundamental make-at-home dish—something you'd cook in the wok after school or a long night out. The appeal comes from the way it's seasoned (not too salty or too sweet), the way it uses pantry staples that almost every Thai home cook has on hand, and the slick, bouncy texture of the fried noodles.

If you can't get hold of Mama brand noodles, you can use any pork-flavored instant ramen, although I'd suggest adding ½ teaspoon Roasted Chile Powder → 304 and Garlic Oil → 311 to compensate for not having the Mama seasoning packets.

In the most basic application, you could leave out the bacon and *gai lan* and enjoy the seasoned fried noodles by themselves. If you're not into pork, the meat options are open-ended—leftover steak or grilled chicken is genius, but you could also go fancy and include things like scallops. Just remember to toss proteins that requiring cooking into the wok first, and add more delicate ones at the end. The same logic goes for vegetables: If they require cooking, thinly slice and add early on.

1.   Open the instant noodle packages and separate out the little packets of joy: bouillon, chile powder, and garlic oil. In a large pot of boiling water, cook the noodles for slightly less time than the package directions indicate. Drain the noodles and set aside.

3 (2.12-ounce) packages pork-flavor Mama Instant Noodles

4 slices thick-cut bacon, diced (optional)

2 tablespoons vegetable oil

1 tablespoon minced garlic

2 cup loosely packed Chinese broccoli (*gai lan*) or broccoli rabe, stems thinly sliced on an angle into 2-inch lengths, and leaves sliced into 2-inch pieces (optional)

2 eggs

1½ tablespoons sugar

2 tablespoons Thai seasoning sauce

Ground white pepper

2 green onions, sliced on an angle into 2-inch lengths

½ cup roughly chopped cilantro, with stems

Lime wedges, for serving

recipe continues

2.   Heat a wok over high heat and add the bacon (if using). Stir-fry until the fat is rendered and the bacon is slightly crispy. (If you're not using bacon, add the oil here and heat until shimmering.) Add the minced garlic, broccoli (if using), and the garlic oil packets and stir-fry until the greens are slightly wilted and the garlic is fragrant, about 1 minute. Crack the eggs into the wok, let them cook for 10 seconds, then break them up into the rest of the mixture. Throw in the noodles, along with the sugar, seasoning sauce, a dash of white pepper, and the remaining seasoning packets. Toss to coat and stir-fry for another 30 seconds or until the seasonings are all absorbed, then sprinkle in the green onions and cilantro and remove from the heat. Transfer to a plate and serve with lime wedges.

STIR-FRIED GREENS
WITH GARLIC AND CHILES

Serves 2 to 4

2 tablespoons vegetable oil

1½ tablespoons
minced garlic

2 fresh bird's eye chiles (or
other hot peppers to taste),
thinly sliced on an angle

6 cups loosely packed
Chinese broccoli (*gai lan*),
broccoli rabe, or other
robust leafy green, stems
thinly sliced on an angle into
2-inch lengths, and leaves
sliced into 2-inch pieces

2 tablespoons Stir-Fry
Sauce → 306

3 to 4 anchovy fillets,
chopped (optional)

Ground white pepper

The same advice for noodle
stir-fries in the first chapter
applies to these stir-fries
too. If you're making greens
for a large group, cook
them in batches rather than
overloading the wok all
at once.

Serve with Steamed
Jasmine Rice → 296 or
as part of a larger meal.

This is something you'd expect to see at any Thai restaurant: stir-fried Chinese broccoli (*pad pak kanna*) cooked in the wok and doused with soy sauce. Greens that were formerly tough and fibrous wither under the heat of the wok until they become soft and silky with slightly crunchy stems, soaking up just enough of the salty sauce to season them. They don't need much embellishment except for chiles and minced garlic.

You could eat it with curry as a side dish, with a plate of noodles to balance out the meal, or just on a bowl of rice. Instead of seeing stir-fried Chinese broccoli as a single dish, it's better to see it as a technique you can apply to any seasonal leafy green or, even more broadly, any vegetable you pick up from the farmers' market that could benefit from a trip into a wok.

A good rule of thumb is that almost anything you could sauté in a pan becomes even better when cooked in the wok: kale, bok choy, romaine lettuce, snap peas, mushrooms, cabbage, Chinese celery, lettuce, peppers, baby corn. (Not green beans, though. For those, see page 228.) If necessary, cut the vegetables into small bite-size pieces so they'll cook evenly and quickly. If the greens are especially tough or hardy like kale, consider cutting them into even thinner pieces. If you're using vegetables that are denser, like broccoli, squash, Brussels sprouts, or carrots, you'll also need to blanch them in boiling water for 30 seconds to 1 minute before stir-frying so they'll be crisp-tender and then cook all the way through in the wok. And make sure everything is well drained before it goes into the wok. If not, the vegetables will steam rather than stir-fry.

If you're sticking with leafy greens (we use *gai lan* at Night + Market), I find the best way to measure out chopped leaves is to fill a roughly 10-inch-wide, 4-inch-deep bowl to the brim, which is equivalent to about 6 loosely packed cups. That amount should provide enough greens for two people, generally speaking. A classic Thai variation on pad pak kanna is to toss in salted fish at the end—if you're down with salty and funky, adding a few chopped anchovies right as the greens wilt hits a similar note.

1. Heat the oil in a wok over high heat until it starts to shimmer. Add the garlic and chiles and stir-fry until fragrant, then toss in the greens and stir-fry sauce. Cook, stirring or tossing the greens, until they are tender and wilted. Depending on the kind of greens you use, this might take 1 minute or it might take 5 or more. If you're using hardier, tougher greens like kale or collard greens, splash in 2 tablespoons water at a time to help them wilt. Once the greens are wilted, stir in the anchovies (if desired).

2. Remove from the heat and add a dash of white pepper before serving.

STIR-FRIED GREENS WITH MUSHROOMS AND TOFU

Serves 2 to 4

If you want to bulk up stir-fried greens into a full vegetarian meal, you have options. The idea is to use the Thai stuff in your pantry as accents (fried shallots, fried garlic, fish sauce, chile powder, rice powder) and then to include other items that are good at soaking up those flavors, which in this case might be mushrooms and tofu. Vegetarian stir-fries might sound boring, but if you liven them up with bold flavors and interesting texture, they become more than the sum of their parts.

This particular stir-fry leans as much Chinese as it does Thai due to the use of sesame oil, but the oil's velvety richness adds a roasted nutty flavor you can't achieve with anything else.

1. In a wok, heat the sesame oil over high heat until it starts to shimmer. Add the garlic and chiles and stir-fry until fragrant. Throw in the chard, mushrooms, sugar, and seasoning sauce. Cook, stirring or tossing the greens, until they are tender and wilted. If you are using other kinds of greens, this might take 1 minute or it might take 5 or more. If you're using hardier, tougher greens like kale or collard greens, splash in 2 tablespoons water at a time to help them wilt. Once the greens are wilted, gently fold in the ginger and tofu and cook until warmed through.

2. Remove from the heat and sprinkle with sesame seeds. Serve with steamed jasmine rice or alongside a bowl of Thai Rice Porridge.

2 tablespoons sesame oil

1 tablespoon minced garlic

1 teaspoon minced fresh bird's eye chiles, or to taste

6 cups loosely packed rainbow chard or other leafy green, stems thinly sliced on an angle into 2-inch lengths, and leaves sliced into 2-inch pieces

1 cup oyster mushrooms (or any meaty-textured mushroom like wood ear, chanterelle, hen-of-the-woods, king trumpet), tough stems removed, torn into bite-size pieces

1 teaspoon sugar

1 tablespoon Thai seasoning sauce or thin soy sauce

2 tablespoons peeled and julienned fresh ginger, soaked in cold water for 10 minutes, then shaken dry

6 ounces medium-firm tofu, cubed

Sesame seeds, for garnish

Serve with Steamed Jasmine Rice → **296** or Thai Rice Porridge → **215** as a meal.

GARLIC GREEN BEANS

Serves 2

Vegetable oil, for deep-frying

2 heaping cups trimmed green beans, about 3 inches long

1 tablespoon minced garlic

½ teaspoon sugar

1½ tablespoons Stir-Fry Sauce → 306

Ground white pepper

Serve with Steamed Jasmine Rice → 296 and grilled meats.

There's a simple reason green beans weren't included as a possible substitute in the stir-fried greens recipe: You have to deep-fry them first. I know it probably seems like an inconvenience, but that's truly the only way they'll measure up to the snappy, beautifully saucy green beans that are a timeless menu staple at American Chinese or Thai restaurants. At Talésai, my grandmother would serve these green beans underneath a slab of seared filet mignon seasoned in the same way as Prakas's Rib Eye → 54 and at Night + Market we occasionally offer a special of green beans with wild shrimp, but they're great even unadorned. As with other stir-fries in this chapter, you could tweak the seasonings and additions based on what you have in your pantry, but I tend to think because this dish is so classic and iconic, it doesn't require much beyond stir-fry sauce and garlic.

1. Pour about 2 inches of oil into a wok and heat over high heat to 350°F. (Throw in a grain of uncooked rice; if it pops up and starts sizzling right away, the oil is ready. Or use a thermometer.)

2. Working in batches of ¼ cup, fry the beans until they begin to wrinkle, 30 to 40 seconds. Drain on paper towels.

3. Pour out almost all the oil into a heatproof container (and reserve for another use), until just a thin coating remains (about 1 tablespoon or so). Heat the wok over high heat until the oil is shimmering, then add, in this order, the garlic, green beans, sugar, and stir-fry sauce. Stir-fry until the green beans have absorbed the sauce and the garlic is fragrant and lightly browned, 1 to 2 minutes. Remove from the heat and add a dash of white pepper. Serve immediately.

GRILLED SWEET CORN WITH COCONUT GLAZE
KHAO POTE PING PING

Serves 6

When summer corn is in season, the best way to prepare it, hands down, is to char it on the grill. In Thailand you'll see vendors selling fresh grilled corn, brushed with coconut milk and sugar, which intensifies the sweet corn flavor and forms this beautiful caramelized glaze. The irony is that the corn in Thailand is pretty terrible—yellow, mealy, sort of bland—so this dish actually becomes infinitely better when you use quality sweet corn grown in the States. As far as grilled vegetables go, it's the epitome of high pleasure, low hassle, especially if you make the glaze beforehand and stash it in the fridge.

Brushing peak-season sweet corn with a creamy sweet glaze is decadent in a more-is-more way, but another approach is to use the glaze as an enhancement for less-sweet vegetables that lend themselves well to grilling like squash, zucchini, or yams. This is especially true when those vegetables are out of season, as it can add a needed boost to their natural sweetness.

If you're using other vegetables that are too thick to be grilled whole, prepare them by slicing into ¼-inch-thick planks and brushing liberally with the glaze. Grill over medium-low heat, basting occasionally, until the vegetables are tender and slightly charred.

1 (13½-ounce) can coconut milk

1 tablespoon coconut or palm sugar

2 teaspoons kosher salt (see → 26)

2 teaspoons ground turmeric

6 ears of corn, husked

1. In a small saucepan, combine the coconut milk, coconut sugar, salt, and turmeric. Bring to a boil, stirring to dissolve the sugar. Cook until slightly thickened, about 10 minutes.

2. Preheat a well-oiled grill to medium-high heat.

3. Brush the corn with some of the coconut glaze and grill, turning and basting occasionally, until the exterior is charred and crisp-tender, about 20 minutes. Brush the corn with more glaze and serve warm.

SEASONAL CREAMY YELLOW VEGETABLE CURRY

Serves 4

1½ (13-ounce) cans coconut milk

2 tablespoons All-Purpose Curry Paste → 303

2 tablespoons coconut or palm sugar

3 tablespoons fish sauce or thin soy sauce

1 tablespoon ground turmeric or grated fresh turmeric

4 cups bite-size pieces of seasonal vegetables (see Note)

½ to 1 cup chicken or vegetable broth, or less to taste

⅓ cup shredded *grachai* (Thai wild ginger) or peeled and shredded fresh ginger

OPTIONAL GARNISHES:

½ cup Fried Shallots → 311 or Fried Garlic → 311

2 or 3 fresh bird's eyes chiles or other hot peppers to taste, thinly sliced on an angle

5 or 6 kaffir lime leaves, deveined and finely julienned

Thai basil leaves

Most of this book approaches curries the way they're served in Thailand, which is basically in soup form, but another way to think of them is as a sort of seasoned, emulsified sauce on the same level as hollandaise or beurre blanc. One unconventional combination I came up with for a party for a friend was to pour this thick yellow curry sauce over a bed of roughly smashed roasted potatoes. You could do the same thing with grilled or poached salmon, broccoli, asparagus, or any other meat or vegetable that jumps to mind. That said, if you're craving a more conventional curry, consider this a multipurpose foundation to highlight whatever vegetables are in peak season. It's pretty much foolproof—over 99 percent of vegetables lend themselves well to creamy yellow curry. If you find one that doesn't, let me know.

This recipe is deliberately an open-ended endeavor. You can use the homemade All-Purpose Curry Paste → 303, the Green Curry Paste → 303, or whatever store-bought curry paste you'd like. Adjust the amount of stock added based on whether you're using the curry as a soup or a sauce. The vegetable element has the most flexibility. Unlike meats, the Thai method is to parcook the vegetables before adding them to the curry so that they retain their individual character and don't soak up so much of the curry as to become indistinguishable. How to cook them is up to you. Blanching in boiling water is the most common Thai practice, but roasting or sautéing with a splash of oil are valid options as well. A general rule of thumb is to undercook the vegetables slightly, so that they'll be just right after simmering in the curry for a few minutes before serving.

1. In a large saucepan, heat the coconut milk over medium heat until bubbling. Add the curry paste, coconut sugar, fish sauce, and turmeric and stir until everything is dissolved. Reduce the heat to a simmer.

2. If you're planning on blanching the vegetables, bring a large pot of water to a boil over high heat. If you're roasting the vegetables, preheat the oven to 375°F.

3. Either blanch the vegetables for 1 minute or roast for 15 to 25 minutes (exact times will vary based on the vegetable). You'll want them mostly cooked but still slightly firm, so that they'll finish cooking in the curry.

4. Meanwhile, thin out the curry with the broth to achieve the desired thickness. Use closer to 1 cup if you want a soup-like curry, but closer to ½ cup if you want a sauce-like curry you can pour over vegetables and proteins. You can also use reserved blanching water instead of broth, though consider seasoning it with a little extra salt to taste if that's the case.

5. Once the vegetables have finished cooking, stir them into the curry along with the ginger and simmer for a minute or two more until warmed through and combined. Alternatively, add the ginger and simmer, then pour the thickened curry over the vegetables like a sauce.

6. If desired, garnish with fried shallots or garlic, sliced chiles, lime leaves, or Thai basil.

Serve with Steamed Jasmine Rice → 296, Cucumber Salad → 181, egg omelet → 214, and/or Thai Beef Jerky → 188.

Some vegetables you can try this with: broccoli, snap peas, zucchini, squash blossoms, green beans, peppers, potatoes, butternut squash, kabocha squash, pumpkin, cabbage, turnips, parsnips, leafy greens, tomatoes, cauliflower, celery, eggplant, corn, bok choy, carrots, mushrooms, asparagus, yams.

BOON, VICKIE, ALEX

COLD SUMMER VEGETABLE CURRY
GAENG LIENG

Serves 2 or 3

BASE:

1 large shallot, peeled

3 or 4 fresh bird's eye chiles, or to taste, stemmed

2 tablespoons shrimp paste

½ teaspoon ground white pepper

1 teaspoon sugar

2 tablespoons fish sauce

VEGETABLES (SEE NOTE):

8 fingerling potatoes, quartered

8 whole cherry tomatoes

½ cup zucchini wedges

½ cup sliced yellow squash

½ cup sliced okra

1 cup fresh corn kernels (cut from about 1 ear)

½ cup lemon basil leaves, or equal parts mint and sweet basil

Use the standard options in the recipe, or any of the items suggested in the Note on → 233, or whatever you have on hand. You just need 1½ pounds total.

This is an old-fashioned curry, which means it's basic. The curry paste, like a lot of primitive Central Thai curry pastes, is about as minimalist as it gets: shrimp paste, shallots, and chiles blended together. What you're really doing is creating a funky, salty, slightly spicy bath for whatever vegetables you have sitting around. I've included standard options with this recipe, but you can get creative with things like peeled watermelon rinds, daikon radish, or chayote squash. Throw all of them into the pot—you can't go wrong. Just make the recipe through the first step, add whatever vegetables you have, cook them until tender, and you're done.

Usually this curry would be eaten hot, and you can certainly do that, but since we're in LA, I find myself craving chilled things the majority of the year. Having eaten enough leftover *gaeng lieng* straight out of my parents' fridge, I find it to be excellent when served chilled, almost like a more pungent and exciting gazpacho.

If you can't find any lemon basil to finish this curry with, the refreshing aroma is what really makes it—you could also use a combination of sweet basil and mint to achieve roughly the same effect, or experiment with other leafy fresh herbs.

1.   For the base: In a medium pot, bring 3 cups water to a boil.

2.   Meanwhile, in a blender or food processor, pulse together the shallot, chiles, and shrimp paste until a rough paste forms.

3.   Once the water is boiling, reduce to a simmer. Add the curry paste, white pepper, sugar, and fish sauce.

4.   Add the potatoes and simmer for 5 to 7 minutes. Add the tomatoes, zucchini, squash, okra, and corn. Simmer until the vegetables are tender, another 5 minutes or so. Remove from the heat and stir in the lemon basil while the broth is still hot; the herbs will wilt slightly and become fragrant.

Serve chilled or hot with a side of Steamed Jasmine Rice → 296.

"THAI" STEAK SALAD

Serves 4

1½ pounds thin-cut skirt steak or hanger steak

¼ cup black soy sauce

2 tablespoons Thai seasoning sauce

4 tablespoons olive oil

Ground white pepper

1 medium sweet white or yellow onion, cut into 8 wedges

3 green onions

2 tablespoons fish sauce

1 teaspoon sugar

1 teaspoon Roasted Chile Powder → 304

2 fresh bird's eye chiles (or other hot peppers), or to taste, thinly sliced on an angle

1 large heirloom tomato, cut into 6 to 8 wedges

Handful of torn mint or other herbs

½ lemon

1 teaspoon Toasted Rice Powder → 299

Serve with brown rice or over a bed of robust mixed greens.

The origin story of this recipe involves a backyard dinner party with a bunch of chef friends I hosted at my house for a *Vogue* article in 2016. The theme was grilling outdoors, and the writer's challenge to me was to shop for everything at Whole Foods, a limitation that shaped the dish in a way that made it different from most of the food served at Night + Market (though I did use some restaurant staples I had stashed in my pantry).

The result was a Thai guy doing an impression of the Thai beef salad you'd find at most American Thai restaurants, but filtered through the lens of the LA summer backyard barbecue. It was a hit. The centerpiece, of course, was the grilled steak. I use hanger steak or skirt steak, but any cut that you might imagine making carne asada with works well, and you could experiment with thin cuts of pork or chicken. Beyond the two types of charred onions, you can throw in whatever grilled vegetables sound appetizing (shishito peppers are brilliant if they're in season). Use good olive oil to add a luxurious quality, and make sure to save any juices and charred bits from the steak to amp up the beefy flavor of the salad dressing. A healthy squeeze of lemon rather than lime, since we're going for a less traditional approach, and a light pinch of rice powder complete the picture.

Interestingly enough, this is the only dish in the book that I would suggest eating with brown rice. We don't serve brown rice in the restaurant because I find the nuttiness and texture too much of a distraction usually, but here it works as a low-key "healthful" foil to the heartiness of smoky beef and olive oil. A bed of robust mixed greens like arugula or dandelion greens is a nice option too.

1. Preheat a well-oiled grill to very high heat.

2. While that's happening, coat the steak with the black soy, seasoning sauce, 2 tablespoons of the olive oil, and a dash of white pepper.

3. When the grill is hot, cook the steak, flipping once, until the outside is charred but the inside is still pink, 2 to 3 minutes per side. Let the meat rest for 5 minutes. Grill the sweet onions and

green onions over high heat until wilted and charred on all sides, 2 to 3 minutes, then move them to a cooler part of the grill or turn the heat to medium-low after the steak is off and cook for another few minutes, until softened.

4.   Meanwhile, in a small bowl, whisk together the fish sauce, sugar, remaining 2 tablespoons olive oil, chile powder, and chiles.

5.   Once the meat is rested, cut it across the grain into ¼-inch-thick slices. Reserve any meat juices or charred bits and transfer them, along with the sliced steak, to a large bowl. Pour the dressing over the steak and mix and massage it into the meat. Add the grilled onions, tomato, and fresh herbs, then toss everything lightly to coat. Transfer to a plate and just before serving, squeeze the lemon over the top to taste and sprinkle with the rice powder.

POMELO OR OTHER FRUIT SALAD WITH COCONUT AND PEANUTS
YUM SOM-O

Serves 4

2 tablespoons coconut or palm sugar, or to taste

½ teaspoon minced fresh bird's eye chiles, or to taste

1 teaspoon minced garlic

¼ cup lime juice

3 tablespoons fish sauce

Kosher salt (see → 26)

½ cup sweetened shredded coconut

½ cup vegetable oil, for frying

2 shallots, thinly sliced, or 2 tablespoons Fried Shallots → 311, plus 1 shallot, thinly sliced

2 tablespoons dried shrimp

2 large pomelos (or other fruit; see Note)

¾ cup roughly chopped cilantro, with stems

¼ cup Seasoned Fried Peanuts → 309

Handful of mint leaves

Some fruits you can try this with: grapefruit, tangerines, navel oranges, mandarins, mango, cucumber, jicama, apple, watermelon, or Asian pears. You just need 1¼ pounds total of prepared fruit.

For this classic sweet-savory salad, the focus is citrus, specifically pomelo. If you can't find pomelos, you can use any sweet-tart citrus or go further afield and use any fruit or sweetish vegetable that can hold its shape while being tossed into a salad. You could even try a mix of fruits, like the Thai equivalent of Mexican fruit cart vendors, who can chile-lime anything and make it taste amazing.

You can always tweak some components based on personal preference. The dressing part—sugar, chile, lime, garlic, fish sauce—is fairly set in stone, but the rest of the toppings are open to interpretation. Things that are sweet, salty, crunchy, or fried work especially great, but you could also toss in Roasted Chile Powder → 304, Crispy Rice → 301, or thinly sliced lemongrass → 25. Basically anything you can sprinkle from the basics chapter → 294 is fair game.

1. In a bowl, whisk together the coconut sugar and 1 tablespoon water to dissolve. Whisk in the chiles, garlic, lime juice, fish sauce, and salt to taste. Taste and season with more sugar, lime juice, or fish sauce and salt if needed.

2. In a dry saucepan, toast the coconut over medium heat, stirring occasionally, until golden brown, about 4 minutes.

3. In a wok or skillet, heat the oil over medium-high heat until shimmering (if you're using fried shallots you can skip this step). Add half the shallots and fry, swirling, until golden brown and crisp, 3 to 4 minutes. Drain on paper towels and season with salt. Repeat the frying process with the dried shrimp.

4. Remove the peel and white pith from the pomelos. Tear the membrane off and separate the segments into pieces, transferring them to a large bowl. Add the cilantro, the remaining raw shallots, and half of the dressing. Toss to coat. Add the coconut, peanuts, and dried shrimp, then toss again. Divide among plates, drizzle with the remaining dressing, and top with fried shallots and mint leaves.

CANNED TUNA (OR OTHER MEAT OR FISH) YUM

Serves 4

The best metaphor for how to make *yum* (Thai salads)—and really, most Thai food in general—is to imagine building a house. You wouldn't just throw up the walls and the roof and everything else at once; you'd start with the foundation. The same goes for yum: You start with a central ingredient and build around it, adjusting and tasting and seasoning as your salad takes shape. The idea is to achieve a sort of customized balance.

In this case, the spotlight is on canned tuna (yes, people love eating canned fish in Thailand). Start with making a basic dressing to season the fish, then use everything else to further "season" the seasoned fish. You might not immediately think of onion, tomatoes, and herbs as seasonings, but in the Thai repertoire that's what they are. My suggestion is to use this recipe as a basic blueprint for whatever you want to build a salad around (poached salmon, grilled chicken, pork, tofu, canned meats) and then make adjustments based on what is on hand (onions, cucumbers, tomatoes, carrots, lettuce, herbs, crispy things, etc.). What you'll end up with is a versatile salad that could be highbrow or lowbrow, with enough heft to serve as a post-drinking snack (consider adding a fried egg) but refreshing enough to work as a light lunch.

In a medium bowl, whisk together the fish sauce, sugar, lime juice, garlic, and chiles until the sugar is dissolved. Add the tuna to the bowl and toss lightly—you want the tuna to remain in medium to large chunks. Taste and tweak the seasonings, as desired, until balanced. Add the onion, tomatoes, and chopped herbs and toss again to coat. Transfer to a plate and garnish with dill sprigs.

1½ tablespoons fish sauce

2 teaspoons sugar

1 tablespoon lime juice

½ tablespoon minced garlic

½ tablespoon minced fresh bird's eye chiles, or to taste

2 (5-ounce) cans water-packed solid white tuna, drained

½ medium sweet white or yellow onion, thinly sliced (root to stem)

½ cup halved cherry tomatoes

½ cup roughly chopped fresh herbs: any combination of green onion, cilantro, *rau ram*, and sawtooth (culantro)

Dill sprigs, for garnish

Serve with Sticky Rice → 296–299, Steamed Jasmine Rice → 296, or Thai Rice Porridge → 215; and cucumber slices, lettuce leaves, and cold beer.

MARINATED TOMATOES (AND A LESSON IN BALANCING THAI FLAVORS)

Serves 4

2 large heirloom tomatoes, cut into wedges

1 cup halved grape or Sun Gold tomatoes

¼ cup fish sauce or thin soy sauce

2 fresh bird's eye chiles, or to taste, thinly sliced on an angle

1 tablespoon toasted sesame seeds

1 tablespoon Fried Garlic → 311

Handful of mint leaves

Serve alongside *larb*, grilled meats, or any type of curry. Or eat as a snack.

This low-effort, high-flavor tomato salad isn't Thai per se, but it does demonstrate how the Thai concept of balancing flavors can be achieved in different combinations. Let's say you find yourself with some excellent peak-season heirloom tomatoes, the kinds that are juicy and plump and incredibly tasty on their own. Since the tomatoes already have the inherent sweetness and acidity found in good ripe tomatoes, you're basically just balancing them out with fish sauce and fresh chiles.

Imagine the most basic Thai dressing as a square, with the sides labeled "lime," "sugar," "chile/garlic," and "fish sauce." When the main ingredient of the salad is mild or blandish, the sides should be more or less the same size. But once you use an ingredient that has more pronounced flavors—sweet, sour, salty, pungent—you cut back on the corresponding seasoning based on that (i.e., if the salad ingredient is sour, then the "lime side" shortens up) and the square turns into a weird customized trapezoid.

As for this salad, since the best tomatoes can be found in warmer months, this works well as a quick appetizer or snack on a hot day, ideally with a refreshing beverage nearby.

In a medium bowl, lightly toss the tomatoes with the fish sauce and chiles. Let stand for 5 minutes or so at room temperature, then transfer to a plate or bowl and sprinkle with the sesame seeds and fried garlic. Garnish with the mint leaves.

CRISPY FRIED EGG
KHAI DAO

Serves 1 or 2

1 cup vegetable oil

2 eggs

Serve with Steamed Jasmine Rice → **296**, Prik Nam Pla → **306**, and some sort of stir-fry.

A heavily browned, crisp-bottomed Thai fried egg is a magical thing when done right, but it can be tricky if you've only ever made Western fried eggs before. Think of it as shallow-frying an egg in your wok. You'll want an inch or so of oil heated in the wok over very high heat, which will help produce fried eggs that are puffier, crispier, lacier, and, despite the extra oil, somehow lighter than any fried egg you've ever had.

Unlike the other egg recipes, you wouldn't normally eat this type of egg with rice alone, but ideally enjoy it atop a stir-fry served with steamed rice, or a noodle stir-fry that doesn't already have eggs mixed in. Grapow Chicken → **46** with a fried egg is probably the most beloved example among Thais, but in my experience you can put a fried egg over anything and it will become better. Go crazy.

If you're going to make a crispy fried egg to eat alongside a stir-fry, the most efficient way to go about it is to fry the egg in the wok first, transfer it to a plate or paper towel, pour out the excess oil, then cook the stir-fry as directed using some of the reserved frying oil. The eggs will be fine resting until you finish the stir-fry.

1. Heat an empty wok over high heat until it begins to smoke, then swirl in the oil. Once the oil is shimmering, crack the eggs into the wok, one at a time, as low to the oil surface as possible. Fry the eggs, spooning oil over the top, until the white is opaque and the yolks begin to set, about 1 minute. The underside and edges should be browned and crispy. Lift the eggs out with a spoon or spatula and transfer them to a plate or paper towel to drain.

2. Serve atop steamed rice and a stir-fry, or whatever else inspires you.

SEASONED HALF-SCRAMBLED EGG
KHAI KHON

Serves 1

This style of egg is meant to be sort of runny—almost like a soft-cooked egg but half-scrambled, half-fried. It's the ultimate eat-something-before-you-pass-out meal. Dump it straight from the pan onto a waiting plate of rice. If you wanted to expand beyond dorm-room style, you could class it up by topping it with a handful of chopped mellow herbs or thinly sliced raw vegetables right as the egg finishes cooking. Master this recipe and you will never be without grateful friends at the end of the night.

In a wok, heat the oil over medium heat until it starts to shimmer. Crack in both eggs and let them fry for 10 to 15 seconds before using a fork or spatula to break up the yolks. Sprinkle on the sugar, seasoning sauce, green onions, and a dash of white pepper and reduce the heat to low. Cook, without flipping, until the top layer is set but still looks moist and creamy, 20 to 30 seconds. Remove from the heat and dump the eggs immediately over rice.

2 tablespoons vegetable oil

2 eggs

1 teaspoon sugar

1½ teaspoons Thai seasoning sauce

¼ cup thinly sliced green onions

Ground white pepper

Serve with Steamed Jasmine Rice → **296** and Prik Nam Pla → **306**.

THAI PUFFY OMELET
KHAI JIEW

Serves 1

For Thais, the recipe for a puffy fried omelet is almost too basic to say. It's made from ingredients that all Thai people have in their fridge or pantry—eggs, sugar, fish sauce, herbs, and ground pork or crab if you want—and if you cook at all, then of course you can make it. Even if a restaurant doesn't list it on its menu, it's assumed that it can be whipped up at any time. The texture of this style of egg is almost like a frittata more than a traditional omelet, though you do achieve that same fluffy-inside effect but with the added bonus of crispy browned edges. The technique is essentially a shallow-fry, which causes the eggs to puff up as they quickly cook.

    Using pork and/or crab can add richness, but ultimately they're optional. This is just as good without any type of meat. I find that including some sort of onions or shallots adds body, but if you wanted to go even simpler you could always make the omelet with just eggs.

1. In a small bowl, beat the eggs with the fish sauce, then fold in the sugar, red onion, crab or pork, and a pinch of white pepper.

2. Heat an empty wok over high heat until it begins to smoke, then swirl in the oil. Once the oil is shimmering, pour in the egg mixture using one swift motion. You're basically making a deep-fried egg pancake, so the oil should be hot and plentiful. The egg will crackle and sizzle at first, but after about 20 seconds it will have died down enough that you can flip it over. Don't worry about executing the perfect flip; this isn't meant to be a flawless French omelet. Cook the other side for 20 seconds or so, until golden, then remove it from the pan and let it briefly drain on a paper towel. Garnish with herbs, if desired, and serve Sriracha on the side.

3 eggs

2½ teaspoons fish sauce

½ teaspoon sugar

½ cup thinly sliced (root to stem) red onion or shallot

¼ cup (1½ ounces) lump crabmeat or ground pork (optional), at room temperature

Ground white pepper

⅔ cup vegetable oil

Handful of roughly chopped cilantro, with stems (optional)

A few torn Thai basil leaves (optional)

Sriracha sauce, for serving

> Serve with Steamed Jasmine Rice → **296**, Prik Nam Pla → **306**, and/or any type of curry.

A note on ground pork: Thai-style is to mix it into the egg raw so that it cooks together with the egg (bring the raw pork to room temperature first). If you're worried about undercooked pork, you can also parcook the meat beforehand.

CHAPTER 5
T.G.I.F.

I've occasionally described Night + Market as like T.G.I. Friday's, but with waterbug relish. I imagine most people find that strange. The truth is, I've never been to T.G.I. Friday's but I've seen the ads. There's always a big group of people huddled around a table and they're having an absolute blast. Maybe the guy on the left is trying to hook up with the girl across the table, maybe they're coming from the office after an exhausting week and want to get messed up on bottomless Mudslides. If I actually went to the restaurant, I'm sure that image would deflate pretty quickly in a sea of soggy mozzarella sticks, but that's why I choose to never go there. I don't want to ruin my personal fantasy.

What T.G.I. Friday's symbolizes to me is a place that exists for your pleasure. That's what I want Night + Market to be—a pushback against the oppression and solemnity that's become so pervasive in dining culture. Eating in an "authentic ethnic" restaurant shouldn't feel like an ethnography course. When it comes to my own food and culture, I find that level of seriousness to be a tough pill to swallow. Most Thai food wasn't conceived cerebrally—the basis of the cuisine, whether street food or royal food, is about bringing pleasure to people. I want to be proof that having fun doesn't involve sacrificing identity.

Over the years our restaurants have existed, the number of non-Thai (or loosely Thai) dishes we cook has grown and evolved. It's become part of who we are. If you want to watch Netflix and eat solid Thai-ish takeout on your couch, we've got that. If you want chicken wings and a Northern Thai dish you may have never heard of, we've got that too. It's more important to be known as a reliable neighborhood spot to me than as a place that does super-regional Thai specialties. The food we make is intended to please people, most of all me. Really, I tried to build the restaurant that I wanted to eat and hang out at.

I think about one of my biggest heroes, Wolfgang Puck. When he opened Spago, he was cooking Austrian food, but then realized he was feeding Californians and they were into Californian food, so he started putting smoked salmon on pizzas and making Chinese-ish chicken salad. How can you not adapt to what's going on around you? The cliché is that in Hollywood, you can be anyone you want, but my theory is that the city helps you become yourself. As a student of delicious food, there are endless stimuli. Whether it's tacos or fried chicken or patty melts, the city is riddled with source material, and you can't help but soak up the influence and come out a little richer and more wide-ranging.

When I was attending Beverly Hills High, there was this sushi restaurant called Crazy Fish that was the certified chill spot, like our version of the Max in *Saved by the Bell*. It was the cream of the crop when it came to Americanized sushi—Superman roll, Jewish roll, Spider roll, Philly roll. Crispy, crunchy, salty, sweet; they had it all. That's inspiration. My favorite Korean barbecue place in LA is the one where they give you a vat of molten orange cheese to dip your grilled meat into—why isn't this everywhere? That's inspiration.

My personal barometer for cooking dishes that I'm not an expert in is: Do I have something to say about it? Do I have something to add? I remember when I was attending NYU I took a music business class from a professor who sort of rubbed me the wrong way. He was known for pushing his students, and I was a smug college kid who thought he knew better. For an end of semester term paper, I wrote about the Rolling Stones. He pulled me aside after I turned it in and pressed me on the thesis—the point it basically amounted to was "Keith Richards is cool." I get that the Rolling Stones are cool, he told me, but that's not a thesis. You have to complicate it; you have to add depth; you have to espouse an opinion as to why they are cool. I know that everyone loves fried chicken sandwiches, but what makes my fried chicken sandwich worthy of existence? Whether we're cooking chicken satay or tuna noodle casserole, everything we make should in some way reflect that specific Night + Market sensibility of pleasure.

What makes a great meal to a Thai chef is balance, and part of what that means to me is combining so-called silly dishes with more serious ones.

When chefs come in to eat at Night + Market, they're ordering the tostadas, crab wontons, and party wings as often as they are the more "authentic" upcountry dishes.

The recipes in this chapter aren't bound by the burden of tradition. On a basic level they're foods meant to encourage drinking and socializing, which obviously Thai cooking does not monopolize. Eating and partying is universal. That means deep-fried things, beef tartare, spring rolls—whatever else fills your nightly food fantasies. I hope you experience the same amount of whole hearted and unbridled satisfaction cooking these dishes that I get from serving them.

HEY-HA PARTY WINGS AND PARTY SAUCE
PEEK GAI HEY-HA

Makes 12 wings

12 chicken wings

1 cup fish sauce

1 teaspoon ground white pepper

Vegetable oil, for deep-frying

½ cup tempura flour

Hey-Ha Party Sauce (recipe follows)

Roasted Chile Powder → 304

½ cup thinly sliced green onions, for garnish

In Thai, the onomatopoeia for having fun is *"hey-ha."* If someone asks you what you got up to last night, you might say, *"Sang san, hey-ha,"* which is a little expression that basically means we got together, had some fun, etc. When Night + Market started, the thing that I cared about as much as the food and wine was capturing that sort of party vibe. So we served chicken wings, of course, because they are the ultimate party food. There were two styles, the first being straight-up fried chicken with a side of *nam prik noom* (Roasted Green Chile Dip → 191) and the second being those same wings doused in what Thais call "three flavor sauce," which is an extremely addictive sweet/salty/spicy glaze made from coconut sugar, vinegar, and fish sauce. It's intended to go over deep-fried stuff like whole fish. I didn't want to call them "three flavor wings," though, so they became known as hey-ha wings, as in *Do you want your wings regular style or hey-ha style?* As you can imagine, most people said yes to sticky wings. As they took off in popularity, we actually stopped serving the plain version altogether. The hey-ha wings were king.

If you don't want to go to the effort of deep-frying the wings yourself, you can always start with frozen wings heated up in the oven, or ones you picked up from Popeyes. Just toss them with the sauce in a wok. You could also make just the sauce and serve it with other fried or grilled things: tempura cauliflower, crispy green beans, seared scallops, fried fish, popcorn shrimp. Remember: It's the sauce that brings the party—well, actually half the party is in the sauce and the other half is in the alcohol you're drinking.

1. In a large bowl, toss the chicken wings with the fish sauce and white pepper. Let them marinate for 10 minutes at room temperature, then rinse off and pat dry with paper towels.

2. Meanwhile, pour enough oil into a wok or deep pot to come halfway up the sides. Heat the oil over medium-high heat to 350°F.

recipe continues

(Throw in a grain of rice; if it pops up and starts sizzling, the oil is ready. Or use a thermometer.)

3. Spread the tempura flour in a shallow dish and lightly coat each wing. Working in batches to keep from crowding the pan, fry the wings until golden brown, 6 to 7 minutes. Transfer to paper towels or a wire rack.

4. Measure out ¼ cup of the frying oil and pour the remainder into a heatproof container (for another use). Use the reserved oil to make the party sauce (see below).

5. Toss the wings in the party sauce, adjusting the amount to your liking. Garnish with the chile powder to taste and the green onions. Serve with wet wipes and beer.

HEY-HA PARTY SAUCE

Makes about 1½ cups

¼ cup vegetable oil (or frying oil reserved from the wings)

½ cup diced red bell pepper

½ cup diced white or yellow onion

¼ cup diced jalapeños

½ cup distilled white vinegar

⅓ cup fish sauce

¾ cup coconut or palm sugar

¼ teaspoon paprika

In a wok, heat the oil over high heat until shimmering. Throw in the bell pepper, onion, and jalapeños and cook until softened and fragrant, 2 to 3 minutes. Add the vinegar, fish sauce, coconut sugar, and paprika and stir until the sugar is dissolved. Reduce the heat to low and cook, stirring occasionally so it doesn't burn, until the sauce is slightly thickened and has a deep reddish-amber hue, 8 to 9 minutes. If you're not planning to use the sauce right away, it will keep in the fridge in an airtight container for up to 1 month.

ARON

UNI GARLIC FRIED RICE

Serves 2

I love things that bring me pleasure. Really great *uni* (sea urchin), especially the stuff from Hokkaido or Santa Barbara, is one of those things. It doesn't matter whether it's on sushi, on pasta, whatever. The sweet, briny flavor is decadent in a way that makes it hard to believe you're eating something that comes from a spiky prehistoric ocean creature that eats algae all day.

Is sea urchin popular with chefs? Of course it is—it's wonderful. What I figured was if every fancy chef in town was putting uni on everything, I should be able to use it too. I mean, I love it just as much as them—let me in on that uni action.

After many experiments, I decided that the perfect vehicle for uni and *ikura* (plump salt-cured salmon eggs that resemble tiny rubies) was a big soft bed of garlicky fried rice with fresh herbs. It was well seasoned but not a flavor bomb, ideal for highlighting that briny sweetness. As you'd expect from a dish topped with a trendy thing, what began as a nightly special at Night + Market quickly evolved into something everyone was ordering.

Most reputable seafood markets these days, especially Asian ones, will carry uni preshucked and packaged in small wooden boxes. It will cost a premium, but it will also be far cheaper than what you'd pay in a restaurant. At that point, the question then becomes *How can I use this awesome sea urchin without messing it up?* That is where the simple brilliance of garlic fried rice slides in—it's a talented supporting actor that makes other actors that much better without overshadowing them.

1. Heat an empty wok over high heat until it begins to smoke, then swirl in the oil. Once the oil is shimmering, add the garlic and stir-fry until fragrant, a few seconds, then add the rice and sugar. Stir-fry until the rice develops a slight toasted color, which should take no more than a few minutes. Remove from the heat and fold in the fish sauce and a dash of white pepper.

2. Once the rice has cooled slightly, transfer it to a plate and top with the salmon roe, spread evenly down the middle. Gently lay the sea urchin on top and sprinkle with the green onion and cilantro. Serve with a small cup of *nam jim* seafood on the side.

2 tablespoons vegetable oil

2 tablespoons minced garlic

2 cups Steamed Jasmine Rice → 296, preferably day-old

1 heaping teaspoon sugar

2 tablespoons fish sauce

Ground white pepper

¼ cup cured salmon roe (*ikura*)

8 sea urchin lobes (*uni*), or more to taste

¼ cup thinly sliced green onion

¼ cup roughly chopped cilantro, with stems

2 tablespoons Nam Jim Seafood → 177

SUBTLE TRANGRESSIONS

I used to never think of myself as Asian-American, or even Thai-American. The way I saw it, I was a Thai kid who happened to be living in Los Angeles. I didn't like the idea of checking a box on a census form and having your identity defined for you. I imagine it's the same for someone who was born in Mexico but grew up in LA—you're not quite Mexican in the same way as more recent immigrants, but you're not quite *Chicano* either.

When Night + Market was in its early days, I felt I had something to prove, as if showing that I was aware of "what Thai people really eat" was an affirmation that I was truly, seriously Thai. Part of that was a way of pushing back against the things my parents had achieved (as children often do) at Talésai, where my dad and my grandmother had achieved a certain level of fame by getting influential and famous (mostly) white people to eat upscale, refined, and sometimes fusion-y Thai food. I mean, my grandma once showed Wolfgang Puck how to make green curry pizza.

When I took over the reins at Talésai, I was stubbornly determined to do it differently. But I tried to split the baby. I tried to implement what I considered "real Thai food" while preserving Talésai's classic dishes. Nobody was happy; the regular Talésai customers were pissed off because I cut things from the menu, and the crowd that frequented spots in Thai Town still weren't coming because Talésai was still seen as the place that served poached salmon with lemongrass sauce (which, although perfectly delicious, was deemed outdated). My vision was running the restaurant into the ground; it almost closed, but Night + Market somehow emerged and transitioned from a smoldering failure into a success story.

I feel extremely fortunate that our team has gotten the recognition we have, and that people seem to be paying attention on some level. But now that we aren't fighting for survival, I've also been able to reflect what that experience all meant, in terms of what I was trying to do. There's an idea in movies or music that Asians are less marketable. The one field where we're actually well represented is the food world, which means, like it or not, that Asian chefs have been shifted into being spokespeople for their culture. This is not something I'm whining about: I was reluctant at first but now I relish the challenges and benefits of that reality. You have to own it and deal with the good and the bad.

As I've met other Asian chefs, I've started to realize that we face similar issues. You get saddled with the pervasive idea of "ethnic food" as something that's inherently cheap. You deal with the inevitable comments of *Why would I pay $10 for your pad Thai when I can get it for less in Thai Town?* When I first started serving the *uni* garlic fried rice, I remember reading an incredulous Instagram comment on a photo of the dish, which read [sic] *"that's not Thai???"* That's part of cooking so-called ethnic food: Officers of the Authenticity Police are always ready to pop out and tell you what you can and can't serve, and how much you can charge.

Once that happens, you start to get a sense that the fetishization of "authentic food" is actually kind of messed up.

Authenticity is, in its own way, a prison, a type of confinement. You are limiting your creativity based on what other people tell you is the right way. Who was I trying to prove my Thai bona fides to? If anything, by being Thai-American, I actually have access to a creative freedom many people don't. I can walk in both worlds.

There was a review in which Jonathan Gold, the food critic for the *Los Angeles Times*, called my cooking transgressive—I think he was referencing the Blood Dipping Soup → 114—and while I'm not sure how broadly he meant it, I started to embrace it in a much wider context. I wanted to subvert the ideas people had of what it means to cook authentic food, a subversion of the militancy imposed by food nerds.

But there's another way I think about it: When was the last time eating food at a restaurant was fun? Like theme-park fun? In my opinion, it was the '80 and '90s, when Asian fusion was king. Everyone was less obsessed with authenticity, and not just because they were too coked-out to notice. For example, consider Nobu Matsuhisa, the Japanese chef who opened Nobu restaurants all over the world with help from, of all people, Robert De Niro. Nobu-*san* is a hero of mine, a true genius and visionary. There's one dish on the menu called Rock Shrimp Tempura with Creamy Spicy Sauce. It's amazing, very popular, and tastes just like it sounds. It is the dish that launched a thousand imitators, though haters gonna hate, and in this case they hate on the fact that the flavors are almost too pleasurable (yes, there are people who say stuff like that). I doubt Nobu-*san*, or most of his customers, loses sleep over the fact that there isn't a dish in Japan called Rock Shrimp Tempura with Creamy Spicy Sauce.

In every field of art, there are always people who vilify going for broad appeal. We make fun of the latest installment of a superhero franchise. We make fun of the latest bubblegum pop single that repeats on the radio all summer long. Even if, you know, they're actually pretty good. Over the past decade or two, it has started to happen with food too. There is a certain type of restaurant snob who turns a nose up at the mention of "Asian fusion." These are the people who dismiss any type of sushi drizzled with eel sauce or spicy mayo. These people are not fun.

What those people don't realize is that when you criticize a chef for going broad, for expanding that small window of authenticity someone tells them they should be aiming for, you're holding them back in the same way as the people who scoffed at Talésai making Thai food with Dungeness crab and filet mignon in the '80s. That's the same line of small-minded thinking that led people to be pissed at Bob Dylan when he went electric. Is fusion

food occasionally bad? Sure. But there is bad so-called authentic food too. Maybe just aim for delicious food and move on from there.

Is this the cliché ending where I make peace with the Thai-American identity I once resisted? Is this the part where I realize that Talésai and Night + Market have a lot more in common than I once realized? I guess so, but if the result is that it inspires you to cook a batch of Thai party wings, I'm cool with it.

SCALLOP TOSTADA

Serves 1

The Night + Market tostada is another dish that grew out of a particular obsession. In this case, it was scallops. I ordered a case of good ones—maybe the night after a blowout oceanfront meal at Nobu Malibu—and decided I was going to make a killer scallop dish. I tried out *Mama pad* (Stir-Fried Instant Noodles with Bacon, → 221) topped with paper-thin scallop slices. I tried out a sort of crudo showered in *furikake.* Nothing quite struck that right chord.

But then I started thinking about tostadas at Mexican seafood places like Mariscos La Playita in Venice or La Guerrerense in Ensenada, places where the tostada acts as a vessel for good seafood. Not to make a blanket statement, but the loose connection between Mexican and Thai drinking food—salt, chiles, some type of souring agent—kind of jumped out at me. Using a crispy fried tortilla as a vessel for a spicy, tart Thai-Mexican ceviche tossed in Nam Jim Seafood → 177 kind of fell into place naturally.

If you don't want to go to the trouble of deep-frying corn tortillas, fresh tostada shells work in a pinch, as do tortillas brushed with oil then toasted in the oven until crispy. I think the slick richness of raw scallop works well specifically, but you could also use raw shrimp.

1. In a small bowl, combine the scallops, red onion, and carrot, then toss with the *nam jim* seafood until mixed. Add the cilantro last and gently toss to coat.

2. Use a spoon to scoop out a few curls of avocado and layer them on the base of the tostada. Season with a pinch of salt. Top with the scallop mixture and, if you so desire, neatly arrange sea urchin or salmon roe on top like jewels. Serve with a lime wedge.

¼ cup bay scallops, or 3 ounces sea scallops cut into marble-size chunks

⅓ cup thinly sliced (root to stem) red onion

¼ cup shredded carrot

3 tablespoons Nam Jim Seafood → 177

⅓ cup roughly chopped cilantro, with stems

½ avocado

1 tostada shell

Kosher salt (see → 26)

2 or 3 sea urchin lobes (optional)

1 tablespoon salmon roe (optional)

Lime wedge, for serving (optional)

FRIED CHICKEN SANDWICH

Serves 1

1 white burger bun

3 tablespoons Ranch Dressing (recipe follows)

4 slices Roma (plum) tomato (¼ inch thick)

1 boneless fried chicken thigh (Chiang Rai Fried Chicken, → 104)

½ cup Green Papaya Slaw (recipe follows)

¼ cup roughly chopped cilantro, with stems

½ jalapeño pepper, cut lengthwise into strips

Our "world famous" fried chicken sandwich evolved out of a problem: too much fried chicken and not enough applications. When we opened Night + Market Song, we would prep huge amounts of brined chicken and batter every day, and even though we sold a lot of chicken, there always seemed to be extra. As with any professional kitchen, leftovers and extra stuff usually turn into a staff meal. Somewhere along the line the fried chicken made its way onto a white squishy hamburger bun from my wholesale guy, which I later learned was the same brand In-N-Out uses. It got topped with a loose riff on our papaya salad, as well as chopped herbs and a thick spread of ranch dressing. The sandwich started out as a staff meal, but it became an off-menu thing people had to ask for—I guess you can't keep something that wonderful bottled up.

One of our regulars came in and ordered the sandwich right before we closed; he told me later that he was pretty wasted after barhopping, and the chicken sandwich gave him a second wind. He ended up getting a girl's number at the next bar. This is that kind of food.

1. In a dry skillet, toast both sides of the bun over medium heat until crispy. Slather half the ranch dressing onto the bottom bun. On top, in this order, stack the tomato slices, fried chicken, and papaya slaw (shake out the excess liquid). Spread the rest of the ranch onto the top bun and top with cilantro and jalapeño.

2. Flip the top bun onto the bottom and gently press it down so it compacts. Spear the sandwich with a frilly club sandwich toothpick and serve.

recipe continues

GREEN PAPAYA SLAW

Makes about 2 cups

2½ tablespoons coconut or palm sugar

2½ tablespoons fish sauce

1½ tablespoons lime juice

1½ cups shredded green papaya or green cabbage

½ cup shredded carrot

In a bowl, combine all the ingredients and use your hands to massage the dressing into the papaya for a few minutes until it seems saturated and absorbed.

RANCH DRESSING

Makes about 1 cup

½ cup mayo

½ cup Mexican crema

1½ tablespoons ranch seasoning powder

1½ teaspoons ground white pepper

Put the mayo, crema, ranch seasoning, and white pepper in a small bowl and stir until combined.

FRESH VIETNAMESE SPRING ROLLS

You probably already know what's up with fresh spring rolls (or summer rolls, as they're sometimes called). They're like salad, but more fun. They're finger food, but refreshing and elegant. Even though they aren't specifically a Thai thing, I think they have a universal appeal as a self-contained unit of flavor and texture, one that you dip into sauce no less.

What makes these suitable for cooking at home is also what makes them efficient at restaurants: You can set up a station and crank out a million rolls once you've gotten set up. It's a shrewd way to feed a lot of people.

Following are my three favorite takes on the spring roll. The first is classic Thai–Vietnamese style. The second two—crab and avocado with a creamy-spicy mayo dip and grilled *unagi* with eel sauce—are more my tribute to a sort of '90s California fusion vibe. If you're planning on going big for a get-together, I'd suggest making all three variations and laying them out on a platter. Since the basic ingredients are the same, it doesn't require much extra effort.

IRMA (OPPOSITE), TUNG

GRILLED SHRIMP SPRING ROLLS

Makes 8 rolls (serves 4 to 8)

1. In a small bowl, toss the shrimp with 1 teaspoon of the sugar, the white pepper, and the seasoning sauce. Let marinate for about 10 minutes at room temperature. Meanwhile, preheat a well-oiled grill pan or broiler to high heat.

2. In a small saucepan, stir together the remaining ½ cup sugar, the vinegar, fish sauce, and 5 tablespoons water over low heat until the sugar dissolves. Remove from the heat to cool. Place the shredded carrot in a small bowl and cover with ½ cup of the fish sauce mixture plus another 5 tablespoons water. Let the carrots marinate for at least 10 minutes. The rest of the fish sauce mixture will be used a dipping sauce for the spring rolls.

3. Remove the shrimp from the marinade and cook them over high heat until just opaque, 1 minute.

4. Build your *mise en place*: Fill a wide shallow dish with faucet-hot tap water and arrange containers or small piles of shrimp, basil, cilantro, chiles, cucumber, carrots, romaine, noodles, and bean sprouts around a large cutting board or dry work surface. Submerge a rice paper wrapper in the water until it's soft and pliable, around 10 seconds. Shake off the excess water and spread the wrapper out flat on the work surface.

5. Start by laying 3 basil leaves on the bottom third of the rice wrapper, near the center, followed by 3 shrimp halves (if the grilled shrimp don't lie flat, use a paring knife to flatten them). You'll want to leave about 1 inch of space on either side of the shrimp from the wrapper's edge. Work quickly to stack on one-fourth portions of the cilantro, chile, cucumber, carrot, bean sprouts, and noodles, spreading each ingredient out evenly along the length of the roll. Cap it off with a strip of romaine, then fold the bottom part of the wrapper up over the filling. Holding the whole thing firmly in place with your fingers, fold the sides in like you would when rolling a burrito. Wrap it tightly, but not so tight that it tears.

6. Once you've repeated the process to produce 8 rolls, place them on a platter along with the reserved fish sauce mixture for dipping. Dollop the sambal into the sauce just before serving.

12 large shrimp, peeled, deveined, and halved lengthwise

1 teaspoon plus ½ cup sugar

½ teaspoon ground white pepper

2 tablespoons Thai seasoning sauce

½ cup distilled white vinegar

½ cup fish sauce

1 cup shredded carrot

24 Thai basil leaves

16 cilantro sprigs

8 fresh bird's eye chiles, or to taste, thinly sliced on an angle

1 cucumber, peeled and cut into 2 × ¼-inch sticks

4 romaine lettuce leaves, ribs removed, cut into 4 × 2-inch strips

2 cups cooked rice vermicelli noodles (follow the package directions)

1 cup bean sprouts

8 round rice paper/spring roll wrappers (8 inch)

2 tablespoons sambal oelek

CRAB AND AVOCADO SPRING ROLLS

Makes 8 rolls (serves 4 to 8)

2 tablespoons sugar

2 tablespoons fish sauce

2 tablespoons distilled white vinegar

1 cup shredded carrot

2 cups shredded lump crabmeat

16 slices avocado

16 *rau ram* leaves

16 cilantro sprigs

1 cucumber, peeled and cut into 2 × ¼-inch sticks

2 cups cooked rice vermicelli noodles (follow the package directions)

4 butter lettuce leaves, ribs removed, cut into 4 × 2-inch strips

8 round rice paper/spring roll wrappers (8 inch)

Yuzu Kosho Mayo (recipe follows)

1. In a small bowl, whisk together the sugar, fish sauce, vinegar, and ¼ cup water until combined. Add the shredded carrot, making sure it's completely covered by the liquid, and let marinate for at least 10 minutes.

2. Build your *mise en place:* Fill a wide shallow dish with faucet-hot tap water and arrange containers or small piles of crabmeat, avocado, *rau ram*, cilantro, cucumber, carrots, noodles, and lettuce around a large cutting board or dry work surface. Submerge a rice paper wrapper in the water until it turns soft and pliable, around 10 seconds. Shake off the excess water and spread the wrapper out flat on the cutting board.

3. Lay 2 slices of avocado on the bottom third of a rice wrapper, near the center. You'll want to leave about 1 inch of space on either side. Follow that with ¼ cup crabmeat and one-quarter portions of the rau ram, cilantro, cucumber, carrots, and noodles, spreading each ingredient out evenly along the length of the roll. Cap it with a strip of butter lettuce, then fold the bottom part of the wrapper up over the filling. Holding the whole thing firmly in place with your fingers, fold the sides in like you would when rolling a burrito. Wrap it tightly, but not so tight that it tears.

4. Once you've repeated the process to produce 4 rolls, place them on a platter and serve with a side of yuzu kosho mayo.

YUZU KOSHO MAYO

Makes about 1 cup

1 cup mayo

1 tablespoon yuzu kosho (Japanese citrus-chile paste)

2 teaspoons sugar

Squeeze of lime juice

In a small bowl, mix together the mayo, *yuzu kosho*, and sugar. Mix in lime juice to taste.

ROASTED UNAGI SPRING ROLLS

Makes 8 rolls (serves 4 to 8)

1. Build your *mise en place:* Fill a wide shallow dish with faucet-hot tap water and arrange containers or small piles of warmed *unagi*, mint leaves, green onion, cilantro, chiles, tomato, cucumber, bean sprouts, and lettuce around a large cutting board or dry work surface. Submerge a rice paper wrapper in water until it turns soft and pliable, around 10 seconds. Shake off the excess water and spread the wrapper out flat on the cutting board.

2. Lay an unagi fillet on the bottom third of a rice wrapper, near the center. Leave about 1 inch of space on either side. Follow that with one-fourth portions of the mint leaves, green onion, cilantro, chiles, tomato, and bean sprouts, spreading each ingredient out evenly along the length of the roll. Cap it with a strip of lettuce, then fold the bottom part of the rice paper wrapper up over the filling. Holding the whole thing firmly in place with your fingers, fold the sides in like you would when rolling a burrito. Wrap it tightly, but not so tight that it tears.

3. Once you've repeated the process to produce 4 rolls, place them on a platter and serve with a side of eel sauce for dipping.

EEL DIPPING SAUCE

Makes about 1½ cups

2 teaspoons tapioca flour

1 cup Japanese soy sauce

1 cup sugar

1 cup mirin (Japanese sweet wine)

In a small bowl, whisk the tapioca flour with just enough warm water (start with 2 teaspoons) to dissolve without clumps. In a saucepan, combine the soy sauce, sugar, mirin, and tapioca flour slurry and cook over medium heat, stirring occasionally, until reduced by half. Remove from the heat to cool slightly before using.

1 pound roasted *unagi* (see Note), reheated according to package directions and cut into four 4 × 2-inch fillets

24 mint leaves

4 green onions, halved lengthwise and cut crosswise into 2-inch lengths

16 sprigs cilantro

8 fresh bird's eye chiles, or to taste, thinly sliced on an angle

8 tomato slices, cut into half-moons

1 cucumber, peeled and cut into 2 × ¼-inch sticks

1 cup mung bean sprouts

4 leaves romaine lettuce, ribs removed, cut into 4 × 2-inch strips

8 round rice paper/spring roll wrappers (8 inch)

Eel Dipping Sauce (recipe follows)

Look for roasted *unagi* (freshwater eel) in the frozen section of a Japanese market.

CRAB MENTAIKO WONTONS

Makes about 16 wontons (serves 4)

Vegetable oil, for deep-frying

½ cup whipped cream cheese

½ cup shredded crabmeat
(use claw meat; it's cheaper)

Kosher salt (see → 26)

16 (4-inch) wonton wrappers
(with yellowish dough),
thawed if frozen

3 tablespoons mentaiko
(Japanese marinated cod roe)
or other small fish roe

¼ cup Sweet 'n' Sour Sauce
→ 308 (optional)

Serve with Cucumber
Salad → 181.

Hats off to the guy who invented the crab and cream cheese wonton. It's been a flagship appetizer for mom-and-pop Chinese and Thai restaurants for decades, relying on the theory that no matter where you're from, creamy stuff inside crispy deep-fried stuff is appealing on a primal level.

A 1:1 ratio is what you want here: the saltiness of crabmeat melded with the richness of cream cheese. The briny pop of fish roe is just icing on the cake.

1. Pour enough oil into a deep pot or wok to come halfway up the sides. Heat the oil over medium-high heat to 350°F. (Throw in a grain of uncooked rice; if it pops up and starts sizzling right away, the oil is ready. Or use a thermometer.)

2. While the oil is heating up, in a bowl, stir together the cream cheese and crabmeat until incorporated. If you're using canned or frozen crabmeat it will be a little salty already, but season with a touch more salt if desired. Spoon a tablespoon or so of the filling into each wonton wrapper, then top with slightly more than ½ teaspoon of the mentaiko. To fold the wrappers, use your fingers to grab the midpoint of each side and carefully pinch upward like your hand was one of those metals claws from an arcade machine. Use your fingertips to pinch together the skin well so it sticks together. Don't worry about sealing the edges too much; the sticky filling will help form a natural seal. Just make sure the points of the skins stick to each other well, so no oil seeps into the wonton.

3. Working in batches of one or two, carefully lower the wontons into the oil and fry until they're deep golden brown, 30 to 40 seconds. Let them cool on paper towels or a wire rack.

4. Arrange the fried wontons over a bed of cucumber salad, or serve with the sweet 'n' sour sauce for dipping.

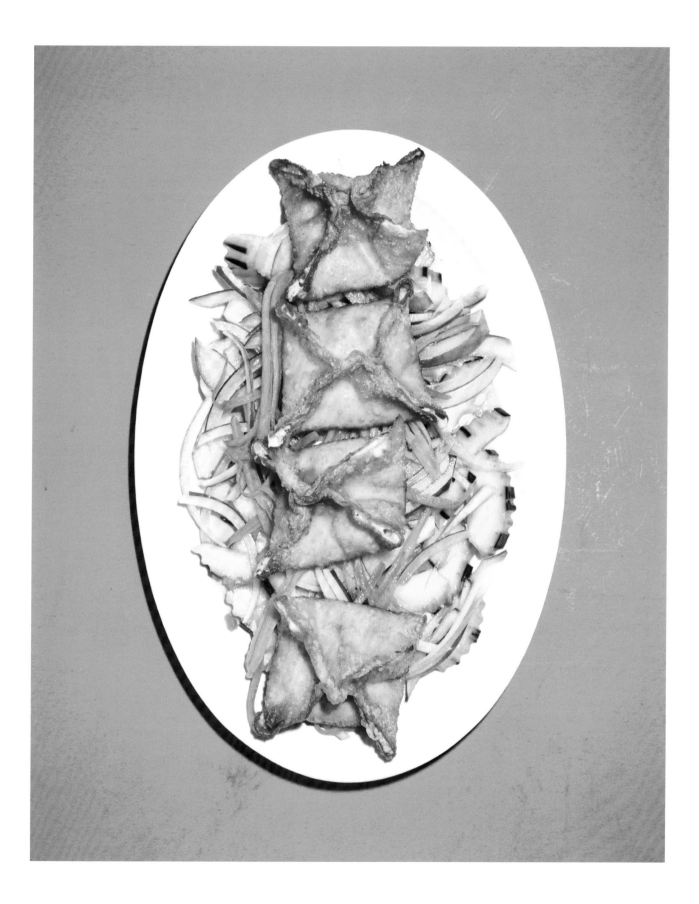

CORN FRITTERS

Serves 4

This recipe is based on an appetizer from Café Talésai, which was a casual spin-off of Talésai that my family ran in Beverly Hills for a little over a decade. Their basic version of this fritter is essentially a warm, puffy, corn-filled hush puppy—which is a fantastic drinking snack all on its own—but it becomes a little more special when you mix in different textures and flavors. In this case it's crabmeat and collard greens, but the potential for riffing is endless—shrimp, ground pork, cilantro, green onion, or anything else in your accumulated Thai pantry.

    Given that I'm a prototypical extra-sauce-with-my-McNuggets-please type of person, I serve this with two dipping sauces for variety: one creamy, one sweet-sour. Double-dip between them and enjoy the spice of life.

1. Pour enough oil into a deep pot or wok to come halfway up the sides. Heat the oil over medium-high heat to 350°F. (Throw in a fleck of batter; if it pops up and starts sizzling right away, the oil is ready. Or use a thermometer.)

2. In a large bowl, stir together the tempura flour, club soda, salt, and white pepper until something approaching pancake batter forms. Fold in the corn, crabmeat, and greens.

3. Once the oil is hot, use a large dinner spoon to carefully dollop the batter in (each scoop should be about 3 tablespoons in size). Fry small batches of fritters until they are a deep golden brown, about 3 minutes. Let cool on paper towels or a wire rack.

4. Garnish the fritters with the lime leaves (if using) and sweet 'n' sour sauce and yuzu kosho mayo.

Vegetable oil, for deep-frying

1 cup tempura flour

¾ cup club soda or seltzer

½ teaspoon kosher salt (see → 26)

½ teaspoon ground white pepper

2 cups fresh corn kernels (cut from 2 to 3 ears)

¾ cup lump crabmeat

½ cup chopped collard greens or other leafy greens, stems removed

3 kaffir lime leaves (optional), deveined and julienned

Sweet 'n' Sour Sauce → 308, for serving

Yuzu Kosho Mayo → 266, for serving

Serve over a bed of Cucumber Salad → 181.

THAI-STYLE KOREAN SHORT RIBS

Serves 2 to 4

⅓ cup peeled and grated fresh ginger

¼ cup minced garlic

⅔ cup Japanese or Korean soy sauce

½ cup sesame oil

3 tablespoons sugar

1 tablespoon ground white pepper

1½ pounds beef short ribs, cut into ½-inch slices across the bones

4 green onions, cut lengthwise into thin strands

2 tablespoon toasted sesame seeds

Serve with Steamed Jasmine Rice → 296.

A more accurate name for this recipe might be "Korean Short Ribs as Made by Thais Who Have Never Been to Korea." Generally, when Thai people think about Korean barbecue, they think about sesame oil—which is because it adds a very specific rich taste you don't find in Thai barbecue. I remember eating dinners with my family in Mae Chan where we'd fire up a little charcoal dome grill, gnaw on smoky short ribs, and open (without a corkscrew) a few bottles of wine my parents brought from the States. I distinctly remember it being Opus One, which was probably one of the gaudiest "status" wines in the '90s, which only further amplified the surreal quality of sipping wine and eating Korean barbecue in rural Northern Thailand.

The Korean-style marinade that I use is basic, but infinitely applicable and totally delicious in an uncomplicated and direct way. At the restaurant, we use bone-in short ribs sliced in long strips because a) they cook superfast and b) you get that chewy, charred texture that makes them excellent finger food. If you want to experiment with other cuts—hanger steak, thin pork chops, chicken thighs—I'd recommend letting the meat marinate for another hour or two.

1. In a small bowl, mix together the ginger, garlic, soy sauce, sesame oil, sugar, and white pepper until the sugar dissolves. Place the short ribs in a large zip-top plastic bag or shallow dish and cover with the marinade. Let marinate for 1 hour in the fridge (if using a dish, cover it with plastic wrap), then remove and let stand at room temperature for 30 minutes.

2. Meanwhile, preheat a well-oiled grill to very high heat.

3. When the grill is hot, cook each short rib for 2 minutes on each side (they cook fast). A little char is a good thing. Arrange the grilled short ribs on a plate and top with the green onions and sesame seeds. Serve with steamed jasmine rice.

ORANGE CHICKEN NIGHT + MARKET

Serves 2 to 4

Another thing I love: Panda Express. When I see that logo inside an airport food court, it's like manna from heaven. When I go to food conferences and corporate chefs from Panda are attending, I pick their brains about honey walnut shrimp theory. They're the Michael Jordans of casual Asian food—no one can even touch what they do. But what I admire most about Panda is that they took food that used to be seen as non-American and helped make it mainstream. They turned it into fast food, which is for better or worse the most American thing ever. That's a huge accomplishment.

This is my humble tribute to orange chicken, and in particular Panda Express's extra-crunchy, tangy orange chicken: probably the best of all time. Mine is second-best, though: I use fish sauce to add a salty/funky punch to the sweet glaze.

1. Pour enough oil into a deep pot or wok to come halfway up the sides. Heat the oil over medium-high heat to 350°F. (Throw in a fleck of batter; if it pops up and starts sizzling right away, the oil is ready. Or use a thermometer.)

2. In a large bowl, stir together the tempura flour, club soda, salt, and white pepper until a thick batter forms. Fold in the chicken until coated.

3. Once the oil is hot, remove the chicken from the batter, letting the excess drip off. Working in batches of 6 or 7, fry until the nuggets are golden brown on all sides, 4 to 5 minutes. Let cool on paper towels or a wire rack while you make the sauce.

4. To make the sauce: In a small bowl, whisk the tapioca flour with just enough warm water to dissolve with no clumps. In a small saucepan, combine the fish sauce, vinegar, sugar, marmalade, orange juice, tapioca flour slurry, and salt and stir over medium-low heat until bubbling and slightly thickened.

5. Pour the oil from the wok into a heatproof container for future use. Add the orange sauce to the empty wok over medium heat. Once the sauce is bubbling and syrupy, add the chicken and toss to coat. Transfer the chicken to a plate and garnish with the orange zest, green onion, and chile powder.

Vegetable oil, for deep-frying

1 cup tempura flour

¾ cup club soda or seltzer

½ teaspoon kosher salt (see → 26)

½ teaspoon ground white pepper

1 pound Brined Chicken thighs → 313, cut into nuggets

SAUCE:

1 heaping teaspoon tapioca flour

¼ cup fish sauce

¼ cup distilled white vinegar

¼ cup sugar

¾ cup orange marmalade

¼ cup orange juice

Pinch of kosher salt

1½ tablespoons thinly sliced orange zest

1 green onion, slivered

1 teaspoon Roasted Chile Powder → 304

If you decide to skip the chicken frying, consider using KFC popcorn chicken or something nugget-size from your favorite fast-food spot.

Serve with Steamed Jasmine Rice → 296.

BEEF TARTARE NIGHT + MARKET

Serves 4

Kosher salt (see → 26)

1 pound beef top round steak, cut into 1-inch cubes and trimmed of any fat or sinew

Vegetable oil, for frying

½ cup capers, drained and patted dry

¾ cup Seasoned Mayo (recipe follows)

2 hard-boiled eggs, peeled and finely chopped

½ cup Italian parsley leaves

½ cup minced red onion or shallot

½ cup Crispy Rice → 301 or Rice Krispies cereal

Ground pink peppercorns

Wasa rye crispbreads, toasted white bread, or Chicken in a Biskit crackers

The weeklong trip I took to Copenhagen in 2015 was wild. I was so hungover for my meal at Noma, I came close to disrobing at our table. I opted for the (fantastic) juice pairing instead of the wine pairing, which was against character because I love wine and they have one of the best wine programs in the world, but that's how hungover I was. The rest of the trip was a blur of hay-smoked duck and bacon-wrapped Danish hot dogs.

But the thing that captivated me most on the trip was the beef tartare at Manfred's, a cross between a bistro that serves three or four things and a wine bar, from chef Christian Puglisi. There was a lot of wine happening, but I remember being blown away by how assertively seasoned the tartare was, especially compared to the delicate cooking that's pervasive in Copenhagen. As someone who consumes an above average amount of raw meat, I was enthralled. I would hop on a plane just to eat it again. I decided that I was going to re-create the dish—or how I remembered it, more or less—as a tribute and serve it one night at the restaurant.

The more I delved into making it myself, the more illuminating the flavor combinations became. There was the salty pop of fried capers, the lushness of fresh mayo and hard-boiled eggs, the sharpness of red onion, peppercorns, and parsley. It struck the same balance of robust flavors that you'd look for in a Thai salad. And the meat: It was freshly ground instead of hand-chopped, which breaks down the muscles fibers in a way that gives it a unique silky, extra-luscious, almost creamy texture. It didn't rely on a superluxurious cut of beef, but instead used salt and a freezer to preseason and tenderize the meat. It was highbrow, yet visceral—heady, but results-oriented.

I've never seen the exact recipe for chef Puglisi's tartare (and the version they serve changes all the time anyway), but in the process of tweaking things to my personal taste (extra seasoning in the mayo) and using stuff I have on hand (like crispy rice), I ended up with a version that achieved what I loved so much about the original, but was distinct enough to call our own.

recipe continues

"Tosca Cerrada" Palamino Fino en Rama, Mario Rovira, Spain

This wine is essentially an unfortified sherry, which means it's a white wine that has tremendous savory and herbal qualities with a nice texture (like a skin-contact wine) that comes from aging. In my opinion it offers the best of both worlds between sherry and table wine: You get a fresh and direct snapshot of the grape itself, but you get all the interesting and complex yeasty flavors that come from hanging out in sherry casks. I'd suggest trying this with dishes that toe the line between mellow and bold, like some milder salads and curries.

A meat grinder is essential to achieve silky raw beef in this recipe, so if you don't have one I'd suggest buying one of the tabletop ones for thirty dollars. If you're opposed to purchasing a grinder, you can substitute a very tender cut like filet mignon, salt it and freeze it, then hand-chop it into small ¼-inch cubes.

In Thai culture, raw dishes are traditionally enjoyed with alcohol (to kill the germs?), and I think the same logic applies here. Consume with a glass of slightly chilled, chugable wine that's light on its toes.

1. In a bowl, sprinkle 1 tablespoon salt over the cubed meat and toss to coat evenly. Arrange the meat cubes in a single layer on a sheet of foil and place in the freezer until the cubes are firm and sticky to the touch, but not rock-hard, 30 to 45 minutes. They should look slightly dried out on the surface.

2. Pour about 1 inch of oil into a wok or deep saucepan and heat over medium-high heat to 350°F. (Throw in a single caper; if it pops up and starts sizzling right away, the oil is ready. Or use a thermometer.) Deep-fry the capers until they start to blossom, about 20 seconds. Be careful, they burn quickly. Remove from the heat. Drain the capers on paper towels. If you haven't already, make the seasoned mayo.

3. Remove the meat cubes from the freezer and run them through a meat grinder set to fine (between ¼ and ⅜ inch). Divide the ground beef evenly among four serving plates, arranging it into loose mounds placed in the center of the plate. In little piles around the beef, spoon on 2 tablespoons each of capers, egg, parsley, red onion, and crispy rice. Dollop about 2½ tablespoons of seasoned mayo wherever there is room. Sprinkle with ground pink pepper to taste and serve with either Wasa crispbreads (fancy), toasted white bread cut into triangles (less fancy), or Chicken in a Biskit crackers (least fancy, but most addictive).

SEASONED MAYO

Makes about 1¼ cups

I will admit to using Best Foods (Hellmann's) mayonnaise on most occasions, but in this situation homemade mayo is worth the effort. I go back and forth between spiking the mayo with pungent additions like horseradish, *yuzu kosho*, or Dijon mustard. Use whichever flavor speaks to you most.

2 egg yolks, at room temperature

Kosher salt (see → 26)

Dash of ground white pepper

½ teaspoon distilled white vinegar

1 teaspoon lemon juice

1 cup canola oil

½ teaspoon extra-hot ground horseradish, ½ teaspoon *yuzu kosho*, or 1 teaspoon Dijon mustard

1.　In a blender or food processor, blend together the egg yolks, a pinch of salt, the white pepper, vinegar, and lemon juice. Then, while the motor is running on low, pour the oil in at a very slow, steady stream and continue blending until the mayo is thick and smooth. You can also use an immersion bender for this step.

2.　From here, choose your own adventure: remove the mayo from the blender and stir in the horseradish, yuzu kosho, or mustard (adding more or less to taste). You can also season a smaller portion of mayo just for the tartare (you'll need ¾ cup) and reserve the plain mayo for later use. Refrigerate the leftovers in an airtight container for up to 1 week.

SAM

ROYAL TUNA TARTARE

Serves 4

There's a Thai dish called *miang kham*, made by wrapping aromatics and crunchy things like dried shrimp inside betel leaves—the name essentially means "little bundles you eat in one bite." It's often lumped in with so-called royal Thai cuisine, a way of cooking associated with the aristocratic class, which emphasizes subtle flavors and elegant presentation. My grandmother cooked this style of food at Talésai, and although it's not what the majority of Thai people eat, it's what you'll find at most upscale Thai-American restaurants.

    The genius idea my grandmother had when serving miang kham was to strip out the betel leaves and slap that same royal flavor palette onto tuna tartare. The result was protofusion in its highest state—a dish that's clean and modern but distinctly Thai. It also involves fried wonton chips.

    As an appetizer, this recipe is charming in all ways. It's delicate, it looks gorgeous, it takes 20 minutes to make, and it's fun to eat whether you serve it as a dip or a canapé.

Vegetable oil, for deep-frying

16 wonton wrappers

1 cup unsweetened shredded coconut

2 tablespoons sugar

1 pound fresh tuna steak, cut into ¼-inch cubes

⅔ cup minced shallots

⅓ cup very finely diced lime (flesh and peel)

8 fresh bird's eye chiles, or to taste, thinly sliced on an angle

⅓ cup crushed Seasoned Fried Peanuts → 309

⅓ cup thinly sliced lemongrass (see → 25)

12 kaffir lime leaves, deveined and finely julienned

High-quality finishing salt, like Maldon or Himalayan pink salt

1. Pour enough oil into a wok or large saucepan to come halfway up the sides. Heat the oil over medium-high heat to 350°F. (Throw in a grain of uncooked rice; if it pops up and starts sizzling right away, the oil is ready. Or use a thermometer.) Fry each wonton wrapper one at time until golden brown, for 5 to 10 seconds. Drain on a paper towel.

2. In a dry skillet, toast the coconut over medium heat, stirring occasionally, until a slight amount of color forms. Stir in the sugar and continue toasting until golden brown. Remove the coconut from the pan and spread out on a paper towel to dry.

3. In a large bowl, combine the tuna, shallots, lime, chiles, peanuts, lemongrass, and lime leaves. Gently toss everything to combine. Spoon the tartare onto the fried wonton wrappers and season with a pinch of finishing salt. Alternatively, serve the tartare in a bowl (season with salt to taste) and use the fried wonton wrappers for dipping.

SALMON POKE

Serves 2 to 4

1 pound skinless thick salmon fillets, cut into roughly ¾-inch chunks

3 tablespoons Japanese soy sauce

3 tablespoons sesame oil

¼ teaspoon sugar

¾ teaspoon sambal olek

½ cup julienned jicama

2 green onions, cut lengthwise into thin strands

2 fresh bird's eye chiles, or to taste, thinly sliced on an angle

2 tablespoons *furikake* (preferably nori-tamago)

½ tablespoon toasted sesame seeds

½ avocado, cubed (optional)

Snack on this by itself, or serve with warm rice for a quick meal.

I'm a notorious latecomer when it comes to trends. It took me until 2002 to find out why people were so into Nirvana (I bought the album *Bleach* on a whim while I was studying abroad in Paris and finally acquiesced to Cobain). So when poke, a traditional Hawaiian dish of cubed raw fish marinated in soy and other stuff, became a trendy thing in LA and poke shops began appearing in every neighborhood, I was all but oblivious. That changed when I took an overdue vacation to Waikiki a few years ago. I put on board shorts, I took surf lessons, I lay on the beach and got tan—stuff I never do—and most important, I ate lots of delicious poke, which can be found everywhere from liquor stores to sushi bars in Hawaii. The island bug bit me. After that, I finally "got" poke. It made sense why everyone was nuts about it.

So when I got back to LA, I started reading up on the stuff and came up with my own enhanced version for the restaurant. The centerpiece is the buttery salmon, of course, but there is also the snap of jicama, the salty-sweet *furikake* (an addictive Japanese seasoning mix made from seaweed and other sweet-salty things; if you can find it, get *nori-tamago*, the furikake made with dehydrated egg yolk), and a slight crunch from the sesame seeds.

In a medium bowl, toss the salmon with the soy sauce, sesame oil, sugar, and sambal. Let marinate at room temperature for 10 minutes. Add the jicama, green onions, chiles, furikake, sesame seeds, and avocado (if using) and toss to coat. Serve immediately.

NIGHT + MARKET TACOS

When I visited Copenhagen last year, my pal Rosio Sánchez—the former Noma chef who runs the city's best taqueria—and I had planned to do a taco pop-up together. A few weeks before I flew out, I started to mess with the idea of putting *sai uah* sausage and *nam prik* in a tortilla. After a rigorous testing period and many taco runs, taco-making became a personal hobby; I was assembling tacos in my spare time the way people build treehouses or knit sweaters. It was a satisfying way to flex my creativity and use a different part of my brain.

But let me step back for a minute: I am not Diana Kennedy, I am not a *taquero*, and I don't plan on ever opening a Mexican restaurant. I actually debated omitting these recipes altogether because I understand that by putting something in a cookbook, you're implying that the version offered is meant to be a standard-bearer in some way. These are not that. I made these tacos as a learning exercise, and what I've included is more a record of something that transpired than a statement about Mexican cooking.

Why should you care, then? Well, the way I see it, there are two ways to learn things you don't know. The first is to study and obsess and hand-wring about the right way to do it even before you've done the thing. If you concern yourself too much with mastery, you'll never start. The second approach, my approach, is to view challenges with the freedom of being an idiot. It's the idea of using urgency and enthusiasm as the impetus to create something pleasurable, without getting hung up on authenticity. These might not be the best tacos in the world, but they are tacos that can offer a worthy amount of enjoyment if you're interested.

There are two essential recipes for these tacos that function as building blocks: a smoky red salsa made from dried chiles, and velvety refried black beans cooked with lard and herbs. The third building block is really nice corn tortillas—try to find thick handmade ones, or visit a Mexican supermarket where they are cranking out fresh batches. A good tortilla elevates the whole taco. Beyond that, you can play around with toppings and proteins. I've included blueprints for two veggie tacos, a fried fish taco, and the original Night + Market taco, which repurposes Northern Thai sausage into a chorizo-like stir-fry. For that one, you could just as easily swap in any grilled meats from this book, like Pork Toro → 178 or the Thai Boxing Chicken → 141, and add the same toppings.

SALSA ROJA

Makes about 2½ cups

6 dried guajillo chiles, stemmed

4 dried pasilla chiles, stemmed

2 small tomatillos, husked

6 fresh bird's eye chiles, or to taste, stemmed

¼ large white or yellow onion

2 large garlic cloves, peeled but kept whole

1 tablespoon dried oregano

1½ tablespoons kosher salt (see → 26)

1 tablespoon sugar

2 tablespoons vegetable oil

1. In a dry heavy skillet, toast the dried chiles (guajillo and pasilla) over high heat. Flip them every once in a while until they're fragrant and slightly blackened, about 5 minutes. The timing might be different for each chile, so keep an eye on them while they cook. Remove the chiles. Add the tomatillos and char them on all sides until their outer skins are blistered and start to blacken. Once the chiles are cool to the touch, use a pair of scissors to trim them into 1-inch segments. Cut the tomatillos into quarters.

2. In a blender or food processor, combine 2 cups water, the toasted chiles, tomatillos, bird's eye chiles, onion, garlic, oregano, salt, and sugar and blend until smooth.

3. In the same pan you used to toast the chiles, heat the oil over medium heat until it starts to shimmer. Pour in the salsa and stir over medium heat for a few minutes, until you can smell the toasted chiles once again (heating the finished salsa helps the flavors mingle). Remove from the heat to cool. The salsa will keep in the fridge in an airtight container for about 2 weeks.

Piège à Filles, Les Capriades, Loire, France

This is one of the wines I go back to year in, year out. Pascal Potaire, the winemaker, is a somewhat legendary figure and makes ebullient wines that have a knack for sparking romance. In fact, the phrase *piège à filles* translates roughly to "girl trap." It's simple and refreshing but there's something deeper to it. It's intriguing and has real energy. This was the first pét-nat I ever tried back in France, and we were the first restaurant in LA to pour his wines a little less than a year later. The wine itself has the right amount of fruity sweetness to help with some of the more scorching dishes, like the crispy rice salad.

REFRIED BLACK BEANS

Makes about 4 cups

½ **pound dried black beans**

½ **large white or yellow onion**

2 **sprigs fresh oregano**

3 **sprigs epazote or bay leaves**

½ **tablespoon kosher salt (see → 26), plus more to taste**

3 **tablespoons lard**

1. In a large saucepan, combine the beans, onion, herbs, and ½ tablespoon salt and add cool water to cover by at least 2 inches. Bring to a boil over high heat. Let boil for 5 minutes, then reduce the heat to a simmer, cover, and cook until the beans are very tender, 1½ to 2 hours. (Or use a pressure cooker to cut the time in half.)

2. Discard the herb sprigs and onion. Carefully drain off the cooking liquid into a bowl and set aside. Set the pot of beans over medium heat, stir in the lard, and sauté the beans for a few minutes until combined. Pour in 1 cup of the reserved bean cooking liquid, then use a potato masher or the back of a wooden spoon to smash the beans into a thick paste. Splash in more bean water if the mixture seems chunky. Keep stirring and mashing until a smooth puree forms, then season with salt to taste.

AND OUR
WORLD FAMOU
IED CHICKEN SAND

SAI UAH TACOS

Makes 8 tacos (serves 2 to 4)

1. In a skillet or wok, heat the oil over high heat until it starts to shimmer. Add the onion and sauté until soft. Add the garlic and crumbled sausage and stir-fry for a minute or two until you can smell the sausage. Add the oregano and ¼ cup water. Continue to cook until the water has mostly evaporated and you're left with a thick ragu.

2. To assemble the tacos: In a dry pan over medium heat, warm up the tortillas until they're soft and pliable. Use a spoon to spread 2 tablespoons of the black beans onto each tortilla as a base, then top with slightly less than ¼ cup of the sausage mixture. Garnish each taco with an equal portion of shallots, cilantro, salsa roja, Cotija cheese, and a slice or two of avocado. Serve with lime wedges.

2 tablespoons vegetable oil

¼ large white or yellow onion, diced

1 tablespoon minced garlic

2 cups loose Northern-Style Herb Sausage → 162, casing removed

1 tablespoon fresh oregano leaves

ASSEMBLY:

8 corn tortillas

1 cup Refried Black Beans → 286

¾ cup thinly sliced shallots or red onion

½ cup roughly chopped cilantro, with stems

½ cup Salsa Roja → 285

½ cup crumbled Cotija cheese

1 large avocado, sliced

Lime wedges

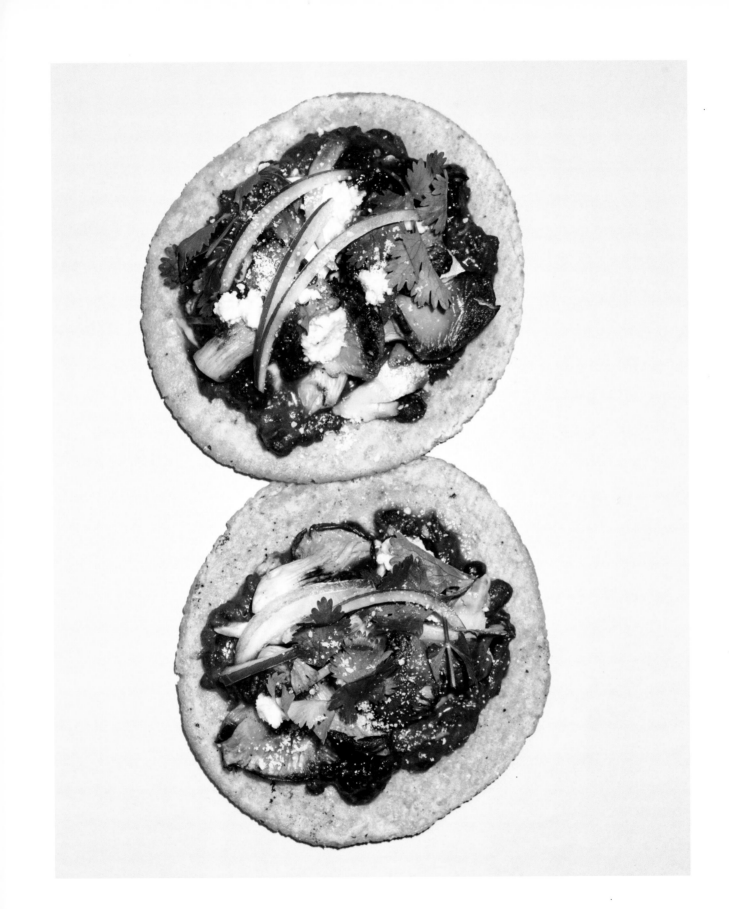

OYSTER MUSHROOM
AND STRING CHEESE TACOS

Makes 8 tacos (serves 2 to 4)

1. Preheat the oven to 450°F.

2. Spread the mushrooms over a large rimmed baking sheet in a single layer. Drizzle on the oil and toss to coat. Season with salt and white pepper to taste. Roast the mushrooms until softened, but slightly crispy around the edges, 15 to 18 minutes, stirring halfway through.

3. To assemble the tacos: In a dry pan over medium heat, warm up the tortillas until they're soft and pliable. Use a spoon to spread 2 tablespoons of black beans onto each tortilla as a base, then top with 3 or 4 mushrooms. Garnish each taco with an equal portion of queso Oaxaca, pickled onion, cilantro, salsa roja, Cotija cheese, and a slice or two of avocado. Serve with lime wedges.

1 pound fresh oyster mushrooms (25 to 30 count)

2 tablespoons olive oil

Kosher salt (see → 26) and ground white pepper

ASSEMBLY:

8 corn tortillas

1 cup Refried Black Beans → 286

½ pound queso Oaxaca or mozzarella string cheese, torn into thin strips

½ cup drained Quick-Pickled Onions/Shallots (recipe follows)

½ cup roughly chopped cilantro, with stems

½ cup Salsa Roja → 285

½ cup crumbled Cotija cheese

1 large avocado, sliced

Lime wedges

QUICK-PICKLED ONIONS/SHALLOTS

¼ cup distilled white vinegar

2 tablespoons sugar

1 tablespoon fish sauce

½ teaspoon kosher salt (see → 26)

½ medium red onion, or 1 large shallot, thinly sliced

In a bowl, whisk together ¼ cup water, the vinegar, sugar, fish sauce, and salt until dissolved. Add the red onion, making sure the slices are completely covered by the liquid. Cover and refrigerate for at least 30 minutes before using.

KUNG PAO EGGPLANT TACOS

Makes 8 tacos (serves 2 to 4)

Vegetable oil, for deep-frying

2 small Japanese eggplants, cut into 1-inch chunks (about 3 cups)

1½ teaspoons sugar

2 tablespoons minced garlic

1 teaspoon Prik Tum → 308 or minced fresh bird's eye chiles, to taste

2 tablespoons Stir-Fry Sauce → 306

1 tablespoon Roasted Chile Powder → 304

1 tablespoon Fried Shallots → 311

¼ cup crushed Seasoned Fried Peanuts → 309

2 teaspoons toasted sesame seeds

½ cup Thai basil leaves

ASSEMBLY:

8 corn tortillas

½ cup crumbled Cotija cheese

¾ cup thinly sliced shallots or red onion

1 large avocado, sliced

Lime wedges

1. Pour enough oil into a wok to come halfway up the sides. Heat the oil over high heat to 350°F. (Throw in a grain of uncooked rice; if it pops up and starts sizzling right away, the oil is ready. Or use a thermometer.) Working in two batches, fry the eggplant chunks until golden colored and slightly wrinkled, 20 to 30 seconds. Drain on a paper towel or wire rack.

2. Transfer the frying oil to a heatproof container. Heat the empty wok over high heat until it begins to smoke, then swirl in 1½ teaspoons of the reserved frying oil. When the oil is shimmering, add the eggplant, sugar, garlic, and *prik tum*. Stir-fry until the garlic and prik tum are fragrant, a few seconds, then toss in the stir-fry sauce, chile powder, fried shallots, peanuts, and sesame seeds. Stir-fry until the eggplant is completely coated in sauce, then remove from the heat and toss in the Thai basil.

3. To assemble the tacos: In a dry pan over medium heat, warm up the tortillas until they're soft and pliable. Spoon a heaping ⅓ cup or so of the eggplant onto each tortilla and garnish each taco with equal portions of Cotija, sliced shallots, and a slice or two of avocado. Serve with lime wedges.

CRISPY CATFISH TACOS

Makes 8 tacos (serves 2 to 4)

PICO DE GALLO:

4 jalapeño peppers, seeded and diced

½ medium white onion, diced

2 Roma (plum) tomatoes, diced

2 tablespoons lime juice

1½ teaspoons sugar

¾ teaspoon kosher salt (see → 26)

CRISPY CATFISH:

1 cup tempura flour

¼ cup white rice flour

1 cup club soda or seltzer

4 teaspoons hot Chinese mustard

1 teaspoon Lawry's seasoning salt

½ teaspoon ground white pepper

Vegetable oil, for deep-frying

¾ pound catfish fillet, skin removed, cut into 1-inch-wide strips

Kosher salt (see → 26)

SAUCE:

½ cup Mexican crema (or crème fraîche)

½ cup mayo

This taco recipe is a bit different from the ones that precede, which makes sense because a good fish taco is conceptually a very specific combination: crispy fried fish, the bland richness of *crema*, and the spicy pungency of salsa verde.

In Thailand there is a spicy dip called *nam prik khee ga* ("crow shit *nam prik*," named I guess because the charred and light bits create a mosaic that resembles the fecal matter of crows), which is essentially *nam prik noom* (Roasted Green Chile Dip, → 191) thinned out with lime juice, fish sauce, and fresh bird's eye chiles. It's the perfect Thai stand-in for salsa verde, and takes only a few seconds to make if you have leftover nam prik noom on hand.

I also feel that fish tacos, for whatever reason, don't demand super-nice tortillas in the same way as the other tacos. Whatever white corn tortillas you can pick up at the supermarket are fine in this case.

1. For the pico de gallo: In a medium bowl, combine the jalapeños, onion, tomatoes, lime juice, sugar, and salt. Refrigerate for 30 minutes to chill.

2. For the crispy catfish: In a large bowl, stir together the tempura flour, rice flour, and club soda to form a batter. Season with the mustard, seasoning salt, and white pepper.

3. Pour 2 to 3 inches of oil into a wok or deep saucepan with several inches of clearance and heat over medium-high heat to 350°F. (Throw in a fleck of batter; if it pops up and starts sizzling right away, the oil is ready. Or use a thermometer.) Working in batches, dip the catfish into the batter, then quickly and carefully slip it into the hot oil and fry, turning occasionally, until golden brown on all sides, about 3 minutes. Drain on paper towels and season with salt to taste.

4.   For the sauce: In a bowl, whisk together the *crema* and mayo and set aside.

5.   To assemble the tacos: In a dry pan or griddle, toast each tortilla until warm and softened. Top each tortilla with a bed of shredded cabbage, 1 or 2 strips of fish, pico de gallo, a splash of *nam prik khee ga*, the crema sauce, and chopped cilantro. Serve with lime wedges.

ASSEMBLY:

8 corn tortillas (or 16 if you like to double-stack)

1 cup shredded green cabbage

Nam Prik Khee Ga (recipe follows)

½ cup roughly chopped cilantro, with stems

Lime wedges

NAM PRIK KHEE GA

Makes 1¼ cups

¾ cup Roasted Green Chile Dip → 191

8 fresh bird's eye chiles, or to taste, stemmed

⅓ cup lime juice

3 tablespoons fish sauce

In a blender or food processor, combine the green chile dip, chiles, lime juice, and fish sauce and blend until combined. If it seems thicker than a salsa should be, thin it out with a little water and blend it some more.

STEPH

The Thai pantry is built to survive the apocalypse. Dried chiles, rice, garlic, shrimp paste, fish sauce—most building blocks of Thai cuisine have the ability to last for weeks, if not months or years, inside a dark cupboard. This is good news for the home cook too, since you'll be able to stockpile essentials and stash them away until needed.

If you've gotten this far in the book, you've realized by now I'm not exactly a diehard make-everything-from-scratch kind of guy. If there is a Thai ingredient that's a) delicious, b) long-lasting, and c) available at the store, you can weigh the scales you and determine if you want to simplify the process by buying premade stuff. There is absolutely no shame in going down that route. But some of those sauces/seasonings/pastes/toppings in the Thai repertoire *are* worth preparing yourself, or are at least worthy of consideration.

The subject of this chapter is how to DIY those important staples, along with handy shortcuts on stuff you'll probably end up making often (like sticky rice). My advice is to not try to scale down *these* recipes so you can make just enough for what is called for in another recipe. Having leftover pantry items leads to flexibility, versatility, and creativity. Nearly everything in this section will stay fresh for weeks at least, and each has enough applications to keep you from getting bored.

CHAPTER 6
BASICS THAT ARE WORTH
MAKING YOURSELF

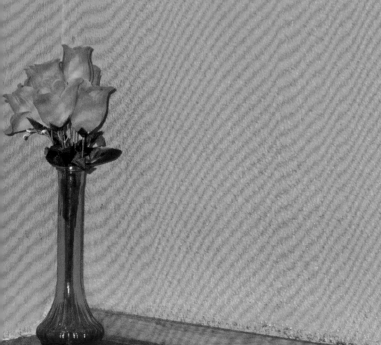

STEAMED JASMINE RICE

Makes about 5½ cups (serves 4)

What can you say about making rice? Well, first, invest in a rice cooker if you don't already own one. It's an indispensable tool found in any Thai kitchen, and even buying a cheap one will make your life much easier. Remember to wipe it down every so often so the starchy steam doesn't clog up the vents. If you're opposed to the rice cooker idea, or you don't have one quite yet, I've included stovetop instructions here as well.

As mentioned in "Get the Necessities" → 23, you should be using long-grain jasmine rice from Southeast Asia, ideally Thailand. Most jasmine rice imported into the United States is "new crop," meaning it absorbs less water than the rice sold in Thailand, which has often been aging in bags for a matter of months. What this means for you in the kitchen is that each brand or producer of rice might vary slightly for how much water is required. A good place to start is a 1:1¼ rice-to-water ratio (ignore the markings in your rice cooker). From there you can adjust based on whether your rice tastes too dry or too mushy. The sweet spot is when the grains are soft and fluffy, but still retain their individual texture.

Before cooking, rinse the rice three times with cold water to remove some of the starch (until the water is no longer cloudy, more or less), then drain well in a sieve.

2 cups jasmine rice
2½ cups water (see Note)

RICE COOKER METHOD

1. Transfer the rinsed and drained rice to a rice cooker and spread it out in an even layer. Add the water, cover, and press whatever button makes the rice.

2. Once the timer is done, let the rice sit for 5 to 10 minutes with the cover closed to let the steam inside cool and absorb back into the rice. Use a large spoon or fork to gently fluff the rice from the bottom, separating and breaking apart the grains without smashing them. If your cooker has a "Keep Warm" setting, you can use that to keep the rice warm for a few hours if not serving immediately.

STOVETOP METHOD

1. Transfer the rinsed and drained rice to a medium saucepan with a tight-fitting lid. Add the water and bring to a boil uncovered over high heat, stirring occasionally.

2. Once the water is boiling, stir a few more times, then cover the pan and reduce the heat to as low as possible. Simmer for 15 minutes. Try not to lift the lid during this part, since it will cause the rice to cook unevenly. After 15 minutes, check the rice: There should be no water left and the grains should be tender but a little firm. (If they are still hard or there is still water visible, keep cooking for another few minutes.)

3. Remove from the heat and let the rice sit uncovered for a few minutes to cool. Use a large spoon or fork to gently fluff the rice from the bottom, separating and breaking apart the grains without smashing them. Serve as soon as possible.

If you're making freshly cooked rice for the fried rices (pages 207–213)—rather than the more-ideal situation of using day-old leftover rice—scale back the water by ½ cup or so.

MICROWAVE STICKY RICE

Makes about 5 cups (serves 4)

Given how essential sticky rice (or glutinous rice, as it's often labeled) is to the Thai diet, making *khao niew* the traditional way is kind of a hassle. At the restaurant, we cook 200 cups at a time. The rice is soaked overnight in big plastic containers, wrapped in cheesecloth, and then steamed in these conical bamboo steamer baskets. It's a process.

That's not to say you shouldn't attempt sticky rice the traditional way at home, but I would recommend saving that method → **299** for occasions where you're making sticky rice for a big group rather than one to four people.

For me, the best way to make sticky rice in a pinch involves the microwave (you know you grew up in a Thai-American household when your mom made sticky rice in the microwave). It's a product of immigrant ingenuity. While microwaved sticky rice won't produce exactly the same tacky texture as steamed sticky rice, the results are close enough to make the time and effort trade-off worth it. Since microwave wattage varies, I'd suggest microwaving the rice in increments rather than all at once, stirring and checking for doneness in between.

2 cups Thai glutinous rice

1. Add the rice to a largish microwave-safe bowl or container. Rinse and drain with cold water three times, using your fingers to massage and stir the rice. When the water becomes less cloudy, you're good. Drain the rice thoroughly and cover it with 1½ cups warm water and let soak for at least 30 minutes (longer is better).

2. Cover the bowl with plastic wrap (or a lid) and microwave on high for 5 minutes. Carefully remove the plastic wrap and fluff thoroughly with a fork. The water level should have gone down and the rice should resemble risotto slightly. Loosely cover and microwave for another 5 minutes, then fluff again. Depending on how dry the rice looks, microwave for an additional couple minutes if necessary, checking the doneness every minute or so until the desired softness and chewiness is achieved. Transfer to a sealed container (a thermos is perfect, another Thai-American trick) to keep warm until serving.

TRADITIONAL STICKY RICE

Makes about 10 cups (serves 8)

For this method, you'll need an 18-inch (or so) square of cheesecloth and either a metal colander or some sort of steamer basket, which could be the traditional Thai bamboo variety or a large metal one.

4 cups Thai glutinous rice

1. Rinse and drain the rice with cold water three times, using your fingers to massage and stir the rice. Drain thoroughly, then soak the rice in cold water for at least 6 hours (overnight is best).

2. Place a steamer basket on top of a small rack or metal cup positioned in the center of a tall pot filled with 3 inches of water; the water level should be at least 3 inches below where the rice will sit. If you're using a mesh colander, select a pot that is just wide enough for the colander to fit inside without falling in (and you can also skip the cheesecloth wrapping—see next step—and just add the rice directly to the colander).

3. Drain the soaked rice into the cheesecloth and squeeze to remove the excess liquid. Wrap the rice tightly in the cheesecloth, place it in the steamer, and cover with a lid or thick cloth (but don't let the cloth hang over and catch on fire) so that steam doesn't escape out the edges. If you're using the colander, cover that as well. Steam for 30 minutes, flipping the rice bundle once halfway through, until you achieve a consistency that's soft but not mushy. Transfer to a sealed container to keep warm until serving.

COCONUT STICKY RICE

Serves 4

At most Thai restaurants, sweet coconut sticky rice is dessert. You could easily top this with very ripe (as ripe as possible) sliced mango and a little more of the sweet-salty coconut cream you stir into the rice, but in my opinion the best way to experience the sheer pleasure of coconut rice is as a foil to spicy/pungent/salty dishes like *moo sadoong* (Startled Pig → 94). The creaminess of the coconut milk mellows out the chile firestorm just enough to keep your pain sensors from overloading. Beyond that, try it with anything you would normally eat with sticky rice: grilled meats, salads (including the Crispy Rice Salad, → 101), *larb*, or *nam priks*.

1 (13½-ounce) can coconut milk
½ cup sugar
1½ tablespoons kosher salt (see → 26)
4 cups cooked Sticky Rice → 296–299

1. In a small saucepan, bring the coconut milk, sugar, and salt to a boil. Reduce the heat and simmer for 10 minutes, stirring occasionally. Remove from the heat and let cool slightly.

2. If you're using sticky rice that's been in the fridge, pop it in the microwave for a couple minutes so it's warm and pliable. In a large bowl, pour the warm coconut mixture over the rice and stir with a large paddle or spoon until totally incorporated. Allow to sit for 10 minutes before serving, then transfer to a sealed container to keep warm.

TOASTED RICE POWDER

Makes about 1 cup

Made from uncooked rice that's been toasted in the wok and ground, rice powder is something you'd traditionally find in Isaan-style *larb* and *yum* (salads). Its subtle nutty flavor and crunchy, pleasantly sandy texture make certain dishes sing.

I find the applications for rice powder go way beyond Thai food. You could experiment in any situation you would use bread crumbs— sprinkled over pasta, for instance—or use it instead of sesame seeds when you're dressing sautéed vegetables or marinated greens. It also functions as a mild thickening agent: A pinch or

RICE POWDER, BEFORE AND AFTER

two adds some body to clear soups or non-coconut milk curries.

Every Thai cook has a preference for using sticky rice or jasmine rice in rice powder, but both are suitable in my opinion. Use whatever is on hand. Much like other toasted preparations in this chapter, the key to rice powder is low heat, patience, and a lot of stirring. I've included some aromatics in the recipe below. These additions lend flavor but aren't strictly essential—even plain rice powder is terrific.

1 cup uncooked glutinous rice or jasmine rice

¼-inch piece fresh galangal, cut into thin coins

1 tablespoon thinly sliced lemongrass (see → 25)

2 kaffir lime leaves

1. In a dry wok, brown the rice over medium heat, stirring occasionally at first and more frequently as it browns. Once you smell the toasting rice, stir in the galangal, lemongrass, and lime leaves. Continue to cook until the rice develops a deep amber-golden hue, about the same color as brown rice, 15 to 20 minutes total. Remove from the heat and let cool completely.

2. Once cooled, run everything through a food processor or spice grinder until you reach the consistency of granulated sugar. Store in an airtight container in a cool, dry place for up to 1 month—any longer than that and you'll start to lose the nutty aroma.

CRISPY RICE

Makes about 2½ cups

Making crispy rice involves a bit of drying time and oil for deep-frying, but once you've made it you'll be glad you did. The stuff stays crunchy for a few weeks, and is delicious enough to eat by the handful. It also makes a very practical addition to your pantry. The most straightforward application is as a base for Crispy Rice Salad → 101, but you can use it as a topping for anything improved by an element of crunch (see the Beef Tartare Night + Market, → 276). As with fried rice, the best practice is to use leftover rice rather than fresh if you have some on hand.

2½ cups Steamed Jasmine Rice → 296, preferably day-old

1 teaspoon kosher salt (see → 26)

1½ tablespoons All-Purpose Curry Paste → 303

½ cup white rice flour

Vegetable oil, for deep-frying

1. If using leftover rice, break up the grains and spread them evenly over a baking sheet. If the rice is fresh from the steamer, fluff it with a fork, then spread it over a baking sheet and chill it uncovered in the refrigerator to dry for at least 1 hour before using.

2. Season the rice with the salt and curry paste, mixing it in by hand (use gloves if you want) to coat the individual grains. Sprinkle a few tablespoons of rice flour over the rice and continue mixing by hand, rubbing the rice to further separate it out. Add the remaining rice flour a little more at a time until it's all incorporated. The rice should feel very dry by the end and should not clump together.

3. Meanwhile, pour enough oil into a deep pot or wok to come halfway up the sides. Heat the oil over medium-high heat to 350°F. (Throw in a grain of rice; if it pops up and starts sizzling right away, the oil is ready. Or use a thermometer.)

4. Working in batches of a handful at a time, sprinkle the rice into the hot oil. The oil will bubble as the rice fries to a light golden color, so don't add too much at once or it will boil over. When the bubbles have subsided and the rice is golden brown, about 45 seconds, transfer to paper towels to drain. When fully cooled, store in an airtight container.

A.P.C.P. (ALL-PURPOSE CURRY PASTE)

Makes about 2 cups

If you tried to catalogue every variety of curry paste in Thailand, you'd probably end up with a book thicker than a September issue of *Vogue*. There is a lot of complexity down that road, and it's a topic that far more masterful chefs than myself have dedicated their careers to illuminating.

For this book, I've devised a handy all-purpose curry paste meant to serve as a baseline, one that's customizable based on whatever specific curry you're cooking. The philosophy behind it is a "more is better" approach: Not every curry paste is traditionally made with lemongrass and galangal for instance, but in my opinion adding those extra aromatics only makes the final product better.

The undoctored recipe below, which is basically a red curry paste, is suitable for making Crispy Rice → 301 or for use in milder curries or stir-fries. If you wanted to increase the heat level, you could swap out a portion of the milder large chiles for smaller, hotter ones. Or you can turn it into a green curry paste (see Variations) and use it as the base for any creamy curry. Beyond that, you can spike it with various additions like cilantro stems, fresh turmeric, or toasted cumin or coriander—some of which are detailed in the curries found in "Grandma" → 29.

Kosher salt (see → 26)

½ cup thinly sliced lemongrass (see → 25)

¼ cup roughly sliced galangal

10 large dried chiles (New Mexico or ancho chiles), stemmed

4 kaffir lime leaves, deveined and julienned, or grated zest of 2 key limes

½ cup roughly sliced shallots

¾ cup garlic cloves, peeled but kept whole

1 teaspoon shrimp paste

⅓ cup vegetable oil

1. In a food processor or blender, process the ingredients in this order (starting with the hardest and adding them one by one), sprinkling each with a pinch of salt to help break them up: lemongrass, galangal, chiles, lime leaves, shallots, garlic, and shrimp paste. Blend until each ingredient is totally incorporated before adding the next, stopping as needed to scrape down the sides with a spatula. By the end, you should end up with a thick semi-dry paste.

2. In a wok or small skillet, heat the oil over medium-low heat until shimmering. Stir in the curry paste and cook until the oil is combined and the mixture is very fragrant, 5 to 10 minutes. This part helps the paste keep longer and become more *hom* (the Thai word for the savory fragrant aroma that happens when you toast/roast something). Let cool completely before transferring to an airtight container. The paste keeps in the fridge for up to 3 weeks, or in the freezer for up to 3 months.

GREEN CURRY PASTE VARIATION
Add 1 tablespoon toasted ground coriander. Omit the dried red chiles and substitute an equal amount of fresh green chiles: use half bird's eye chiles and half shishito peppers, long peppers, or any mild green chile that is not too fleshy.

VEGAN CURRY PASTE VARIATION
To make a vegan version, omit the shrimp paste and season with extra salt or thin soy sauce to taste.

CHILE OIL

Makes ½ cup (or more)

½ cup dried whole chiles, roasted (see → 304)

¼ cup vegetable oil, plus more to taste

Kosher salt (see → 26)

1. In a blender or food processor, combine the chiles, oil, and a pinch of salt and blend on low speed until the chiles have broken down into coarse shards. Tweak the oil-to-chile ratio to your liking— you can add up to a cup of oil

without diluting the potency too much—and adjust the salt level to taste. Transfer to an airtight container and store in a cool, dry place for up to 6 months. When serving, you can either spoon out only the oil or scoop up some of the chile shards that have settled to the bottom.

ROASTED CHILE POWDER

Makes about 1 cup

You can't talk about Thai flavors without mentioning the spicy punch of roasted chile powder. Its inclusion is nonnegotiable. And since the fresh stuff is far brighter and more fragrant than anything found in a bag, I consider this a situation where you'll want to make it yourself. It's that important.

The key to roasting chiles is maintaining the correct heat level. The flame should be low enough so the chiles don't burn, but high enough so that the chiles darken and develop flavor. The sweet spot is when you end up with a dark red color and a powerful fruity aroma. Once you've roasted the chiles but before you've pulverized them, you can set a portion aside to make a simple chile oil, which can be served with Thai Dim Sum → 60 or used as a topping for *khao soi* (Chiang Mai Curry Noodles, → 107).

2 cups dried Thai bird's eye chiles, pulla chiles, or árbol chiles, stemmed

1. In a dry wok, roast the chiles over medium-low heat, stirring occasionally, until they turn a deep, dark crimson (almost brown) and give off a sweet and earthy smell (not burnt). The process shouldn't take more than 10 minutes, but it pays to be vigilant in making sure the chiles toast evenly and slowly.

2. Remove the chiles from the heat and let them rest until cool enough to handle. Transfer to a food processor, blender, or spice grinder and grind until the mixture is slightly finer than the crushed red pepper you'd find at a pizza shop. Be careful not to breathe in any chile dust when you remove the lid. Store in a sealed container in a cool, dry place for up to 3 months.

CHILE JAM
NAM PRIK PAO

Makes about 2 cups

The beauty of chile jam is its sweet/spicy/umami versatility. You can scoop it up with shrimp chips, toasted white bread, or grilled meats. You can thicken it with crushed pork rinds or fried chicken skin to create a heartier, crunchier, saltier dip (I've seen my aunt blend in dried shrimp too) that pairs well with vegetables. It tastes good with rice, and you can mix it into stir-fries, soups, salads, or curries to lend a deep, tangy edge.

As the Thai name—*nam prik pao*—implies, chile jam is technically a type of *nam prik*, or chile dip → 190. But out of all nam priks, this is the one that benefits most from being made in a blender. That's because you want the texture to be sticky, like something out of the La Brea Tar Pits. Achieving that gluey jam-like texture with a mortar and pestle is laborious; doing it with a blender is not.

Experiment with any dried chile you prefer, hot or mild, just keep in mind the final product will reflect the characteristics of that chile, i.e., using dried chipotles will produce a smoky jam, or using dried árbols will make it spicier.

2 cups vegetable oil

1 cup peeled and halved garlic cloves

¾ cup sliced shallots

10 to 12 dried New Mexico chiles (or any dried chile), stemmed, seeded, and trimmed into 1-inch segments

¼ cup coconut or palm sugar

1 tablespoon shrimp paste

2 teaspoons kosher salt (see → 26)

2 tablespoons fish sauce

¼ cup Tamarind Water → 313

1. In a wok, heat the oil over medium heat until it starts to shimmer. Add the garlic and fry until browned and slightly softened, 20 to 30 seconds. Skim out the garlic and let drain on a paper towel. Repeat the process with the shallots. Add the chiles to the oil and fry until they puff slightly and become fragrant and dark red, 10 to 15 seconds. Be careful because they cook quickly—if you burn the chiles, the entire jam will taste burnt. Drain the chiles on a paper towel. Turn off the heat and reserve the frying oil.

2. In a small saucepan, combine the coconut sugar and ¼ cup water and stir over low heat until dissolved. Remove from the heat.

3. In a food processor or blender, pulse the chiles until pulverized. Add the garlic, shallots, and shrimp paste, blending until they form a thick paste. Transfer the mixture to a medium bowl and stir in the sugar syrup, salt, fish sauce, tamarind water, and ¼ cup of the reserved frying oil until totally combined. Store in an airtight container and pour on another ¼ cup of the reserved frying oil as a cap to help it stay fresh longer. The chile jam will keep in the fridge for up to 1 month.

STIR-FRY SAUCE

Makes 2½ cups

At Night + Market we make large batches of what I call stir-fry sauce, a stupidly simple sweet and salty mixture stashed next to the wok in squeeze bottles. We use it to season noodles, fried rice, vegetables, or anything else that goes into the wok. I recommend taking a minute to make it after you hit the supermarket so it's ready once you start cooking—having everything prepped and ready is half the battle with wok recipes.

1½ cups Thai seasoning sauce
1 cup oyster sauce
1½ tablespoons sugar

Combine everything in a bowl and whisk until the sugar has dissolved. Keeps in an airtight container indefinitely.

PRIK NAM PLA

Makes about 1¼ cups

Prik nam pla (or *nam pla prik*, since the Thai language sometimes lets you flip words around and achieve the same meaning) is a universally beloved Thai condiment made from fish sauce, chile, garlic, and lime. It's something you will find on nearly every Thai table, whether it's at home or a restaurant. The tangy/salty/spicy flavors act as an addictive flavor enhancer for anything starchy, which makes it brilliant for splashing onto fried rice (the greatest application, in my opinion) or more generally, seasoning anything that has been stir-fried in a wok, whether it be meats, eggs, noodles, or vegetables.

The exact ratios involved in prik nam pla—like most Thai dressings—are heavily based on personal preference, so use this as a rough guideline rather than an absolute; tweak and taste until you find a balance of tangy/salty/spicy that strikes you the right way.

1 cup fish sauce
¼ cup lime juice
1½ tablespoons minced fresh bird's eye chiles, or to taste
3 tablespoons minced garlic

In a small bowl, whisk together the fish sauce, lime juice, chiles, and garlic, tasting and adjusting as needed. Store in an airtight container in the fridge for up to 1 month. When serving, the idea is that you can scoop out as much chile and garlic as you want, or you can use only the slightly-less-intense liquid.

SWEET 'N' SOUR SAUCE

Makes about 2 cups

I use this dipping sauce for anything deep-fried, but it can also accompany grilled meats and other crispy things. Ideally, you'll want to pick up Chinese pickled (also labeled salted or preserved) plums in brine, or in a pinch Japanese *umeboshi*, which provide that specific tart flavor.

1½ cups sugar

2 cups distilled white vinegar

7 Chinese pickled plums, pitted and finely minced

    In a small saucepan, combine the sugar, vinegar, plums, and ½ cup water and bring to a simmer over medium-high heat, stirring occasionally. Adjust the heat to maintain a simmer, until thickened slightly, about 20 minutes. Remove from the heat and let cool before serving. Keeps in an airtight container in the fridge indefinitely.

PEANUT SAUCE

Makes about 3½ cups

Peanut sauce isn't as prevalent in Thai cooking as you might think—it's mainly used as a dipping sauce for grilled pork satay or grilled chicken, or spooned atop a simple home-style dish known as "Bathing Rama" (see Seasoned Boiled Pork, → 217). Traditionally it's made by grinding roasted peanuts and cooking them down with coconut milk, but I've always preferred the quicker Thai-American method involving supermarket peanut butter. Skippy is a good standard.

    Beyond grilled meats, use peanut sauce as a dip for toast, a sandwich spread, or thinned out with water and vinegar to make salad dressing. I don't personally endorse slathering it on your pad Thai (as I've seen some people do at the restaurant), but, hey, whatever you're into.

1 (13½-ounce) can coconut milk

1 cup creamy peanut butter

1 tablespoon All-Purpose Curry Paste → 303, or more to taste

2 tablespoons coconut or palm sugar

2 tablespoons fish sauce

1½ tablespoons distilled white vinegar

1 teaspoon kosher salt (see → 26)

    In a medium saucepan, combine ½ cup water, the coconut milk, peanut butter, curry paste, coconut sugar, fish sauce, vinegar, and salt. Simmer over medium heat, stirring often, until the oil has started to separate out (which means it's done). Store in an airtight container in the fridge for up to 2 weeks, reheating as needed. Before serving stir the separated oil back in as you rewarm.

GARLIC-CILANTRO PASTE

Makes about ⅔ cup

This is what most Thai cooks consider the foundation of a basic marinade for pork, chicken, or shrimp—and really, there isn't any protein that suffers from a 30-minute bath in the stuff. At the restaurant we sneak it into other dishes too, like Golden Triangles → 59 and Thai Dim Sum → 60 because it adds fragrance and complexity without being overpowering. Think of it as a Thai sofrito: a spoonful in rice, soups, or stews adds immediate depth.

⅔ cup roughly chopped cilantro stems

⅓ cup garlic cloves, peeled but kept whole

2 teaspoons ground white pepper

½ teaspoon kosher salt (see → 26)

    In a blender or food processor, combine all the ingredients and puree until a rough paste forms. Transfer to an airtight container and store in the fridge for up to 1 week.

PRIK TUM

Makes about 2 cups

Prik tum is a hot-garlicky paste made by mashing and cooking down chiles and garlic. The most essential application for prik tum is in spicy stir-fries such as Grapow Chicken → 46 and Drunken Noodle Pastrami → 45. In a wider sense, it's useful any time you want to impart the flavor of roasted garlic and chiles, and at Night + Market we use it like a shortcut: Instead of stir-frying fresh chiles and garlic for each order of noodles, we add a spoonful of prik tum. We cook this in large industrial-size batches, which require an hour or more of standing over a stove inhaling spicy fumes—it's like preparing a hollandaise that can make you cry. Cooking small batches is less painful, but be forewarned that simmering raw chiles are very potent.

If you don't have prik tum on hand, you can always substitute equal amounts of minced garlic and bird's eye chiles when starting off a stir-fry. But cooking everything together beforehand yields a deeper and more intense flavor, a combination of what Thai people call *hom* (fragrant) and *choon* (zesty).

3 large jalapeño peppers, stemmed

¾ cup fresh bird's eye chiles, stemmed

¾ cup garlic cloves, peeled but kept whole

½ tablespoon kosher salt (see → 26)

1 cup vegetable oil, plus more as needed

2½ teaspoons ground white pepper

1.   In a blender or food processor, puree both types of chile, the garlic, and salt until everything is finely minced. Transfer to a small saucepan and add the oil. Simmer over low heat, stirring often, until the liquid released by the chiles has evaporated and the mixture has transformed into a sticky paste, with the oil taking on the color of the chiles, 30 to 45 minutes.

2.   At this point your nose might itch and eyes water—this means you're on the right track. If at any time the paste seems too viscous or dry, add more oil as needed. Remove from the heat, stir in the white pepper, and let cool. Store in an airtight container in the fridge for up to 1 month.

SEASONED FRIED PEANUTS

Makes 2 cups

If you want to substitute dry-roasted peanuts any time this book calls for fried peanuts, no big deal. However, I've always found that fried skin-on peanuts offer a major upgrade in terms of crunch and flavor—plus they make for an addictive snack. You can season these peanuts with just salt, of course, or since you're heating up the oil anyway, you can boost them with an array of fried aromatics. If you want to go all in, stir in 2 tablespoons each of Fried Garlic → 311 and toasted shredded coconut → 281 into the finished fried peanuts to create the most addictive nut mix of all time.

Vegetable oil, for deep-frying

2 cups raw peanuts, skin-on, if possible

Kosher salt (see → 26)

12 kaffir lime leaves

2 tablespoons thinly sliced lemongrass (see → 25)

8 small dried chiles (bird's eye chiles, pulla, or árbol), or to taste

1.   Pour enough oil into a wok or deep saucepan to come halfway up the sides. Heat the oil over medium-high to 350°F. (Throw in a grain of uncooked rice; if it pops up and starts sizzling right away, the oil is ready. Or use a thermometer.) Add all the peanuts and fry until they turn golden-brown and become fragrant, 45 seconds to 1 minute. Drain on paper towels, spacing out the nuts so they stay crisp. Sprinkle a teaspoon or so of salt over the nuts while warm.

2.   Repeat the frying process in the same oil with the lime leaves, lemongrass, and chiles, cooking each separately until fragrant and golden brown (less than a minute), then draining on paper towels. Transfer the peanuts to an airtight container and crush the fried aromatics over the top, tossing to mix. Store in a sealed container in a cool, dry place for up to 1 month.

SEASONED FRIED PEANUTS

FRIED SHALLOTS

Makes about 2 cups

I've messed up a lot of batches of fried shallots. If you're not paying attention to the fine line between golden brown and black, they'll burn quickly and taste awful. That said, when they're done right, there is nothing more mouthwatering than the sweet, oniony crunch of fried shallots. Showering them over sticky rice makes a dynamite meal in itself, but there is literally nothing they don't improve—grilled fish, fried chicken, creamy curries, salads, stir-fried veggies. I often have to cook three times more than I need because I eat so many as a snack.

There are two secrets to perfectly crisp (non-limp) shallots. First, you'll want to slice your shallots fairly thin, but not *Good-fellas* razor thin—somewhere between ⅛ and ¹⁄₁₆ inch thick. If you have a mandoline slicer, it will make the task even easier. Second, the heat should be low but steady, ensuring that the shallots have enough time to crisp up. It can take a couple of batches to get the hang of it, so persevere.

Vegetable oil, for deep-frying

16 medium shallots, peeled and halved lengthwise, cut into thin slices to make rings

Kosher salt (see → 26)

1. Pour 3 inches of oil into a wok or large saucepan with several inches of clearance. Heat the oil over medium-low heat to around 275°F. (Use a thermometer.) The oil should be hot enough that a shallot slice sizzles immediately when tossed in but doesn't take on color right away.

2. Working in batches, add as many shallots as will fit in a shallow layer and fry until they're dark yellow, almost amber-bronze, 5 to 10 minutes. Sprinkle in a pinch of salt if you'd like—I'm not sure if it keeps them from burning, but it's a trick my grandmother uses. As the shallots cook they'll start to slowly take on color. Stir the oil occasionally at first, but more frequently when they're almost finished to keep the heat even. When done, they might not look totally fried, but they'll take on more color and crispness as they drain. Meanwhile, line a plate with paper towels.

3. Remove the shallots using a slotted spoon or skimmer and let cool on the paper towels in a single layer. Repeat the frying process with the remaining shallots. Transfer cooked shallots to an airtight container and store in a cool, dry place. If fried properly, they should stay crisp for up to 2 weeks.

Bonus: Once the frying oil is cool, strain out any loose bits and store in an airtight container. You now have delicious shallot oil to drizzle over rice, soups, and stir-fries, or to otherwise add depth to any recipe.

FRIED GARLIC AND GARLIC OIL

Makes 1 cup

If you've gotten the knack of fried shallots, fried garlic is a cakewalk. Since the garlic pieces are smaller, they'll cook more quickly and require more frequent stirring, but overall you're looking for the same benchmarks as the shallots: a deep golden color and crispy texture. Avoid burnt garlic.

Much like the shallots, fried garlic is a universally appealing topping—it's not going to make any-thing taste worse. It's particularly crucial in dishes like the Northern-Style Pork Larb → 152, Marinated Tomatoes → 242, and *nam prik ong* (Chiang Rai Pork Chile Dip, → 198), but feel free to sprinkle it over any salad or dip.

Vegetable oil, for deep-frying

1 cup minced garlic

1. Pour 2 inches of oil into a wok or large saucepan with several inches of clearance. Heat the oil over medium-low heat to around 275°F. (Use a thermometer.) The oil should be hot enough that a piece of garlic sizzles immediately when tossed in, but doesn't take on color right away.

2. Add all the garlic and fry until golden and crispy, 4 to 6 minutes. Stir the oil occasionally at first, but

FRYING SHALLOTS

more frequently when it's almost finished. Meanwhile, line a plate with paper towels. Remove the garlic using a slotted spoon or skimmer and let cool on the paper towels. Once cool, break up any clumps that have formed. Transfer to an airtight container and store in a cool, dry place for up to 1 month.

Garlic Oil: To make garlic oil, stir back in as much fried garlic as desired into the reserved frying oil once cooled. (Even without garlic stirred back in it will have great flavor.) Store in an airtight container. Fry eggs with it; drizzle it over rice, soups, or stir-fries; or add it to whatever else requires an extra boost of garlic.

TAMARIND WATER

Makes about 3 cups

Think of tamarind water as you would lime juice or vinegar. It's another Thai method of adding a sour edge to something like curry or *nam prik*. Making it involves extracting that sour flavor from tamarind paste—the fruit from the tamarind pods mashed up and dried into a tangle of membrane and stringy bits—by steeping it in hot water to produce a concentrate. You can find bricks of dried tamarind paste at most Asian markets, or even some Latino markets (just make sure you don't buy sweet tamarind candy).

2 ounces seedless tamarind paste (about one-eighth of a package, usually)

2½ cups boiling water

1. In a large bowl, break up the tamarind paste into small chunks and cover with the boiling water. Use a spatula or masher to break up the tamarind chunks until pulpy and let steep.

2. Once the water is lukewarm, use your hands to squish and mash up the pulp further. Let sit for another 10 minutes or so, then pour everything into a mesh sieve set over a bowl, pressing the pulp and scraping off the flavorful puree that collects on the underside of the sieve.

3. Discard the stringy membrane and any bits of seed left over. Stir the juice and pulp to incorporate and store in an airtight container. The tamarind water will keep in the fridge for about 2 weeks, or in the freezer indefinitely.

BRINED CHICKEN

Makes 1½ pounds

About 90 percent of the chicken we use at Night + Market is brined ahead of time—the exceptions being ground chicken or any chicken that has its own marinade (like Cashew Chicken, → 49, or Thai Boxing Chicken, → 141). We use chicken thighs, because in my opinion dark meat is more delicious and it retains moisture better. We take the time to brine because it means having flavor built-in before you start cooking, which is a tremendous advantage, especially when it comes to quick cooking techniques like stir-frying. Brining your chicken not only adds complexity, it keeps the meat moist too. If you don't plan on cooking the chicken right away, I'd suggest draining off the brine liquid once marinated and storing the thighs in the fridge until you're ready to use them.

1½ pounds boneless, skin-on chicken thighs (4 to 6)

1 tablespoon minced garlic

1 tablespoon minced lemongrass (see → 25)

½ tablespoon kosher salt (see → 26)

½ teaspoon ground white pepper

1. Place the chicken in a large bowl, plastic storage container, or large zip-top bag. Sprinkle on the garlic, lemongrass, salt, and white pepper and add enough cold water to cover.

2. Mix until the seasonings are dissolved and let marinate at room temperature for at least 15 minutes and up to 30 minutes; any longer and the chicken can become too salty. Pour off the liquid and keep the chicken refrigerated until ready to use.

ROTI BREAD

Makes eight to ten 5-inch discs

Making *roti* bread—the croissant of Southeast Asia—is a skill that takes years to perfect. Thailand is packed with street vendors who specialize solely in roti, cooking it to order on hot griddles and serving it with a slick of margarine or sweet condensed milk. You'll find it at some restaurants too, often served with creamy curries for dunking and dipping—my favorite way to eat it.

When done correctly, roti is both buttery and light-as-air, woven together from intricate flaky layers formed by kneading and tossing the dough in just the right way. It can be tricky and temperamental, and even cooks who have been making it forever don't always agree on a single technique. Which is to say, if you can locate frozen roti in the freezer section of your Asian grocery, please buy it. I use frozen roti at the restaurant, since it is consistently awesome and because after a thorough weighing of the options I decided the effort involved in making them was far outweighed by the deliciousness and ease of the frozen ones. I've served frozen roti to pastry chefs and they've gone nuts for it.

But if you are a masochist intent on making your own, there is one ingredient that makes a difference: margarine. Historically, a lot of Thais weren't into butter (they consider it too rich), since there isn't much of a dairy culture, so achieving that certain flavor and texture requires margarine. The traditional method of "casting the dough" requires time spent practicing and honing muscle memory in the same way Pete Sampras spent years as a kid developing his lethal tennis serve. If you're not Pete Sampras, use a rolling pin.

Try serving roti with a scoop of ice cream and a heavy drizzle of sweetened condensed milk. We don't offer many desserts at Night + Market (aside from fortune cookies served with the check), but I make an exception for roti à la mode.

½ tablespoon kosher salt (see → 26)

1 teaspoon sugar

½ **cup whole milk, warmed**

2 cups all-purpose flour, sifted

1 egg, beaten

2 tablespoons softened margarine, plus more as needed for cooking

Vegetable oil, as needed

1. In a small bowl, whisk together the salt, sugar, milk, and ¼ cup warm water. Add the flour to a large bowl and form a little well in the center. Add the egg and 3 tablespoons of the milk mixture to the well, stirring with a fork until the liquid is absorbed. Slowly stir in the rest of the liquid, stirring with your hands once the mixture is doughy enough. Transfer the dough to a stand mixer fitted with the dough hook. Mix for 10 minutes on medium-high speed until the dough turns elastic and stretchy. (If you don't have a stand mixer, knead the dough on an oil-coated surface for 20 to 30 minutes, or until your arms fall off.) Rub the outer surface of the dough with 2 tablespoons of margarine and let it rest, covered, for 30 minutes.

2. Grease a large, clean work surface with oil. Use your fingers to twist off doughnut hole–size knobs of dough and flatten them with a rolling pin until they are as thin as possible until it becomes stretched out (or use your hands to flip and slap it against the work surface as if it was pizza dough, which is called "casting the dough"). Twirl the dough sheet like it was a locker room towel until heavily twisted, then coil the string into a spiral like you were making a flat cinnamon roll. Flatten with a rolling pin (or your hands) to stretch it out once again. Once you've achieved a diameter of 4 to 5 inches, set aside.

3. In a skillet, heat 1 tablespoon of oil and ½ tablespoon margarine over medium heat until sizzling. Cook the roti one at a time until browned and crispy, 2 to 3 minutes per side, replenishing the oil and margarine as needed. Drain on paper towels. Serve immediately.

INDEX

THANK YOU

Grandma, my true north. Without you, none of this would be possible.

Sarah, my love at first sight, my ride or die, my strength, my inspiration, my best friend.

Mom, for teaching me love and compassion.

Dad, for leaving me stranded at that Brazilian restaurant that one time and teaching me how to fend for myself.

Pa Lee and Lung Song, you are everything good and pure.

The Yenbamroong family, I am so proud to tell our story.

Chef Ting and Chef Lek, you raised me. You taught me so much of what I know and watched me grow from a not-so-great cook to a slightly better one. You are the foundation on which Night + Market is built.

Night + Market family, for holding yourselves to such an exacting standard and dedicating yourselves to hospitality day in, day out. You make it look easy. Special nods to Lucy, Zeferino, Lourdes, Boon, Irma, Estela, Pun.

Our amazing guests, for your enthusiastic support. We are humbled. Thank you especially to those who came in the early days when you were likely to be the only patrons in the restaurant!

Francis Lam, for believing in this project, for asking the tough questions, and for keeping us on course.

Kitty Cowles, for your tireless advocacy.

MOM, DAD, ALFIE

Marcus Nilsson, my bro. Your photos are everything. And thanks for getting me hooked on UFC.

Garrett Snyder, for picking my brain, learning my voice, reading my mind, and doing it all so effortlessly.

Juliette Cezzar, I had dreams for what this book would be. You not only took that to heart, but made it better than I could have ever imagined!

Clarkson Potter, for bringing this project to life!

Jonathan Gold, for not allowing me to quit when I was on the ropes. You are the patron saint of young broke chefs.

Andy Ricker, dear friend, brother, teacher, drinking partner, youth hostel, inspiration, foreword writer. Thank you for all that you do.

Wolfgang Puck, Spago always loomed so large on the Sunset Strip for a restaurant brat growing up down the road. You are an LA icon. Thank you for paving the way.

David Chang, Danny Bowien, Aziz Ansari, Gwyneth Paltrow, Shepherd Fairey, James Murphy, thank you for lending your kind words, support, and friendship.

Richard Kern, for taking me under your wing and teaching me how to push boundaries.

Sonny and Alfie, for always making me smile after a tough day.